Financial Regulation and Technology

ELGAR PRACTICAL GUIDES

Rich in practical advice, *Elgar Practical Guides* are handy, concise guides to a range of legal practice areas.

Combining practical insight and step-by-step guidance with the relevant substantive law and procedural rules, the books in this series focus on understanding and navigating the issues that are likely to be encountered in practice. This is facilitated by a range of structural tools including checklists, glossaries, sample documentation and recommended actions.

Elgar Practical Guides are indispensable resources for the busy practitioner and for the non-specialist who requires a first introduction or a reliable turn-to reference book.

Financial Regulation and Technology

A Legal and Compliance Guide

IAIN SHERIDAN
Legal Consultant, Barrister, MBA (Oxon), London, UK

Elgar Practical Guides

Cheltenham, UK • Northampton, MA, USA

Published by
Edward Elgar Publishing Limited
The Lypiatts
15 Lansdown Road
Cheltenham
Glos GL50 2JA
UK

Edward Elgar Publishing, Inc.
William Pratt House
9 Dewey Court
Northampton
Massachusetts 01060
USA

A catalogue record for this book
is available from the British Library

This book is available electronically in the **Elgar**online
Law subject collection
http://dx.doi.org/10.4337/9781802205411

ISBN 978 1 80220 540 4 (cased)
ISBN 978 1 80220 541 1 (eBook)
ISBN 978 1 80220 542 8 (paperback)

Printed and bound by CPI Group (UK) Ltd, Croydon, CR0 4YY

To Anita Hoi-Yin,
for all her love, support and intelligence

Content overview

Table of contents

About the author

Iain Sheridan is a legal consultant covering all aspects of financial regulation and technology, including fundraising, structuring, contracting, documentation, intellectual property and enforcement. His experience covers UK and EU financial regulation relevant to both buy-side and sell-side firms. He also provides advice to industry associations on financial regulation and technology.

Before becoming a consultant, he was Head of Legal Europe and Asia for the financial sector dedicated investment bank Fox-Pitt, Kelton. His consulting projects have included advising ABN AMRO, Bank of America, Barclays, Deutsche Bank, Fidelity Investments and Société Générale. A qualified barrister (England & Wales) and solicitor (New South Wales), Iain has also studied data science at Oxford University and machine learning at Cambridge University.

As well as frequently contributing to seminars, his articles on financial regulation, disruptive innovation, e-commerce, machine learning and smart phones have been quoted authoritatively by other international practitioners.

Foreword

Gordon Brough

Now that TikTok have increased their standard contribution model from 60 seconds to three minutes (to allow for more in-depth analysis) and with many of us starting to look for legal or regulatory advice with a Google search, some might ask if there is any need for a 336 page legal and compliance guide to financial regulation and technology. Even the sparest of readers will quickly put any doubts aside. This is a book every financial services lawyer and compliance officer will benefit from, not because it delivers all the answers but because it makes you think about the problems posed and how an answer might be arrived at.

Mr Sheridan has succeeded not only in covering lots of ground, bringing together a wide range of diverse subjects, but doing so in a way that is both interesting and stimulating. You will find the answer to any number of specific questions here but, more importantly, you will find new ways of thinking. Mr Sheridan's approach to his material is as innovative as some of the technology he explains (not to mention being at the same time readable, entertaining even).

When the scientists involved in new technologies like quantum computing cannot agree on exactly how it works, legislators and regulators are going to be a considerable way behind. This leaves legal and compliance teams trying to guess at how to apply old rules to new problems. Mr Sheridan's work helps to plug that gap. Time is obviously our most precious resource but, as Mr Sheridan suggests, if you can find an hour here or there to dip in to this new treatise it will be time well spent.

Gordon Brough
General Counsel, CQS (UK) LLP

Preface to the first edition

This first edition of *Financial Regulation and Technology* concentrates on recurring issues in financial services law and regulation relevant to the use of technology. I am a financial regulation lawyer who has been tackling technology issues for more than 20 years. My first practitioner-focused article, produced in 2001 whilst working as an associate at Allen & Overy, involved collaborating with IBM engineers and UK financial regulators to examine prosecuting fraud over the Internet. I have since contributed a wide range of financial regulation and technology articles, published by Butterworths, Kluwer Law International, Oxford University Press and the Royal Society, as well as a chapter on commercial contracts and machine learning in another Edward Elgar book entitled *Artificial Intelligence and Law*.

My motivation for writing this guide was the lack of any source providing a comprehensive survey of cutting-edge technologies from the angle of financial regulation. This guide provides an initial one-stop reference source for both legal counsel and compliance officers. Every topic in this guide requires substantial effort to digest, because each involves understanding the relevant financial services law, regulatory guidance and the fundamental aspects of technology. Unsurprisingly, one topic can have several connections to another topic, which can be challenging even for experienced practitioners. My insights derive from completing legal and compliance tasks inside a number of leading asset managers and investment banks. Additionally, I have also advised consumer credit businesses, hedge funds, private equity managers and trading platforms. Legal and compliance professionals analysing these key technology topics within or instructed by any of these regulated firms can gain from reading and referring to it.

For all readers cooperating with or overseeing legal and compliance functions, its contents will also be illuminating, saving many hours of research and analysis. This wider readership includes business strategy directors, entrepreneurs, innovators seeking to protect intellectual property, public service officials, all relevant senior management functions, risk specialists and software engineers. In sum, it is written to benefit experienced legal and compliance practitioners, as well as anyone seeking to expand their knowledge on technology-driven opportunities and risks.

To keep pace with financial regulation requires continuously checking detailed rules, applying the precise rules then re-checking for any subsequent changes. Further, contract clauses need to be regularly updated to reflect changes in both rules and emerging technology. The frequency and size of regulator fines make neglecting these processes an irrational diseconomy to not only the balance sheet, but also the long-term reputation of any asset manager, investment bank, platform or FinTech SME. To spot existing issues and pre-emptively adjust for imminent changes to law and regulation are complex tasks. This guidebook attempts to provide an initial grounding in the main themes. The specific substance includes algorithmic trading, cloud computing, crypto assets, cyber security, databases, data engineering, data protection, machine learning, payment services, quantum computing and trading platforms.

Once the Introductory and Accountability chapters are digested, anyone reading subsequent individual topics should gain a better understanding of how English law and EU regulation treat key technology topics. Many UK financial services transactions are governed by transposed EU directives and regulations, or UK equivalent versions have been implemented. Therefore, EU law also forms a significant part of the analytical framework. Further, when helpful, comparisons are made between the UK and other individual technologically innovative jurisdictions, such as China, Hong Kong, Singapore, Sweden and the US.

From a form and style viewpoint, nearly all statute and case law citations are confined to the footnotes. Thus any chapter can be fluidly read. An initial perusal of each chapter does not get slowed down because of long titles to multifarious legislation and case law names. Each chapter assumes no advanced knowledge of computers and related technology topics, and, where necessary, encapsulates the essential aspects. Any reader should come away with an understanding of the key case law, regulation, authoritative financial services regulator guidance and international standards governing these specific themes.

Given even the most formidable legal memories can be forced to pause for thought to make an impromptu application of all the salient aspects of what can often be complex topics, this guide also attempts to make memorable the essential features of each topic by including diagrams, graphs and also a few simple text formulae to highlight the fundamental elements. As the pioneering Dutch software engineer, Edsger Dijkstra, once said 'a picture may be worth a thousand words, a formula is worth a thousand pictures'.[1]

Finally, I would like to acknowledge my gratitude to the editorial team at Edward Elgar who made this all happen.

The law is stated as of 4 January 2022.

Iain Sheridan
London, UK

---

[1]   Krzysztof, R, and Hoare, T (2021) Edsger W. Dijkstra: a Commemoration, at 5. See www.cs.utexas .edu/users/EWD/commemoration/EWD-commemoration-2021.pdf.

Abbreviations

AEMIs	Authorised Electronic Money Institutions
AFME	Association for Financial Markets in Europe
AI	artificial intelligence
AIFMD	Alternative Investment Fund Managers Directive
AISPs	Account Information Service Providers
AML	Anti-Money Laundering
APAC	Asia Pacific
API	application programming interface
ASIC	Australian Securities and Investment Commission
ASPSPs	Account Servicing Payment Service Providers
ASS	automated surveillance system
ATM	Automated Teller Machine
BIS	Bank of International Settlements
BNPL	buy now pay later
CBDC	Central Bank Digital Currency
CBPIIs	Card-based Payment Instrument Issuers
CCA	Consumer Credit Act (1974)
CCG	Cyber Coordination Groups
CDEI	Centre for Data Ethics and Innovation
CD-ROM	compact disc read-only memory
CERN	The European Organization for Nuclear Research
CFTC	Commodity Futures Trading Commission
CISA	US DHS Cybersecurity and Infrastructure Security Agency

CiSP	Cyber Security Information Sharing Partnership
CJEU	Court of Justice of the European Union
CMA	Competition and Markets Authority
CME	Chicago Metal Exchange
COBs	FCA Conduct of Business Sourcebook
CONC	FCA Consumer Credit Handbook
CP	FCA Consultation Paper
CPU	Central Processing Unit
CSIRTs	Computer Security Incident Response Teams
CTO	Chief Technology Officer
CVV	Card Verification Value
DBMS	database management system
DEA	Direct Electronic Access
DEPP	FCA Decision Procedures and Penalties Manual
DFSA	Dubai Financial Services Authority
DHS	US Department for Home and Security
DLT	distributed ledger technology
DMA	Direct Market Access
DMT	Digital Markets Taskforce
DMU	Digital Markets Unit
DP	Discussion Paper
DPA	Data Protection Act (2018)
DPIA	Data Protection Impact Assessment
EBA	European Banking Authority
EC	European Commission
ECJ	European Court of Justice, informal name of the CJEU
EDPB	European Data Protection Board
EEA	European Economic Area
EMD	Electronic Money Directive
EMI	e-money institutions or small e-money institutions
EMR	Electronic Money Regulations

ENISA	European Union Agency for Cyber Security
EPC	European Patent Convention
EPO	European Patent Office
ERS	enhanced regulatory sandbox
ESG	environmental, social and governance
ESMA	European Securities and Markets Authority
ETF	Exchange Traded Fund
FATF	Financial Action Task Force
FBI	Federal Bureau of Investigation
FCA	Financial Conduct Authority
FICC	fixed income, currencies and commodities
FinTech	Financial Technology
FIPS	Federal Information Processing Standard Publication
FMI	Financial Market Infrastructure
FMLC	Financial Markets Law Committee
FPO	Financial Promotions Order
FSA	Financial Services Authority
FSB	Financial Stability Board
FSCCC	Financial Sector Cyber Collaboration Centre
FS-ISAC	Financial Services Information Sharing and Analysis Center
FSMA	Financial Services and Markets Act (2000)
G20	Group of 20
G7	Group of Seven
GCHQ	Government Communications Headquarters
GDPR	General Data Protection Regulation
GEN	FCA General Provisions Sourcebook
GFIN	Global Financial Innovation Network
GII	Global Innovation Index
GPU	Graphical Processing Unit
G-SIBs	global systemically important banks

GUI	graphical user interface
GWh	Gigawatt hours
HFT	High Frequency Trading
HKMA	Hong Kong Monetary Authority
IaaS	Infrastructure as a Service
IBM	International Business Machines
IBSIG	Investment Banking Information Security Special Interest Group
ICO	Information Commissioner's Office
IDTA	International Data Transfer Agreement
IEC	International Electrotechnical Commission
IOSCO	International Organization of Securities Commission
IoT	Internet of Things
IP	intellectual property or internet protocol
IPO	Initial Public Offering
IRC	Incident Response Company
IRP	Interest Rate Product
ISDA	International Swaps and Derivatives Association
ISO	International Organization for Standardization
KYC	Know Your Customer
LSE	London Stock Exchange
M&A	Mergers and Acquisitions
MAC	material adverse change
MAS	Monetary Authority of Singapore
MFN	most favoured nation
MiFID	Markets in Financial Instruments Directive
MiFIR	Markets in Financial Instruments Regulation
MIT	Massachusetts Institute of Technology
MTF	Multilateral Trading Facility
NASA	National Aeronautics and Space Administration
NCA	National Crime Agency

NCSC	National Cyber Security Centre (UK)
NIS	Network and Information Security Directive
NIST	National Institute of Standards and Technology
NLP	natural language processing
NSIA	National Security and Investment Act (2021)
OECD	Organization for Economic Cooperation and Development
OTC	over-the-counter
OTF	Organized Trading Facility
Paas	Platform as a Service
PFI	Private Finance Initiative
PISP	Payment Initiation Service Providers
PRA	Prudential Regulation Authority
PSD	Payment Services Directive
PSR	Payment Systems Regulator
QC	Quantum Computing
Qubit	Quantum Bit
R&D	research and development
RAO	Regulated Activities Order of FSMA
RM	Regulated Market
RSA	Rivest Shamir Adleman (public key cryptosystem)
RTS	Regulatory Technical Standard (MiFID)
Saas	Software as a Service
SANS	SysAdmin, Audit, Network, and Security
SCA	strong customer authentication
SCC	standard contractual clauses
SEC	Securities and Exchange Commission
SEF	swap execution facility
SEMIs	Small Electronic Money Institutions
SFDR	Sustainable Finance Disclosure Regulation
SHAP	SHapley Additive exPlanations

SI	Statutory Instrument or Systematic internaliser
SII	systemically important institution
SLA	Service Level Agreement
SMCR	Senior Managers and Certification Regime
SMEs	small and medium-sized enterprises
SMF	Senior Management Function
SMR	Senior Managers Regime
SMS	Strategic Market Status
SRC	Systemic Risk Centre
STEM	science, technology, engineering and mathematics
STRIDE	Spoofing, Tampering, Repudiation, Information, Denial, Elevation
SUP	FCA Supervision Handbook
SWIFT	Society for Worldwide Interbank Financial Telecommunications
SYSC	Senior Manager Arrangements, Systems and Controls
ToS	Terms of Service Agreement
TPPs	Third-party Providers
UCITS	Undertakings for Collective Investment in Transferable Securities
UKJT	UK Jurisdictional Taskforce
VASP	Virtual Asset Service Providers
WFE	World Federation of Exchanges
WIPO	World Intellectual Property Organization
WP 248	Working Party of EU Data Protection Authorities
Y2K	Year 2000 problem

Table of cases

Table of legislation

UK Statutes

EU Directives

EU Regulations

EU Draft Legislation

US Legislation

Other International Legislation

Treaties and Conventions

1. An introduction to financial regulation and technology

1.1 English law with an international perspective

The legal and compliance judgement embedded throughout this book derives from over two decades inside the legal and compliance functions of American, British, Dutch, French and German regulated investment banks or asset managers.

Above all, this is a practical book attempting to meet the challenge of blending financial regulation and technology. The law and regulation is based on English law and transposed EU regulation. However, in any global financial services regulated firm, there is a regular need to analyse law and regulation from both common law and civil jurisdictional viewpoints. Frequently, that includes not only the position in the EU and US, but also what is required elsewhere, for example in Australia, China, Hong Kong (SAR), and Singapore, or other dynamic markets.

I am a dual qualified lawyer, originally trained at the London Bar, and then with Paul Phillips at Allen & Overy in its financial regulation practice group. Later I qualified as a solicitor in Sydney. Additionally, I practised for two years in Vienna, which provided insights on the different approaches applied in an EU civil law jurisdiction. My in-house experience has extensively covered both Europe and Asia. My private law firm experience includes attempting to build two China law practices focused on Beijing and North East China. In sum, my practitioner experience and insights are not anchored in the UK, but are also built on ground truths elsewhere.

1.2   FCA versus PRA rules

Predominantly in this book, the key UK regulations referred to are those of the Financial Conduct Authority (FCA). The Prudential Regulation Authority (PRA) is the prudential regulator for a small number of 'dual-regulated' firms, by which is meant firms that are authorised and regulated by the PRA, and regulated by the FCA.[1] A memorable way to grasp what that means is to think about the underlying reasoning for two regulators that seek to avoid duplication of effort. This involves applying a two-limbed test that characterises the FCA as a regulator of integrity to protect consumers, and the PRA as a systemic regulator to protect the safety of the UK financial system.[2] The FCA acts for firms who collectively determine the integrity of the financial system with the key aim of protecting consumers. The FCA is the conduct regulator for approximately 60,000 regulated firms.

The PRA, as an organ of the Bank of England, was formed in response to the perceived poor systemic risk supervision by the Financial Services Authority (FSA), the FCA's predecessor, before and during the Global Financial Crisis 2007–2008. The key regulated firms under the PRA's watch are around 20 systemically important investment firms.[3] Beyond

---

[1] For the full list of businesses that are dual-regulated, therefore also regulated by the PRA, see The Financial Services and Markets Act 2000 (PRA-regulated Activities) Order 2013, SI 2013/556.

[2] The FCA Handbook sets out the two-limbed prudential context test as follows:

    (1) For the FCA, in relation to activities carried on by a *firm*, the context in which the activities have, or might reasonably be regarded as likely to have, a negative effect on:

        (a) the integrity of the *UK financial system*; or

        (b) the ability of the *firm* to meet either:

            (i) the 'fit and proper' test in *threshold condition* 2E and 3D (Suitability); or

            (ii) the applicable requirements and standards under the *regulatory system* relating to the *firm's* financial resources.

    (2) For the PRA, in relation to activities carried on by a firm, the context in which the activities have, or might reasonably be regarded as likely to have, a negative effect on:

        (a) the safety and soundness of PRA-*authorised persons*; or

        (b) the ability of the *firm* to meet either:

            (i) the 'fit and proper' test in *threshold condition* 5 (Suitability); or

            (ii) the applicable requirements and standards under the *regulatory system* relating to the *firm's* financial resources.

[3] The systemically important institutions (SIIs) are determined annually by the PRA. In 2021 these included: Barclays Plc, Citigroup Global Markets Limited, Credit Suisse International, Credit Suisse Investments (UK), Goldman Sachs Group UK Limited, HSBC Holdings Plc, JP Morgan

these very large groups, PRA-regulated activities include deposit taking,[4] insurers,[5] and dealing in investment as principal. Further, approximately 40 or so building societies are also prudentially regulated by the PRA.[6] In total, the PRA is responsible for supervising approximately 1,500 regulated firms. The PRA's veto powers over the FCA include situations when, in the opinion of the PRA, the FCA's proposed action will threaten the stability of the UK financial system.[7]

A helpful explanation on how the two regulators are required to interact is set out in the FCA-PRA Memorandum of Understanding (the 'FCA-PRA MoU').[8] The FCA-PRA MoU states that the regulators will not normally conduct joint supervisory activity. Further, that any relevant findings from supervisory activity will be shared; for example, the FCA would share with the PRA key findings on conduct risk.[9]

1.3   Recurring questions

Increasingly email, encryption, electronic signatures, Internet platforms, smart phones and other technologies embed themselves operationally into financial services. Consequently there is the recurring challenge of understanding technology in the context of legal risk. From hardware or software viewpoints the three key questions are set out below.

- What aspects of technology are relevant to financial services?
- Which financial services laws or regulations apply?
- If there are not yet relevant legal or regulatory rules, which international standards apply?

Capital Holdings Limited, Lloyds Banking Group Plc, Merrill Lynch International, Morgan Stanley International Limited, Nationwide Building Society, Nomura Europe Holdings Plc, The Royal Bank of Scotland Group Plc, Santander UK Group Holdings Plc, and Standard Chartered Plc. Looking back at the SIIs lists for previous years, this collection is fairly static. UBS is absent from 2018.

[4] Article 5 of the Regulated Activities Order, SI 2001/544. Note that also Amended by SI 2002/682.

[5] Article 10 Regulated Activities Order, SI 2001/544.

[6] It is important to note that the FCA is also responsible for the subsidiaries of many building societies. An accurate way to describe this situation is the sharing of systemic risk supervision based on the PRA as an organ of the Bank of England.

[7] Section 31I(2) FSMA 2000.

[8] FCA-PRA (2019) MoU: Between the FCA and the Bank of England (Exercising its Prudential Regulation Functions).

[9] Ibid., at 24–25.

Decision making of legal and compliance risk requires a balanced under-standing of both financial regulation and technology. As a metaphor, the challenge is the sense that legal and compliance risks are at one end of a see-saw. Positioned there are contractual processes, complying with regulations and High Court legal decisions – collectively 'financial regulation'. These legal and regulatory elements are crucial to avoiding fines, litigation and managing reputation. On the other end of the see-saw are cloud computing, cyber security, data protection, machine learning, online platforms and numerous other digital aspects – collectively 'tech-nology'. This book attempts to be at the fulcrum of the see-saw.

1.4   What is potentially at stake?

The words of William Shakespeare spring to mind: 'I hold my duty as I hold my soul'.[10] Legal counsel and compliance officers support a range of talented profit-focused professionals in financial services, and both these risk management functions require a dissenting bravery and focus. It is memorable that a partnership of two Nobel Prize laureates led the hedge fund Long-Term Capital Management which collapsed from flawed deci-sion making. Further, before its collapse, Lehman Brothers was renowned for an abundance of hard working, talented financiers. Unfortunately, across the global financial services sector there are always patterns of commercial over-optimism combined with the blocking of legal and compliance influence. In most situations there is (a) wilful blindness to the probability of a calamitous outcome, and (b) wilful deafness to dis-senting risk management voices. Legal and compliance functions cannot jointly or severally save a whole regulated firm, but both can contribute to mitigating worse case scenarios.

1.5   How does technology function in financial services firms?

In 2019 I took a sabbatical at Cambridge University. Away from both the City of London and Canary Wharf, I was not only able to re-engage with data science methods I had learned many years before, but also to

---

[10]   *Hamlet*, Act 2, Scene 2.

develop a grasp of Artificial Intelligence (AI), especially machine learning (ML). On returning to the financial services sector, my fresh approach was to think more like electrical engineers and software engineers. At an in-depth level, these professionals understand computer technology as a hierarchy of electronic components organised to allow logical processes (logic gates) to be computed within a system that uses operating systems and computer languages to facilitate the processing, retrieving, storing and viewing of data.

Some technological understanding is, in my view, going to result in better financial regulation decision making, especially thinking in terms of architecture made up of network connections, software, computational statistics, plus the interfaces between hardware and software. Table 1.1 captures the key architectural parts with a description of their form and substance.

1.6   Critical thinking for legal counsel and compliance professionals

A legitimate question to ask is where can thinking critically support legal and compliance workloads? There is the understandable first reaction that your own effective methods have worked over numerous instructions, and new ways of thinking through the legal issues are unnecessary. My respectful response to that reaction, although arguably a logical fast thinking viewpoint,[11] is to remain open-minded and consider three points. First, when dealing with technology issues in the financial services sector there is a need for a multi-disciplinary mind-set, because the challenge is often beyond an in-depth practical experience of applying financial regulation and contract law or both. It requires also knowing, among other areas, the relevant cyber security, cloud computing, data protection, intellectual property protection and practical legal risk management factors. Depending on the context, legal counsel may also need to grasp case law relevant to the specific facts. For example, English High Court decisions on derivatives or force majeure.

---

[11]   Fast thinking is a term coined by the psychologist Daniel Kahneman, a Nobel Prize winner in economic sciences. In his best-selling book *Thinking, Fast and Slow* (2011) (Penguin), Kahneman characterises 'fast thinking' as frequent, instinctive or unconscious thoughts. A memorable example is that we use fast thinking to solve 2+2.

Table 1.1   *Key technology in financial services*

Technology	Architecture	What is it? Why does it matter?
Application programming interface (API)	Software	The way data and functionality owned by one business is opened up to external third-party developers. APIs allow both communication and the sharing of data across different services. Standardised definitions and rules allow software engineers to develop a new application or join together data across multiple platforms.
Artificial Intelligence (AI)	Algorithms, hardware and software	In the narrow context of financial services, AI concerns computational statistics, especially machine learning (see below). Through the application of image recognition, neural networks and other machine learning techniques, businesses can gain competitive advantages by more accurately classifying data and images without human input, and also identifying patterns in data to make superior classifications and predictions.
Cloud computing	Hardware	The use of data storage and accessing computing power that is geographically distant from the user. Typically this is an on-demand arrangement with another company, but it can also be intra-group. Cloud computing presents not only security issues but also jurisdictional ones, given that access or use may be outside England & Wales in the EU, in APAC or the US. Cloud computing has been a huge contributor to the growth of machine learning, which often requires computer capacity and data management that cannot be cost-effectively brought in-house.

Technology	Architecture	What is it? Why does it matter?
Cryptography	Computational mathematics and software	Public key cryptography involves the encryption of data that is transmitted then decrypted by a recipient with a private key. Encryption is the process that converts plain text into cipher text, and in turn allows authorised actors to decipher the encoded text back into plain text. Cryptography was invented by the UK Government Communications Headquarters (GCHQ), and its robustness in hiding commercial data from third parties plays a paramount role, including stored data and emails.
Databases	Software	The means by which data is accessed and stored via a database management system (DBMS). In an era when data is a key asset in the financial services sector, the ability to efficiently process, retrieve and store data is a competitive advantage for both buy-side and sell-side firms.
Digital signatures	Algorithms and software	The use of cryptographic protocols (see Cryptography above) to manage contract formation and financial transactions. As well as reducing the costs associated with traditional paper-based contract signing and archiving, digital signatures save time for authorised signatories.[1]
Graphical User Interface (GUI)	Software	A GUI is what the user sees on a computer screen, smartphone or tablet, the human eye's window on all the architecture below. The clarity of envisioning and organising a GUI affects many functions in any regulated firm. The benefits of effective GUIs include summarising strategies to teams, influencing change and allowing compliance officers to spot data anomalies more quickly.

Technology	Architecture	What is it? Why does it matter?
Machine Learning	Algorithms, hardware and software	A sub-branch of AI (see above) that involves statistical computing. Algorithms forming part of software are able to learn from data. The learning means the program improves over time. The time the program takes to become more efficient varies depending on the task, the computer processing power, plus the quality and size of the data sets. If large data sets are relevant to achieving greater performance, these typically rely on cloud computing (see above).
Trading platforms	Hardware, network connections and software	The main way that equity, fixed income and many other asset classes are traded. Thus, they represent one of the key ways both asset managers and investment banks make profits and hedge against potential losses. Given the global reach of these platforms across many counter-parties, commercial clients and retail customers, they are heavily regulated.

Note: [1] Digital signatures must be differentiated from the treatment under English contract law of a sender's email address. Without more, the automatic inclusion of a sender's email address does not qualify as a valid signature: *Mehta v J Pereira Fernande SA* [2006] EWHC 813 (Ch).

Second, the subject matter is often cutting edge so the more angles, techniques and tactics to apply the better. It is easy to invest an hour looking through instructions requiring answers to financial regulation or a draft contract then subsequently make no or slow progress. Third, there needs to be ways to stimulate more critical 'what ifs' and the answers to such questions require careful deliberation.

To illustrate, business continuity planning is just one example of how thinking critically can potentially improve desired outcomes. In most business continuity plans there will be a list of head of function email recipients who will receive an initial notification of a disruptive event. This initial email list is quite different from the list of recipients that subsequently need to be constantly informed as part of operational resilience measures to recover the regulated firm back to before the disruptive event. On an on-going basis, the General Counsel, Head of Compliance, along with a number of supporting compliance officers, legal counsel and technology professionals, will all need to be kept informed.

On first analysis, email is often a good choice for this task. However, thinking critically, the nature of a client email is one of formality which leads to caution and lost time. Further, if the email server itself has been attacked or is malfunctioning there is no practical contingency plan. A more convenient medium might be WhatsApp,[12] the messaging service supporting the leading mobile operating systems Android[13] and Apple iOS.[14] There is no debate that WhatsApp provides a highly efficient medium, especially for short-term scenarios that benefit from constant, succinct updates. For instance, software engineers can provide quick hourly updates rather than be delayed by the need to draft emails.

Thinking critically, WhatsApp has weaknesses. For example, WhatsApp, and indeed several competing services, do not provide end-to-end encryption, and the code is controlled by the provider. One solution is to have a messaging system that is based on open-source code so that there is 100 per cent certainty that malicious third-parties have no back door access to your messages. An example of an open-source messaging service is Signal.[15] This service includes voice recording and can be set up as a desktop application as long as the user has first installed Signal on an Android or iOS smartphone. It is notable that a number of years ago Signal was approved for messaging by senators and staff of the US Senate.[16]

A critically analysed solution will achieve greater efficiency or robustness or both. In this current disruptive event example, the contract clause may require the software engineers tasked with repairing the system to provide hourly voice-recorded updates via a smartphone platform such as Signal or equivalent mobile messaging service. Detailed in a contract, the agreed approach potentially achieves three things at the same time by (a) learning how to better manage future similar events; (b) providing

---

[12] Available at www.whatsapp.com.

[13] Available at www.android.com.

[14] Available at www.apple.com/ios.

[15] Available at www.signal.org.

[16] Available at www.zdnet.com/article/in-encryption-push-senate-approves-signal-for-encrypted-mess aging/.

detailed evidence on how well or not the provider responded; and (c) establishing a record of how the regulated firm mitigated the situation.[17] Arguably, there are additional effectiveness and time-saving benefits of not unnecessarily distracting the software engineers with different forms of impromptu communication.

The above resilience recovery example may well have weaknesses and there will be improved alternative answers. It is merely one example. What matters is the consistent application of thinking critically about issues that have legal and regulatory consequences. In my view, that is a positive contribution to any buy-side or sell-side regulated firm.

1.6.1   An established critical thinking technique

A valuable critical thinking technique is called fishbone analysis, invented by a Japanese engineer called Kaoru Ishikawa.[18] Often when leading engineering companies make a product to a very high quality standard, they invest time in sitting down to analyse what can be done better. Putting the spotlight on every variable, from start to finish, these quality control teams ask themselves: 'Where did things fall below perfection? Even though the users appear satisfied with the final outcome, what could have been done better?' In sum, they incorporate into their busy, budget-conscious schedules the process of continuous improvement.[19]

As shown in Figure 1.1, it provides an opportunity to apply a proven critical analysis technique to, for example, the drafting, negotiation or renegotiation of any contract clause. By which is meant legal counsel can look at what has already been signed with the same party or a similar contract party. This process is a valuable investment of effort and time. Rather than relying solely on a line-by-line checklist of issues, there is an opportunity to think holistically about all the issues, which may have

---

[17]   Under English law, before a known force majeure event and during its disrupting occurring, a contracting party receiving a good or service has a duty to mitigate the situation: *Mamidoil-Jetfoil Greek Petroleum Co SA v Okta Crude Refinery AD* (No. 2) [2003] EWCA Civ 1031. The detailed treatment of force majeure is considered in Chapter 12 Machine learning.

[18]   Ishikawa, K (1990) *Introduction to Quality Control* (Productivity Press).

[19]   In advanced product engineering this cause and effect analysis is part of a post-mortem on how a product worked, and can often be in the context of a product with one defect per 1 million products. The implication of this for legal counsel and compliance officers is that some software engineers they cooperate with have very high professional standards.

interrelated risks, linkages and synergies that would not so easily emerge from a more linear reflection. The question posed at each finer bone connection (topic) of the main fishbone is which contract clause or compliance issue needs modifying to better manage the adverse effects of this specific technology?

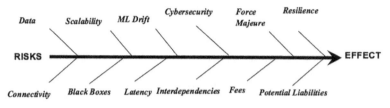

Figure 1.1   *Fishbone risks and effect*

The fishbone analysis starts with topics on the left-hand side tail. The order is irrelevant, but from a logical structure it is easier to start with the treatment of '*Data*', because data will form part of every computer system and is an obvious top priority and getting data management right should avoid dispute resolution costs, any awarded damages, regulator fines or potential loss of reputation.

1.6.2   Thinking critically about data

In the 21st century the value of specific data sets constantly increases, because data is often an appreciating asset. Yet data is also an on-going liability to any business, because its loss or misuse can result in fines, litigation and reputational harm. The purpose here is not to cover the detailed rules that still need be factored in, but to use the example of data as a way of applying fishbone analysis as a critical thinking tool to raise the overall standard of financial regulation advice, drafting and negotiation.

Data can be characterised as possessing three dimensions. First, there is its specific treatment concerning individuals – personal data. Second, there is its general business risk. Third, it has value as an asset – a commodity.[20]

---

[20]   See also Chapter 6 Data protection and Chapter 9 Intellectual property protection.

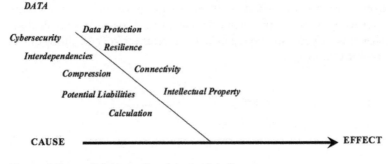

Figure 1.2   *What are the risks to data?*

Breaking down the issue of *DATA*, as shown in Figure 1.2, into sub-branches creates a rigorous way to cover many angles and simultaneously make important risk management and efficiency connections. For instance, if thinking through the sub-branch of *Data Protection*, it is a fast evolving area of regulation that impacts every type of financial services business. The regulator fines are increasingly large and any publicity surrounding data security breaches or lapses are incredibly damaging to brands and corporate reputations. For many years the General Data Protection Regulation (GDPR)[21] of the EU applied to the management and transfer of personal data in the UK, within the European Economic Area (EEA) and its controlled transfer outside of the EEA. Currently, the UK's data protection regulations[22] are an equivalent transposed statute, acknowledging that these UK data protection regulations should be analysed on a case-by-case basis with the broader Data Protection Act 2018.

In many asset managers and investment banks there will often be one legal counsel dedicated to tackling data protection issues on a full-time basis. This individual, if they exist, is an important point of contact, because even a sound grasp of GDPR principles can in certain instances be overtaken by developments. For example, in October 2020, during the Covid-19 pandemic and only eight weeks from the end of the UK's Brexit transition period, the European Data Protection Board (EDPB) issued important supplementary guidance. It is the sort of addition that would

---

[21]   General Data Protection Regulation (EU), 2016/679.

[22]   The full title is the Data Protection, Privacy and Electronic Communications (Amendments etc.) (EU Exit) Regulations 2019.

certainly be picked up by a full-time expert data protection lawyer, but generalists would be forgiven for missing it.

Generally, a 'two heads are better than one' approach is a vital habit for any professional critical thinking. As the brilliant Harvard cognitive scientist, Steve Pinker, put it 'none of us, thinking alone, is rational enough to consistently come to sound conclusions: rationality emerges from a community of reasoners who spot each other's fallacies'.[23]

This section has been entirely conceptual, introducing a proven critical thinking tool to take on the challenges of technology governed by financial regulation in the remaining chapters. Cultivating the habit of including a fishbone analysis requires re-visiting the figures in this chapter. With some time investment there will be an awareness of improved analysis. Readers may choose to use a digital whiteboard, recycled paper, smartphone or tablet. In my experience the investment will be paid many times over, not only for the legal and compliance functions but also in how you are personally valued.

1.7   Recurring themes in this guide

It is evident there are a number of recurring themes throughout this book. These are the priority of learning continuously; algorithms and addressing transparency versus competitive advantages; and understanding financial technology of the past, present and future. Each is dealt with in turn.

First, there is the value of learning continuously. Eric 'Astro' Teller is the Chief Executive Officer of X Development LLC,[24] a highly ambitious research and development (R&D) company set up by Google that focuses on 'moon-shot' innovations. Astro is attributed as drawing Figure 1.3, which illustrates the gap between human adaptability and technological advancement. By which is meant human grasp of technology is always behind the speed of technology. Astro's diagram[25] presents the view that if humans can enhance their ability to adapt even slightly more to techno-

---

[23] Pinker, S (2021) *Rationality: What It Is, Why It Seems Scarce, Why It Matters* (Penguin), at 16.

[24] www.x.company/moonshot/.

[25] Friedman, TL (2016) *Thank You For Being Late – An Optimist's Guide to Thriving in the Age of Accelerations* (Penguin), at 32.

logical advancement, this can reduce some of the gap. The small dotted line simulates not only learning faster, but also governing faster.

For both legal counsel and compliance officers it is inevitable that there will be some technology knowledge gap, given the 'day job' is to advise, draft, negotiate and complete transactions to continuous deadlines. Commuting and lunchtimes may present a chance to keep up-to-date with important High Court cases and regulatory changes. Alternatively, some evening or weekend time is used to get up to date on financial regulation focused solely on or containing significant technological aspects. In sum, keeping up-to-date with the constantly moving target of technology is another task to add to the list of 'must do'.

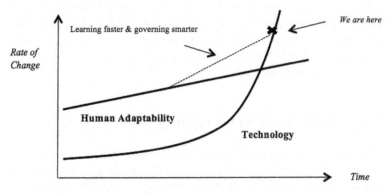

Figure 1.3   Human adaptability and technological advancement

The task requires iron discipline.[26] Yet the rewards are clear. The quality of your advice will shine across your own in-house function, or if you are in private practice with high satisfaction from your clients.

Second, there is the recurring theme of algorithms. Several chapters in this book focus on individual algorithm-based software and network communications protocols. Most pivotally, these are found in cryptog-

---

[26]   My past analysis on this gap-closing challenge has included MiFID II regulation covering algorithmic trading, High Frequency Trading (HFT) and Distributed Ledger Technology (DLT). See Sheridan, I (2017) 'MiFID II in the Context of Financial Technology and Regulatory Technology', *Capital Markets Law Journal*, Volume 12, Issue 4, at 417–427.

raphy, machine learning and trading. Of these algorithms, arguably the one that requires the most scrutiny to understand is algorithmic trading, which concerns computerised trading with no or limited manpower in the trading process. It has been estimated that greater than 75 per cent of equities trading and 40 per cent of foreign exchange trading rely on algorithmic processes.[27] Algorithmic trading is ubiquitous in US equity markets and plays an increasingly important role in debt securities.[28]

Specifically in the Markets in Financial Instruments Directive (MiFID) II rules, algorithmic trading refers to 'trading in financial instruments where a computer algorithm automatically determines individual parameters of orders such as whether to initiate the order, the timing, price or quantity of the order or how to manage the order after its submission, with limited or no human intervention'.[29]

For some lawyers, even very senior highly accomplished partners in London and New York law firms, there is the dreaded thought of a return to high school algebra lessons. Certainly what lies at the heart of most algorithms is algebra and calculus or a mix of these two parts of mathematics with a consistent use of statistics. If you did not enjoy or understand mathematics in the past, my only advice is that the past is another country. In the context of passing numerous law exams and other professional hoops, understanding algorithms is not nearly as daunting as may be imagined. The discipline and logic of thought are remarkably similar. Further, the dedication of frequent time learning the techniques and terminology bring increasing clarity to most algorithms.

Compliance officers in many jurisdictions, including the UK, are already expected to know enough about algorithms used by their business. Given most trading platform contracts and machine learning innovations use algorithms it is logical that both legal and compliance professionals understand how a business automates decision making and how machine learning operates to improve a process or service.

---

[27] Bank of England (2017) 'The Promise of FinTech – Something New under the Sun?' speech by Mark Carney, Governor of the Bank of England, 25 January 2017.

[28] SEC (2020) Staff Report on Algorithmic Trading in U.S. Capital Markets, at 67.

[29] See Article 4 (39) MiFID II.

For instance, MiFID II regulation transposed into UK law requires regulated entities that use algorithms to ensure their compliance function 'has at least a general understanding of the way in which algorithmic trading systems and algorithms operate'.[30]

1.8   Transparency versus competitive advantage

Third, there is the task of addressing transparency versus competitive advantage. At the start of this chapter there was reference to a see-saw where the lawyer has to balance legal advice and skill against varying types of technology, balancing on one end the vital need to avoid misjudging regulatory requirements, and on the other end protecting what commercially matters to the financial services firm. A similar fine-balancing process is occurring with the need for transparency to balance against the protection of hard-earned competitive advantages, typically gained by great expense and time on R&D.

UK and EU laws seek to increase and maintain transparency for the protection of investors. Eminent data scientists have incisively encapsulated the challenge of algorithmic technology in this way:

> Algorithms and machine learning techniques pose big questions around accountability and oversight. How can we achieve true transparency for algorithms written in code that few can understand? Or where constantly changing input data or their 'black box' nature means that it is difficult or even impossible to decipher how algorithms reach decisions? Or where for security or proprietary reasons algorithms cannot be published.[31]

Transparency matters to maintain fairness and integrity in financial services. However, the commercial value of keeping proprietary algorithms confidential is increasingly crucial to sustaining existing businesses and allowing new entrants to grow. Competitive advantages are easily lost by the divulging of algorithmic innovations. For instance, MiFID rules potentially require divulging algorithmic trading strategies to regulators,

---

[30]   See Article 2(1) Commission Delegated Regulation (EU) 2017 589, supplementing Article 48(6) MiFID II.

[31]   Drew, C (2016) Data Science Ethics in Government, *Philosophical Transactions of the Royal Society A, Mathematical, Physical and Engineering Sciences*, published 14 November 2016.

which may in turn be leaked to competitors.[32] Regulators are bound by a duty of confidentiality that would reduce some of the commercial risks.[33] Nevertheless, there would inevitably be some leakage of valuable proprietary strategies because employees move back and forth from regulators to regulated businesses.

The challenge for UK regulated firms is to balance compliance with financial services regulation and simultaneously protect intellectual property (IP) in the form of trade secrets. This commercial point was raised by the International Swaps and Derivatives Association (ISDA) in its response to the FCA's MAR 7A, when it remarked: '*ISDA* members would like to understand if the intention of the FCA is to capture the detailed cases of each type of test ... which may include proprietary information detailing the behaviour of the algorithm'.[34]

1.9   Understanding the past, present and future of FinTech

Fourth, there is a need to understand the past, present and future of Financial Technology (FinTech). Given FinTech is an established competitive advantage, legal counsel and compliance officers need to fully appreciate the legal and risk questions it previously and currently creates, as well as anticipating future regulation and law. FinTech can often be more established in its use than journalists and marketers portray. The phrase 'old wine in new bottles' comes to mind. Journalism about contemporary FinTech can omit reference to the fact that technology has been simplifying financial services for decades to gain a competitive advantage or increase productivity. At the end of the 20th century, it is easy to forget that the Society of Worldwide Interbank Financial Telecommunications (SWIFT) was established in 1973. Further, in the 1990s Reuters launched an automatic matching system of bids and offers.[35] At the beginning of this century the use of the London Transport Oyster electronic payment

---

[32] FCA MAR 7A.3.7R.

[33] Article 76 (1) MiFID II imposes on competent authorities the duty of professional secrecy.

[34] ISDA Response to FCA's MIFID II Implementation under FCA CP15/43 at 21.

[35] See www.thomsonreuters.com/en/about-us/company-history.html.

ticketing card system commenced in 2003.[36] Even the relatively recent astonishing rise of machine learning applied in diverse financial services businesses has to be seen in the time vista of machine learning implemented several years earlier in many hedge funds.

FinTech reflects a change to multiple-layers of technology which are transforming wholesale payments, clearing, settlement and trading. The recurring fundamental characteristics are (a) disruptive innovation,[37] occurring (b) free from legacy technology systems, and with (c) asynchronous compliance.[38]

To this trio might easily be added the elements of scalability achieved via cloud computing, initiatives constrained by low budgets,[39] and a focus on smart phone platforms. However, the core elements are certainly disruptive innovation, legacy-free technology and asynchronous compliance.

The term disruptive innovation is often mentioned, but it is important to have an understanding of the source and spirit of this mind-set. Arguably, the most longstanding contributor to highlighting the critical role innovation plays in capitalist economies is Joseph Schumpeter.[40] His concept of 'creative destruction'[41] captures the evolutionary nature of free-markets where established ways of doing things are replaced by new

---

[36] In fact the origins of the Oyster ticketing card system are Hong Kong's Mass Transit Railway (MTR) which implemented its Octopus card over 20 years ago in 1997, with trials starting three years earlier in 1993.

[37] Disruptive innovation may be either a significant change or improvement primarily achieved with technology. See IOSCO (2016) Securities Markets Risk Outlook, at p.27.

[38] Sheridan, I (2017) 'MiFID II in the context of Financial Technology and Regulatory Technology', *Capital Markets Law Journal*, Volume 12, Issue 4, at 417–427, sets out in detail my original writing on what FinTech encompasses. Available at https://doi.org/10.1093/cmlj/kmx036.

[39] Part of the creative energy of FinTech can derive from low budgets, accepting that innovation has often proven to thrive on paucity. But tight cost-management is hardly unique to FinTech businesses.

[40] See www.econ.univie.ac.at/de/institut/geschichte-des-instituts; and www.iss-evec.de/info. Schumpeter became famous as a Professor of Economics at Harvard University, but he started his academic career reading law at the University of Vienna.

[41] A direct translation from the German *Schöpferische Zerstörung*.

ones.[42] In essence, new entrants to existing markets tend to succeed when introducing significant improvements.[43]

Typically, disruptive innovation involves a new business entering an established market and competing successfully with innovative products or services against the formidable market share and entrenched alliances of incumbents. Looking at the rise of Wise in the foreign exchange market underlines how unintuitive and astonishingly effective disruptive innovation can be.[44] Innovation lies at the centre of modern capitalism, where providers of goods and services seek to take the initiative over competitors. Even when a product or service reaches a high level of refinement, it is often replaced, unexpectedly, with new offerings that cost less, are quicker and are often of higher quality. Throughout this book there are references to IBM, because it is at the forefront of AI, cloud computing and quantum computing. But IBM is also a memorable example of a victim of disruptive innovation. IBM's global success was built around the mainframe computer. During the 1990s IBM profits plunged, partly because of both increased personal computer (PC) use and greater competition from other semiconductor technology businesses. At the beginning of the 1990s these developments were inconceivable.[45]

Legacy-free technology systems tend to be found in small and medium-sized enterprises (SMEs), but even the largest global banks can adapt and choose to 'start up' a new FinTech company autonomous from its group-wide information technology (IT) systems. The repeated pattern in financial services markets is to remember that disruption may also derive from established incumbent firms with the resources and client base to make a long-term success of a new way of doing things, enabled or supported by cutting-edge technology.[46]

---

[42] For example, if we buy a financial regulation practitioner book online we are direct beneficiaries of creative destruction, because capitalist legal systems have allowed consumers to order over the Internet.

[43] Mueller, D, and Cantner, U (eds) (2000) *Capitalism and Socialism in the 21st Century* (Springer Publishing). Also available at www.iss-evec.de/info.

[44] Wise was previously called Transferwise, but rebranded in February 2021. See https://wise.com/.

[45] Gerstner, L (2003) *Who Says Elephants Can't Dance?* (Harper Collins), at 63.

[46] Disruptive innovation may be either a significant change or improvement primarily achieved with technology. See IOSCO (2016) Securities Markets Risk Outlook, at 27.

The term asynchronous compliance characterises the recurring challenge that FinTech companies face, namely business strategies and operations that are developing at markedly different speeds compared with financial regulation. For legislators and regulators globally there is the complexity of keeping pace with rapid change in how technology is deployed for managing, marketing and processing vast amounts of data, money and many different forms of capital market risk. For example, in 2021 JP Morgan conducted a survey of fixed income, currencies and commodities (FICC) traders, 33 per cent of whom believed the use of mobile trading applications was the most important trend.[47] The central challenge for regulators has been memorably encapsulated in the conclusion that they need 'to be willing to experiment quickly and learn from mistakes ... They need to be as innovative as the innovators.'[48]

---

[47]   JP Morgan (2021) FICC e-Trading 2021 Survey See www.jpmorgan.com/solutions/cib/markets/etradingsurvey2021.

[48]   Friedman, TL (2016) *Thank You For Being Late – An Optimist's Guide to Thriving in the Age of Accelerations* (Penguin), at 34–35.

2. Accountability

This chapter addresses the liability of risk managers regulated under the FCA's Senior Managers Regime.[1] The sections on the Senior Managers Regime are of interest to both legal and compliance functions. However, the first section on professional negligence is of specific relevance to in-house legal counsel and externally instructed lawyers.

2.1 English common law professional negligence

For both in-house and private practice legal counsel there is the risk of common law negligence liability in the context of technology operating in or connected to a financial services firm. Liability for negligence can stem from a number of acts or omissions.[2] Lawyers are central to drafting what should be done, not done, audited, checked and monitored. As a frequent task, the drafting, negotiation and signing of contracts can seem to be the beginning of the end. Yet, the networked nature of technology, the immense reliance on trading systems and IT systems generally, mean that the contract is simply recording some of the possible future risk scenarios – the end of the beginning. Subsequent to signing a contract, there are inevitable delays in implementation of systems, errors in data and outages of computer systems that all require gradations of response and expense to correct faults.

---

[1] The FCA is the conduct regulator for all FSMA-authorised firms. To understand the full list of businesses that are dual-regulated, therefore also regulated by the PRA, see PRA-regulated Activities Order 2013, SI 2013/556.

[2] As an important aside, lawyers from some European civil jurisdictions will be used to drafting 'gross negligence' as a defined concept, differentiating it from 'negligence'. However, the English High Courts make no differentiation between the two concepts. In *Camerata Property Inc v Credit Suisse Securities (Europe) Ltd* (Rev 1) [2011] EWHC 479 (Comm), per HHJ Smith at 161, it was observed that the focus is not on whether gross negligence is an accepted concept under English law, but rather on its meaning in the terms and conditions agreed between the parties.

A Supreme Court decision provides a two-stage test on the risk assessments expected from any professional adviser. By which is meant this decision applies across all advisory businesses, and not solely to the financial services sector.[3] In short, the decision can be interpreted requiring quality control tests to check that products recommended by an adviser to an investor include communicating: (a) any material risks in the investment choices, and (b) any reasonable alternative.

While front office managers are interacting directly with clients, legal counsel and compliance officers have responsibilities to ensure contracts, product explanations and websites accurately summarise: (a) material risks, and (b) include information on reasonable alternatives. The Supreme Court interprets that material risks include assessing whether the specific person being advised is likely to see the risks as significant. That interpretation of material risk implies the need for human-based communication between adviser and client, a point followed in an English High Court decision applying the same *Montgomery v Lanarkshire Health Board* two-stage test.[4]

This two-stage test has increasing importance, because material risks include potential biases from the use of AI systems, typically based on machine learning algorithms.[5] There is also the risk of AI systems drifting from what was intended, something that is more likely to occur if on-going checks are neglected. To take an example from Asian jurisdictions, a 2020 survey of 168 banks in Hong Kong and mainland China conducted by the Hong Kong Monetary Authority (HKMA) found that only 68 per cent of regulated firms[6] using AI had regular reviews to identify AI-related risks.[7] Therefore, legal risk analysis has to think through the level of material risk from machine learning algorithms when they initially form part of a financial service, and what risks could emerge over time.

---

[3]   See the two-stage subjective test in *Montgomery v Lanarkshire Health Board* [2015] UKSC 11, at paragraph 87.

[4]   *O'Hare v Coutts* [2016] EWHC 2224 (QB), at paragraph 204.

[5]   Chapter 12 Machine learning considers this sub-branch of artificial intelligence.

[6]   To break down the sample, it was made up of 27 retail banks and 141 non-retail banks.

[7]   HKMA (2020) Artificial Intelligence in Banking – The changing landscape in Compliance and Supervision, at 22. To break down this sample, it was made up of 27 retail banks and 141 non-retail banks.

2.1.1   The rejection of an established objective test

Those familiar with English common law negligence precedent will also be aware that the English High Courts have for several decades applied an objective standard of judgement expected of any professional adviser, namely the *Bolam* test.[8] However, in both the Supreme Court *Montgomery v Lanarkshire Health Board* decision, and in *O'Hare v Coutts*, the *Bolam* test was specifically rejected. The *Bolam* test requires proving that the advice given is on a par with advice expected to be given by a reasonable practitioner at the same level of expertise as the person providing the actual advice. In sum, lawyers now need to also ensure the communication of material risk and alternative options.

2.1.2   Evidential proof for dispute resolution or regulators

Applying the *Montgomery v Lanarkshire Health Board* two-stage test relevant to accusations of negligence, there is corroborative evidential value in recording (a) what was communicated to individual clients, and (b) the written advice and risk warnings supplied. The FCA has record-keeping requirements for written material, but there may need to be extra due diligence required to dig out meeting notes and presentations provided to specific clients. A client may have originated from another division and often made contact with more than one employee in more than one jurisdiction. This due diligence may be time consuming, but it could yield crucial records of what and how the client was cumulatively informed about the terms of product details, risk factors and alternative options.

2.2   The position of FCA rules

The position of FCA rules in the context of common law precedent, statutes and secondary legislation is often confused or at least not communicated with an explicit signalling on the hierarchy and influence of each type of rule. Under pressure of time, it is logical to start with the FCA Handbook. Thereafter, to work backwards, if required, all the way to the primary legislation. In the context of senior managers, the primary leg-

---

[8]   *Bolam v Friern Hospital Management Committee* [1957] 1 WLR 583.

islation is most often the Financial Services (Banking Reform) Act 2013[9] and the Bank of England Financial Services Act 2016,[10] both amending the Financial Services and Markets Act 2000 (FSMA).[11] The short answer to capturing the authority of FCA rules in legal analysis on liability is 'it depends'. When drafting financial services terms of business, whether for an asset manager or bank or other regulated firm, there is often catch-all wording that 'all Applicable Law' applies, which is defined to include, among other things, 'regulations, guidance, usage and custom'. It is timely to summarise what these are, because many issues that legal and compliance functions are asked to advise on are driven by 'regulations, guidance, usage and custom'. It is important to know the limits of corporate and individual liability so that time is spent addressing everything in a proportionate, thorough way.[12]

2.2.1   Statutory interpretation

First, the way to address the validity of any law, regulation, or usage is to start the analysis based on principles of statutory interpretation.[13] It is not necessary to provide an in-depth summary of principles of statutory interpretation, but it is timely to clarify a robust way of applying FSMA and FCA rules so that the right time is spent analysing the most relevant legal references that will ultimately have a potential effect on liability.

FCA Handbook rules derive from secondary legislation, namely numerous statutory instruments providing substantial detail on what is required on specific activities. This secondary legislation is subject to the Interpretation Act 1978. However, case law indicates these secondary regulations can be used to construe the parent Act, here the FSMA, when they come into operation on the same day as the parent Act.[14] The

---

[9]   Specifically Sections 18–38 Financial Services (Banking Reform) Act 2013, amending Part 5 of FSMA 2000.

[10]   Sections 21–25 and Schedule 4 Bank of England Financial Services Act 2016. See www.legislation.gov .uk/ukpga/2016/14/contents/enacted.

[11]   www.legislation.gov.uk/ukpga/2000/8/contents.

[12]   Lomnicka, E, and Powell, J (eds) (2020) *Encyclopedia of Financial Services* (Sweet & Maxwell), is an authoritative, voluminous work on financial services regulation.

[13]   Bailey, D, and Norbury, L (2020) *Bennion, Bailey and Norbury on Statutory Interpretation* (LexisNexis) is a detailed publication covering statutory interpretation.

[14]   *Hanlon v Law Society* [1981] AC 124, per Lord Lowry.

Supreme Court has pointed out that this principle of interpretation[15] can be extended to regulations closely timed with the Act.[16] Therefore, the interpretation of any subsequent post-2001 FSMA regulations requires cautious reading.

Three further points assist the process of interpretation. First, a rational approach when dealing with any later ambiguity in post-2001 FSMA statutory instruments is to read, in order of logic: (a) FSMA; (b) regulations published at or around the same time as FSMA; (c) subsequent post-2001 FSMA statutory instruments; (d) the FCA Handbook. That approach is supported by the fact that any activity-specific rules have to be read in conjunction with rule 2.2.12G of the General Provisions Sourcebook (GEN).[17] GEN 2.2.12R states the expressions used in the Handbook have the same meanings found in the Interpretation Act 1978 'unless the contrary intention appears'.[18]

Second, everything that is in the FCA Handbook provides rules on a specific activity. For example trading or advising on investments has to be read in the context of guidance, simultaneously remembering that guidance sections are only purposive assistance and are not prescriptive rules by another name. The FCA Handbook is labyrinthine in nature, but nearly all rules provide some guidance. GEN 2.2.2G clarifies that '[t]he guidance given on the purpose of a provision is intended as an explanation to assist readers of the [FCA] Handbook. As such, guidance may assist the reader in assessing the purpose of the provision, but it should not be taken as a complete or definitive explanation of a provision's purpose.'[19]

Third, evidential provisions intuitively sound prescriptive, but in fact they serve as a pointer to the FSMA, which states that any rule made by a regulator (FCA or PRA) can set down that:

- contravention may be relied on as tending to establish contravention of such other rule made by that regulator as may be specified, or
- compliance may be relied on as tending to establish compliance with

---

[15] Ibid. There are in fact several principles of statutory interpretation throughout the *Hanlon v Law Society* judgment, so it is a rich seam.

[16] *Deposit Protection Board v Dalia* [1994] 2 All ER 577 at 585.

[17] www.handbook.fca.org.uk/handbook/GEN/2/2.html.

[18] FCA GEN 2.2.12(1)G.

[19] FCA GEN 2.2.2.G.

such other rule made by that regulator as may be specified.[20]

The significance of FSMA, s.138C(2), is that any portion of the Handbook providing evidential provisions, which must be marked with a capital letter 'E',[21] is a potential action for corroborating compliance or a possible rule breach based on an omission. Importantly, GEN 2.2.3R makes clear that FCA Handbook evidential provisions, as allowed under the FSMA, cannot breach any other provisions of the FSMA.[22] In this way the hierarchy of statutory interpretation is not undermined.

The letter 'D' for Directions also deserves brief explanation. Under the FSMA and related secondary legislation, Directions are binding upon the person or categories of persons to whom they are addressed. Further detail on the treatment of Handbook status letters is found in Chapter 6 of the FCA Reader's Guide.[23]

2.2.2   Statutory liability under the FSMA

There is a limited statutory right of action by a 'private person' in the context of a regulated firm breaching FCA rules.[24] Further, High Court case law has reconfirmed that apart from private persons under FSMA, s. 138D, there is no direct right of statutory action for breach of FCA conduct rules for any type of corporate entity.[25]

2.3   Senior managers under the FCA rules

Senior management omitting to do the right thing is a repeated pattern across all recent collapses of financial services firms. To cite just three examples, within Barings Bank (1995), Long-Term Capital Management (1998) and Lehman Brothers (2008), senior managers all played a pivotal or substantial role in their respective failures. Unsurprisingly, the Global

---

[20] Section 138C FSMA 2000.

[21] FCA GEN 2.2.3(2)R.

[22] Section 138C FSMA 2000.

[23] The FCA Reader's Handbook provides explanations on not only D, but also the significance of the status letters R, G, E, UK, EU, P and C.

[24] Section 138D FSMA 2000.

[25] *Target Rich v Forex Capital Markets* [2020] EWHC 1544 (Comm); *Titan Steel Wheels Ltd v The Royal Bank of Scotland plc* [2020] EWHC 211.

Financial Crisis 2007–2008 acted as the specific catalyst to make senior managers more accountable.

2.3.1 Senior legal managers versus the senior managers regime

From the first quarter (Q1) of 2016, dual-regulated banks, those regulated by both the FCA and PRA, have been subject to the new Senior Managers and Certification Regime (SMCR). Since Q4 2019 the SMCR has applied to most solo-regulated firms.[26] Under FSMA, s. 59ZA, the most senior managers in a financial services firm are ultimately responsible for risks that may have serious consequences for an authorised person,[27] another business or other interests in the UK. As an exception, in the opinion of the FCA, FSMA, s. 59ZA, does not include the legal function.[28]

The FCA's current Senior Managers Regime (SMR), has its rules and guidance set out in the Senior Management Arrangements, Systems and Controls (SYSC) part of the FCA Handbook.[29] The FCA's definition of 'legal function', set out in SYSC 26.4.10, includes the provision of legal advice relevant to assisting the regulated firm or with any form of dispute resolution. Further, this definition covers a 'reserved activity' under Legal Services Act 2007, s. 12,[30] when carried out for the firm or intra-group; and any of the activities covered in Solicitors (Scotland) Act 1980, s. 32(1),[31] carried out for the firm or intra-group.

The legal justification for excluding the legal function from the SMR is based on upholding an important part of the rule of law, namely legal privilege. The principle of legal privilege is that legal counsel advice cannot be disclosed unless the advice is to enable the client to commit

---

[26] Section 2(4) Bank of England and Financial Services Act 2016 (Commencement No. 6 and Transitional Provisions) Regulations 2019 provides that for all solo-regulated firms, except benchmark firms, the SM&CR applies to all solo-regulated firms from 9 December 2019. See www.legislation.gov.uk/uksi/2019/1136/regulation/2/made.

[27] Under Section 31 FSMA 2000 'authorised persons' includes both individuals performing a specific regulated role under the FSMA and any regulated firm.

[28] FCA, Optimising the Senior Managers and Certification Regime, Final Rules, PS19/20 at 2.20. See www.fca.org.uk/publication/policy/ps19-20.pdf.

[29] See www.handbook.fca.org.uk/handbook/SYSC/1/1A.html.

[30] www.legislation.gov.uk/ukpga/2007/29/section/12.

[31] www.legislation.gov.uk/ukpga/1980/46/section/32.

a criminal act or a fraud. Lord Scott's analysis in the leading *Three Rivers District Council* judgment encapsulates the reasoning this way:

> in the complex world in which we live there are a multitude of reasons why individuals ... or corporations, whether large or small, may need to seek the advice or assistance of lawyers in connection with their affairs ... they recognise that in order for the advice to bring about that desirable result it is essential that the full and complete facts are placed before the lawyers who are to give it ... and they recognise that unless the clients can be assured that what they tell their lawyers will not be disclosed by the lawyers without their (the clients') consent, there will be cases in which the requisite candour will be absent.[32]

In many boutique and newly formed asset managers, banks, private equity firms and other FCA regulated businesses, the tasks of a General Counsel or Head of Legal is a mix of 'legal and compliance', because a recurring risk is how FCA rules are captured in contracts to operational effect and to ensure processes and policies are congruent with regulation, regulators expectations and to avoid disputes. This triggers the question would a registered compliance oversight senior management function (SMF16) be excluded from simultaneously acting as the legal function? It would not exclude an SMF16 from providing the legal advice and support that the FCA rules under the SYSC view to be legal function work, but clearly it would dilute the effectiveness of obtaining information under the common law principle of legal privilege. Further, the FCA has confirmed that individuals performing both legal function and SMF16 compliance function responsibilities would still need to be registered as SMF16 with the FCA.

Even if the SMR does not apply to a legal counsel directly, there are, in my view, a number of aspects of the SMR to which lawyers need to contribute as part of their professional responsibilities to manage legal risk. Indeed, as part of a regulated firm they are still subject to the FCA Certification Regime and Code of Conduct rules.[33] The individual FCA

---

[32]   *Three Rivers District Council & Ors v Bank of England* [2004] UKHL 48 (11 November 2004), per Lord Scott at 34.

[33]   For an excellent transcript of a video by FCA staff explaining the essential features of SMCR, see www .fca.org.uk/publication/transcripts/senior-managers-certification-regime-video-transcript-july-2018 .pdf.

Code of Conduct rules require, among other things, acting with integrity, due skill, care, diligence and skill.[34]

2.4   Three pillars of accountability

The Head of Legal function remains indirectly accountable as a senior team manager managing risks that affect the regulated firm, its employees and external businesses and other actors. Generally, that requires the legal and compliance functions communicating with the peer heads of compliance, operations and risk on a regular basis. In many instances, given technology is involved, there will be a need to communicate with the head of technology. This most senior technology professional is normally either titled Chief Technology Officer or Chief Information Officer. Further, depending on the size of the firm, there may also be regular contact with the Chief Executive Officer, Chief Financial Officer, Chief Operations Officer and Chief Risk Officer.

The senior management function (SMF) that frequently takes on registered SMF responsibility for technology is the chief operations function (SMF24). However, this is not set in stone, given each regulated firm evolves in different ways. For instance, often FinTech firms are founded by one or more technology professionals, so one of these individuals is often either the Chief Executive Officer (SMF1) or chief finance officer (SMF2). Whether SMF1 or SMF2, he or she is simultaneously leading business strategy and acting as the most senior technology risk manager.[35]

When so many functions and tasks in financial services involve computing systems and data, it is unsurprising that technology risk has risen from a peripheral concern to a core one for all board level executive officers. Before Andrew Bailey became the Governor of the Bank of England he led the FCA. In his capacity as Chief Executive of the FCA he contributed to a UK Parliament report on technology failures in the financial ser-

---

[34]   FCA COCON 2.1.

[35]   Currently, SMF24 applies to a broad range of regulated firms, including banks, building societies, dual-regulated investment firms and solo-regulated firms. However, the SMR does not apply to Financial Market Infrastructure (FMI) firms, for example payment systems. However, it is likely to be extended to FMI firms given disruption to technology can affect significant numbers of customers.

vices sector.[36] In that report there was reference to his oral evidence. He concluded there are two immediate regulator measures to take when IT outages occur. First, the remuneration of the responsible staff, as reflected in the remuneration policies of each regulated firm, should include the consequences of disruptions in the control of IT systems. Second, there will be responsibility under the SMR.[37]

From a senior manager liability perspective, in my view, there are three pillars that require special attention when assisting the individual responsible for technology. These are (a) to know the boundaries, the remit of the SMF responsible for technology; (b) to check the drafting of the Statement of Responsibilities and its practical execution; and (c) to check the drafting of the Management Responsibilities Map and its practical implementation.

Each pillar avoids or mitigates regulatory risks. Further, each provides evidence of a compliance culture. These three pillars can be imagined as a supporting horizontal arch across a firm. On the arch are chiselled the words: 'The Culture of Compliance', reflecting the FCA's expectations that all regulated financial services firms possess it. Failure to support a culture of compliance is treated seriously.[38] To develop the metaphor further, the arch sitting on top of these three pillars is not easily measured and should evolve over time. But the three pillars are recorded evidence of intent, and indeed the regulator will seek to compare how versions of each pillar have improved and become more sophisticated over time to keep pace with market developments, including technological advances. That is implicitly clear by the FCA requirement for most firms to keep certain types of formal SYSC documents for a period of up to 10 years.[39]

---

[36] House of Commons Treasury Select Committee (2019–2020) IT Failures in the Financial Services Sector.

[37] In this context, a clear performance objective criterion is no or minimal disruption to key IT systems. FCA SYSC 19B.1.10R applies specifically to a regulated firm performing AIFM investment management functions, and requires that those performing control functions are remunerated 'according to the achievement of the objectives linked to their functions, independent of the performance of the business areas they control'. Note elsewhere in the FCA SYSC Handbook are set out remuneration codes for other regulated firms, including dual-regulated and UCITs.

[38] FCA Final Notice, *Sonali Bank (UK) Limited*, 12 October 2016, fine of £3,250,600.

[39] FCA SYSC Sch 1.2G, includes guidance to keep past versions of a firm's management responsibilities for 10 years from the date the current registered document is superseded.

2.5   Technological boundaries

First, the remit of the SMF24 is not something that can be based on the logic and general experience of even exceptionally experienced human resources managers. Further, it would be insufficiently diligent to rely on the responsibilities captured in a contract of employment alone, because that might create gaps or simply be too detailed to be of practical significance or become out of date as technology advances or simply changes to become more robust.

Instead, the best legal risk approach is, in my view, to apply the following seven areas to the SMF24 role, provided as guidance by the FCA in its Supervision Manual:[40]

- business continuity, including responsibility for covering specific compliance rules;[41]
- cyber security;
- information technology;
- internal operations;
- operational continuity, resilience and strategy;
- outsourcing, procurement and vendor management; and
- management of services shared intra-group.

If a regulated firm does not have an SMF24, these seven areas of responsibility have to be allocated among its existing SMF managers.[42] The role of legal counsel includes making clear the consequences of inaction by the senior manager responsible for technology used in operations. Under the FSMA the FCA can take disciplinary action against an individual senior manager who does 'not take such steps as [he or she] ... could reasonably be expected to avoid the contravention occurring (or continuing)'.[43] The contravention refers to any relevant regulatory requirement by the senior manager's firm. In short, the senior manager has to apply a standard

---

[40]   FCA SUP 10C.6B.4G. For readers interested in remote working risk management, the Singaporean regulator has collaborated on a paper setting out recommended mitigation practices. See Monetary Authority of Singapore and Association of Banks of Singapore (2021) Risk Management and Operational Resilience in a Remote Working Environment.

[41]   FCA SYSC 4.1.6R and SYSC 4.1.7R are business continuity rules that also have to be covered by the SMF24. However, these rules do not apply to every firm.

[42]   FCA SUP 10C.6B.5G.

[43]   Section 66A(5) FSMA 2000.

of diligence based on taking reasonable steps. Suitable training for the SMF24 and other SMFs on this diligence standard, and all other conduct rules, is a statutory requirement for regulated firms under the FSMA.[44] In many situations legal counsel and compliance officers are the combined means by which code of conduct training occurs.

The FCA Enforcement Division has provided some colour on FCA expectations concerning 'reasonable steps'. There is an expectation of considerable action, whether from personal effort, delegating in-house, outsourcing or instructing external experts. From a transcript of a speech the following comments, among others, were made:

> It has been said that a person who takes reasonable steps is one who does not exhibit a negligent or reprehensible state of mind, who is conscientious ... observing, asking questions and so informed and informing, being vigilant, deciding, guiding and monitoring, oversighting, delegating when safe to do so to those who are well placed, and only acting beyond expertise and experience with competent expert advice.[45]

2.5.1 Statement of responsibilities

In the FCA's guidance on providing a Statement of Responsibilities for each SMF,[46] its rules require that a regulated firm makes appropriate and clear apportionment decisions amongst its senior managers.[47] Further, there are not only general on-going requirements for detailed record keeping,[48] but also a specific statutory duty to update the FCA[49] on any significant changes to any Statement of Responsibilities.[50] The meaning of significant change is set out in the Supervision Handbook (SUP).[51]

Any application for approval of an SMF must be lodged with a Statement of Responsibilities.[52] Detailed guidance on what Statements of

---

[44] Section 64B FSMA 2000.

[45] www.fca.org.uk/news/speeches/tackling-hard-questions

[46] FCA SUP 10C.11G.

[47] FCA SYSC 2.1.1R.

[48] FCA SYSC 9.1R.

[49] For some firms the appropriate regulator to inform would be the PRA.

[50] Section 62A FSMA 2000.

[51] FCA SUP 10C.11.6G.

[52] Section 60(2A) FSMA 2000.

Responsibilities should contain is provided in the FCA SUP.[53] An essential attribute expected of all Statements of Responsibilities is consistency across documentation registered with the FCA. Each Statement of Responsibilities must be consistent with the apportionment of responsibilities given to other SMFs.[54] For example, if there is an ambiguity concerning which SMF is responsible for a specific area of supervision. In the scenario of a planned decision to split a responsibility making two SMFs joint responsibility for something, there needs to be clarity on 'what part of which responsibility or function' is covered by each SMF.[55] Further, each Statement of Responsibilities must be consistent with the regulated firm's Management Responsibilities Map.[56]

2.5.2   Management Responsibilities Maps

Another detailed document required by the FCA is a Management Responsibilities Map. It is not simply a visual overview in the sense of a graphical map or corporate organisation chart. The Management Responsibilities Map is more accurately described as a single gap analysis dossier or manual. It must be a single document, but that document may contain numerous sections.

There is helpful practical feedback from the FCA on Management Responsibilities Maps assessed to be inadequate. Important criticism includes (a) insufficient detail about reporting lines, and (b) lack of clarity on relationships between one firm and another related firm within a group of companies.[57] Every regulated firm to whom SMCR applies must lodge a Management Responsibilities Map with the FCA and keep that document up-to-date. The core aspects required are detail on:

- reporting lines;
- responsibility lines;
- names of the senior managers responsible;
- responsibilities assigned to each senior manager(s);
- indication on how responsibilities are divided or shared.[58]

---

[53]   FCA SUP 10C.11.23G.
[54]   FCA SUP 10C.11.23(1A)G.
[55]   FCA SUP 10C.11.31G.
[56]   FCA SUP 10C.11.23(2)G.
[57]   FCA FS16, at 7.1 to 7.4.
[58]   FCA SYSC 25.2.1R and 25.2.2R.

The specific requirements the FCA expects to find in each Management Responsibilities Map include the reasoning behind any division of responsibility between senior managers, creating joint responsibility.[59] In the context of technology it would be logical for many regulated firms to make key IT systems a joint responsibility. For example, the risk management of business continuity linked to IT migration projects alone is going to be, in my view, of sufficient importance to make both (a) the Chief Operations Officer or Chief Financial Officer, and (b) the Chief Technology Officer or Chief Information Officer, a sensible joint responsibility task force. The Chief Operations Officer or Chief Financial Officer has credibility with the board on issues of group operational, market and strategic risks, and the Chief Technology Officer or Chief Information Officer has the technical grasp to explain how IT projects are planned and implemented.

In a report commissioned by TSB to look into its disastrous decision to have a single event IT system migration, in effect a 'big bang' migration, it is notable that the TSB board was provided with no independent expert advice on its options for migration. A phased migration approach would have been more cautious, but far more expensive. In the opinion of Slaughter and May – the international law firm commissioned by TSB to conduct an independent review of the project's failure, including decision making and governance – at no point before the decision to choose a single event migration did the TSB board or any executive level director request expert external advice.

Incisive observations from the TSB review included that it was 'difficult to see how a single individual would be able to provide all of the advice that the TSB Board needed'.[60] In practice, only an external advisory firm could have mitigated the risks. Further, that 'an external advisory firm would have highlighted to the TSB Board the risk of proceeding with a predominantly single event migration'.[61] Ultimately, the TSB migration failure resulted in extra costs for TSB exceeding £330 million.

---

[59] FCA SYSC Rule 25.2.3.

[60] Slaughter and May (2019) An Independent Review following TSB's Migration onto a New IT Platform in April 2018, at 22.32.

[61] Ibid., at 22.34(C).

Corroborating the lessons from the TSB migration, an FCA review examined how regulated firms implement technological change. The FCA statistical analysis was based on a very small sample of just 23 firms. However, it is notable that the FCA findings included the result that in 24 per cent of high severity incidents the primary cause of operational disruption was technology change failure.[62]

In sum, the Management Responsibilities Map may act as an important governance document for the board of any regulated firm. For technology projects of high risk it is sensible for joint responsibility between two SMFs of which the Chief Operations Officer or equivalent would be included. Further, when the consequences of a failed IT project are high in costs and reputational damage, the reasonable steps expected of a Chief Operations Officer will certainly include seeking external expert advice and sharing that advice with the board. Lawyers play an important role in drafting all the aforementioned reasoning into the Management Responsibilities Map and checking that the Management Responsibilities of all relevant SMFs are clear and consistent on what is required. For example, this task may include ensuring that specific international standards are recorded in contracts and policies; for example, ISO 22301, which specifically focuses on business continuity.[63]

2.5.3 The whole is greater than the sum of its parts

In combination, the importance of both the Statements of Responsibilities and the Management Responsibilities Maps cannot be understated. FCA decision making factors to decide if a senior operations manager was

---

[62] FCA (2021) Implementing Technology Change – Multi-firms Review.

[63] Additionally, for legal counsel there is the crucial task of drafting precise liability clauses for complex technology implementation projects. In a case that ended up in the Supreme Court, a commodities trading software implementation project contract extended to 507 pages. On the interpretation of whether 'negligence' in a clause covering an exception to a cap on the contractor's liability for damages meant the technical tort of negligence or whether it included breach of the contractual duty of skill and care, a majority ruled it covered both. However, there were two dissenting judgments. Further, Lord Sales commented that the whole contract was not well drafted, especially the liability clause. See *Triple Point Technology, Inc v PTT Public Company Ltd* [2021] UKSC 29, 16 July 2021.

responsible for a contravention of a relevant requirement under the FSMA include:[64]

- the SMF manager's Statement of Responsibilities;
- the firm's Management Responsibilities Map;
- how the firm operated, including how responsibilities were allocated in practice;
- the SMF manager's actual role and responsibilities, based on, among other things, emails, minutes of meetings, organisational diagrams, regulatory interviews and telephone recordings;
- the relationship between the SMF manager's responsibilities compared with those of other SMF managers, including any joint responsibilities or matrix management reporting structures.[65]

2.6   Managing conflicts of interest

Accountability for board level decision making, including high value technology procurement decisions, is continually vulnerable to conflicts of interest and needs cautious management. Identifying and preventing conflicts of interest is a principle of MiFID.[66] In my view, legal and compliance professionals are best placed to contribute to avoiding conflicts of interest that breach FCA rules and potentially harm the reputation of the business.

Under the Companies Act 2006 all directors are expected to avoid scenarios in which they have or may potentially have a direct or indirect interest that conflicts with the 'interests of the company'.[67] However, the management of conflicts of interest in all financial services firms goes well beyond board level. Further, not all SMF are directors in this Companies Act 2006 sense of a registered director, so it would never be enough for SMFs to follow UK corporate governance guidance.

Under SYSC there is a requirement for a regulated firm to identify actual or potential conflicts between a regulated firm and clients. Further, the

---

[64]   Section 66A(5) FSMA 2000.
[65]   FCA DEPP 6.2.9C.
[66]   Article 23 MiFID.
[67]   Section 175 Companies Act 2006.

firm needs to spot actual or potential conflicts between its employees, managers and representatives, and clients.[68] The identification process can be viewed as a two-limbed test based on (a) potential damage to the interests of a client, and (b) the regulated firm or its employee, manager or representative having an interest in the outcome. For regulated firms executing orders for clients there are also detailed best execution rules in MiFID.[69]

The types of conflicts that a regulated firm must identify and manage are characterised in SYSC and can be summarised as:

- financial gain or the avoidance of financial loss at the expense of the client;
- an interest in the outcome of a service or transaction provided to the client or which is distinct from the client's interest in that outcome;
- a financial gain or incentive from favouring the interest of another client or group of clients over the interests of the client;
- carries on the same business as the client;
- receipt of an inducement from someone other than the client other than the standard commission or fee for that service.[70]

For certain types of regulated firms, for example Undertakings for Collective Investment in Transferable Securities (UCITS) management companies,[71] practical implementation of the SYSC conflicts rules will include the need to draft a conflicts of interest policy 'appropriate to the size and organisation of the firm and the nature, scale and complexity of its business'.[72] However, drafting such a policy document is a sensible step for any regulated firm.

---

[68]   FCA SYSC 10.1.3R.

[69]   Article 27 MiFID.

[70]   FCA SYSC 10.1.4R. This FCA rule includes a management company under Article 2(1)(b) UCITS, Directive 2009/65/EC, namely 'a company, the regular business of which is the management of UCITS in the form of common funds or of investment companies (collective portfolio management of UCITS)'.

[71]   Under Article 2(1)(b) UCITS, Directive 2009/65/EC, a management company refers to 'a company, the regular business of which is the management of UCITS in the form of common funds or of investment companies (collective portfolio management of UCITS)'.

[72]   FCA SYSC 10.1.10R.

There is a long-established requirement to record conflicts.[73] These records should be kept for five years.[74] Compliance officers or legal counsel should be involved in the setting up and management of that process to ensure consistency of approach with the agreed conflicts policy. It is notable in this context that private equity firms, typically made up of highly competent approved persons, have been scrutinised by the FSA, the FCA's predecessor. Interestingly, that financial services regulator's analysis included a detailed list of potential private equity manager conflicts of interest.[75] A subsequent 2007 FSA thematic exercise on conflicts of interests in private equity recommended the use of a conflicts register.

2.7   Case study: EU ombudsman investigation on EC contract with BlackRock

While not an example of a conflict of interest breach based on technology procurement or use, there is a memorable example of poor conflict of interest management in the EU Ombudsman decision concerning the instruction of BlackRock Investment Management (UK) Limited ('BlackRock') to produce a report for the European Commission (EC).

Before March 2021, environmental, social and governance (ESG) rules were vague.[76] So before the current ESG disclosure rules were formed the EC sought expert insight on how to integrate ESG sustainability factors into EU financial services regulations. The EC produced a tender document. Nine tenderers competed. BlackRock was the only investment manager that submitted a tender bid. Subsequently, the EC awarded the report writing contract to BlackRock. A group of Members of the European Parliament complained to the EU Ombudsman.

---

[73]   FCA SYSC 10.1.6R.

[74]   FCA SYSC Sch 1.2G.

[75]   FSA 2006, Discussion Paper 06/06, Private Equity: A Discussion of Risk and Regulatory Engagement, at 4.59–4.61.

[76]   EU Regulation 2019/2088, on sustainability-related disclosures in the financial services sector, in force in the UK from 10 March 2021.

Facts relied on by the EU Ombudsman in its conflicts of interest assessment included:

- BlackRock is the world's largest asset manager with more than $7 trillion assets under management, and no other asset manager made a tender bid;
- BlackRock offered to complete the report for €280,000, yet the initial estimated total value of the contract published in the EC's tender notice was €550,000 – an offer of just over half the estimated maximum value;
- at the time of the tender submission BlackRock had substantial investments in large fossil fuel companies and systemically important banks. Given the impact of any ESG rules there was a potential motivation to influence ESG policy making to improve or protect its own investments;
- BlackRock was a member of several lobby groups that advocate specific approaches to the application of ESG factors into EU regulation for banks.

The EU Ombudsman investigated the procurement decision making of the EC and concluded that the EC's decision to select BlackRock revealed an inadequate conflict of interest analysis showing a lack of vigilance.[77] The EU Ombudsman found that:

> the Commission should have been more vigilant in terms of verifying that the company was not subject to a conflict of interest that could negatively affect the performance of the contract. The decision to award the contract to the company did not provide sufficient guarantees to exclude any legitimate doubt as to the risk of conflicts of interest that could negatively impact the performance of the contract.[78]

2.8   UK Corporate Governance Code

Finally, a logical question for senior managers, whether working in asset managers, investment banks, platforms or FinTech SMEs, is do they have

---

[77] Blackrock's own conflicts of interest policy and measures were not an issue. Indeed, part of the comfort the EC gained before awarding the contract was from the robust information barriers in place within BlackRock.

[78] Decision of the European Ombudsman 853/2020/KR, at paragraph 61.

to apply the UK Corporate Governance Code 2018 (the 'Code'). Does it still apply to the board given the detailed and formal administrative requirements of the SMCR? The Code[79] continues to apply across all companies listed on the London Stock Exchange (LSE), and is adopted voluntarily by many non-listed UK financial services firms. Moreover, its application is treated by the FCA as corroborative evidence that obligations under the SYSC 3.1.1.R have been met.[80]

---

[79] The current Code is managed by the Financial Reporting Council.

[80] FCA SYSC 3.1.3G.

3. Cloud computing

Roy Amara, a scientist at the Stanford Research Institute and a former president of The Institute for the Future, is attributed with inventing a law of technology – *Amara's law*. More an observation on behaviour and time patterns, rather than a black letter law, it states that in the short term we tend to overestimate and hype new technology; conversely in the long term its effects are underestimated. Cloud computing is a mature but underestimated technology.[1] From a capital markets perspective, there is data evidence to support this view. Since its inception in 2013 to the end of 2020, the BVP NASDAQ Emerging Cloud Index rose over 900 per cent. Over the same period the Dow Jones Index increased by just under 100 per cent.[2]

While accepting *Amara's law* applies to cloud computing, it has limits. For instance, a 2021 FCA survey of regulated firms found that 78 per cent of all production applications are still hosted on-premise.[3] Therefore, while cloud computing use is ubiquitous, it cannot be ignored that it still functions alongside on-premise infrastructure for key production applications. Both *Amara's law* and the moat around certain on-premise applications mean there is growing complexity from constantly assessing risks that are both inward and outward looking, based on a hybrid cloud computing environment that uses on-premise, private cloud or public cloud services.

---

[1] An authoritative practitioner book on cloud computing is Marchini, R (2015) *Cloud Computing: A Practical Introduction to the Legal Issues*, 2nd edn. (British Standards Institute). Additionally, see Ruparelia, NB (2016) *Cloud Computing* (MIT Press).

[2] www.bvp.com/bvp-nasdaq-emerging-cloud-index.

[3] FCA (2021) Implementing Technology Change – Multi-firms Review. It is important to note that the FCA statistical analysis was based on a very small sample of just 23 firms. A future survey based on a much higher sample of regulated firms would be more insightful.

3.1   Introduction

The Chief Technology Officer of JP Morgan Chase has described the cloud as involving 'the delivery of on-demand computing services over the Internet instead of internally hosted hardware'.[4] In short, the remote access of applications, hardware, software or all three. Services that are commonly rented included Infrastructure as a Service (IaaS), Platform as a Service (PaaS) and Software as a Service (SaaS).[5]

A technically authoritative, detailed definition is provided by the National Institute of Standards and Technology (NIST), although it is three pages long.[6] To clarify, NIST is not a regulator but is a highly respected US government agency whose aims are to promote innovation and commercial standards. This definition is widely respected given it covers the key characteristics of any cloud infrastructure. The essential part of the definition describes cloud computing as:

> a model enabling ubiquitous, convenient, on-demand network access to a shared pool of configurable computing resources (e.g., networks, servers, storage, applications, and services) that can be rapidly provisioned and released with minimal management effort or service provider interaction. This cloud model promotes availability and is composed of five essential characteristics.[7]

The five selected characteristics have been pared down in Table 3.1.[8]

3.2   Cloud computing and data control

There is a tendency for cloud computing to seem abstract, because in most instances of outsourced services that is the reality. A memorable analogy can be made between cloud computing and air traffic control. Based on positive feedback from a mixture of nationalities working as

---

4   www.jpmorgan.com/commercial-banking/insights/navigating-the-cloud.

5   FCA FG 16/5 (2016), updated 2019, Guidance for Firms Outsourcing to the Cloud and other Third Party IT Services.

6   Available at https://nvlpubs.nist.gov/nistpubs/Legacy/SP/nistspecialpublication800-145.pdf.

7   NIST (2011), NIST Definition of Cloud Computing. See https://csrc.nist.gov/glossary/term/cloud _computing.

8   Ibid., at 2.

Table 3.1   *NIST's five essential characteristics of cloud architecture*

Characteristic	Description
On-demand self-service	The user triggers the service without any interaction with personnel of the service provider.
Broad network access	The service can be accessed via a laptop, tablet, smart phone or work station.
Resource pooling	The service provider's resources are pooled to serve many users. The users have no or limited control over the precise location of the hardware and other services provided. However, users may have the right to choose the specific jurisdiction or data centre.
Rapid elasticity	Scalability that may or may not be automatic.
Measured service	Some form of metering communication to the user in terms of controlling, monitoring and reporting the precise use of processing, storage and other services.

legal counsel in European central banks and institutional fund managers that I presented to on the topic of financial regulation and data flows, it is a memorable way of thinking about cloud computing.

In summary, any air traffic control system is based on a four-dimensional cube of air space where traffic travels diagonally, horizontally and vertically. Instead of air space, the responsibility is data space.[9] The position of any aircraft is monitored within an air space – at stand, taking off, in flight and landing. With cloud computing the regulated firm is a metaphorical data traffic control tower at the centre of its own four-dimensional data space. Senior managers, including those in the legal and compliance functions, need to be vigilant about all data existing in that data space. Each cloud provider is within the regulated firm's data space, inside and part of the firm's four-dimensional cube of responsibilities. That data space is primarily the UK, but in most cases it is likely to stretch across several international borders. Chapter 6 in this book, covering data protection, provides a visually memorable figure of a regulated firm and its data space (Figure 6.1). That figure may provide a useful means of analysing cloud computing provision both inside the UK and out – a domestic cube

---

[9]   However, note that in commercial computing data space already has more than one precise meaning.

covering a regulated firm's own domestic cloud computing arrangements within an international cube of globally managed data.[10]

3.3   Financial regulation and cloud technology

Cloud computing is increasingly a strategic decision involving board level directors. In my experience, having advised and negotiated as both a full-time IT/IP counsel in global investment banks and as a full-time financial services regulation counsel, lawyers with both technology and in-depth financial services regulation expertise need to be involved. As just one example, ensuring the relevant aspects of MiFID and its related Regulatory Technical Standards (RTS) are accommodated into the Terms of Service and Side Letter Agreement is a multi-faceted task. The costs and risks for any asset manager, bank or trading platform are too high to justify any compromise on financial services regulatory expertise. Simultaneously, the IT counsel provides the full analysis on what technology-linked contractual obligations need to be agreed between the parties.

3.3.1   Cloud computing and MiFID

Turning to specific regulations, firstly MiFID II covers the outsourcing of critical functions.[11] In this context 'critical' means services that are critical to the continuous and satisfactory service of clients. A regulated firm must take reasonable steps to avoid undue additional operational risk from third-party arrangements.[12]

Further, outsourcing of critical functions cannot reduce internal control by the firm's compliance function, including any loss in the ability to supervise which is required to meet the regulated firm's obligations. It is a breach of MiFID II organisational rules to arrange outsourcing that:

- delegates senior management responsibility;
- alters the regulated firm's obligations and relationship towards its clients;

---

[10]   See also Chapter 6 Data protection.
[11]   Article 16(5) MiFID 2014/65.
[12]   Article 16(5) MiFID 2014/65.

- undermines the regulated firm's authorisation conditions;
- changes or removes any other authorisation conditions of the regulated firm.[13]

Other MiFID II organisational rules need to be briefly mentioned because they also have practical relevance to the use of cloud computing services. First, the management of the cloud service provider includes ensuring that periodic testing of the back-up facilities occurs.[14]

Second, outsourced cloud computing arrangements constitute material changes with the regulator in the context of critical and important functions,[15] and outsourcing is specifically flagged up as part of that on-going obligation to notify the regulator.[16] Detail on critical outsourcing would form part of a business plan submitted to the regulator on the original authorisation application. But it is easy to see that as cloud computing takes on increasing importance to regulated firms some material changes will occur as cloud services are expanded.

There are additional rules of specific relevance to the outsourcing of portfolio management services to a service provider in a non-EAA country. MiFID II organisational rules require that in this situation the service provider must be registered in its home country, and there must be in existence a cooperation agreement between that service provider's regulator and the regulated firm's service provider. However, as an exception to these conditions, a regulated firm can decide to outsource as long it has given prior notice to its regulator and that regulator has not objected within a reasonable period of time.[17]

At the date that this book was published, there are no cooperation agreements in place between the UK and other EU country regulators. However, the publishing of cooperation agreements is a requirement of the MiFID II organisational rules[18] for each of the EEA regulators, so the task of finding existing cooperation agreements online is not unduly burdensome.

---

[13] Article 31(1) MiFID Org Regulation 2017/565.

[14] Article 31(2)(k) MiFID Org Regulation 2017/565.

[15] Article 21(2) MiFID 2014/65.

[16] Paragraph 44 MiFID Org Regulation 2017/565.

[17] Article 32 MiFID Org Regulation 2017/565.

[18] Article 32(3) MiFID Org Regulation 2017/565.

3.3.2   EBA and ESMA cloud computing guidelines

If an asset manager, bank or platform is solely operating in the UK and not in the EU, then guidance by the FCA applies.[19] Readers can also find guidance dedicated specifically to all UK banks, building societies and PRA-designated investment firms.[20] However, in most instances asset management, banking businesses and platforms have some activity in the EU. Therefore, for banks in the broader UK plus EC context, the European Banking Authority (EBA) guidelines[21] also apply, and the European Securities and Markets Authority (ESMA) guidelines apply to alternative fund managers as well as investment firms.

Given cloud technology functions uniformly across regulated firms, unsurprisingly the EBA and ESMA guidelines are very similar. Under the ESMA guidelines, the key definition concerns 'critical or important functions' of the regulated firm, which refer to any function whose defect or failure in its performance would materially impair (a) a firm's compliance with its legal and regulatory obligations; (b) financial performance; or (c) the soundness or continuity of a firm's main services and activities.[22]

The EBA guidelines do not use the definition critical or important functions, but refer to the 'criticality and inherent risk profile of the activities to be outsourced'. Logically, the EBA and ESMA guidelines are very similar, given legal obligations, regulatory obligations, financial health and business continuity are all vital aspects.[23] There are also nine principles provided by the ESMA guidelines. In my view, the crucial compliance requirements of each are described in Table 3.2.

3.3.3   FCA SYSC Handbook Rules

Turning to the FCA SYSC Handbook ('SYSC Rules'), a logical question for legal counsel and compliance officers to ask is what in measurable terms does 'critical' mean? SYSC Rules provide that critical operational

---

[19]   FCA (2019) FG 16/5 Guidance for Firms Outsourcing to the 'Cloud' and Other Third-party IT Services.

[20]   PRA (2021) SS2/21 Outsourcing and Third Party Risk Management.

[21]   EBA (2017) Final Report on Recommendations on Cloud Outsourcing.

[22]   ESMA (2021) Guidelines on Outsourcing to Cloud Service Providers, Section II, Definitions, at 7. This definition replicates Article 30(1) MiFID 2017/565.

[23]   EBA (2017) Final Report on Recommendations on Cloud Outsourcing, at Section 4.1.

Table 3.2   *Nine principles in the ESMA guidelines*

	Principle	Description
1	Governance, oversight, and documentation	Must produce a cloud outsourcing strategy that is kept up-to-date.
2	Pre-outsourcing analysis and due diligence	Due diligence on outsourcing critical or important functions to other jurisdictions includes assessing data protection and insolvency laws.
3	Key contractual elements	First, if sub-outsourcing is permitted by the regulated firm, there must be detailed and robust sub-outsourcing conditions. Second, there must be a right to audit for both the regulated firm and its competent authorities.
4	Information security	The regulated firm needs to ensure that contractual obligations on the cloud service provider include the use of encryption technologies with appropriate cryptographic key management both between users and systems.[1]
5	Exit strategies	Cloud service provider arrangements must allow the regulated firm to terminate the agreement without undue disruption to its business activities. Further, termination cannot create any detriment to the regulated firm's compliance obligations.
6	Access and audit rights	The cloud service provider agreement cannot limit access or audit rights for either the regulated firm or its competent authority.
7	Sub-outsourcing	Agreement to specify what, if any, aspects of the regulated firm's data is excluded from sub-outsourcing.

	Principle	Description
8	Written notification to competent authorities	Regulated firm must promptly send written notification to competent authorities about planned cloud outsourcing arrangements that concern critical or important functions. Also need to notify if normal functions become critical ones.
9	Supervision of cloud outsourcing arrangements	Competent authorities need to be confident they can effectively supervise outsourced cloud computing arrangements, especially critical or important functions outsourced beyond the EU.

Note: [1] An appropriate cryptographic key management system may certify its hardware based on the Federal Information Processing Standard Publication 140-2 ('FIPS 140-2'). For example, IBM's cloud computing service hardware is certified on FIPS 140-2. See www.ibm .com/cloud/hyper-protect-crypto.

functions exist when a defect or failure in them would materially impair (a) a firm's regulatory compliance; (b) its financial performance; (c) the competence of its service; or (d) the continuity of its services.[24] In my view, these (a) to (d) critical list criteria are understandably broadly drafted by the regulator but too broad to illuminate a safe path for regulated firms.

There are also fundamental SYSC Rules concerning the management of such operations. Specifically, regulated firms that decide to outsource are subject to the following four conditions: (a) senior personnel cannot delegate their responsibility; (b) outsourcing must not alter the obligations and relationships with clients; (c) compliance rules on regulator authorisation must not be undermined; and (d) other conditions of regulator authorisation must not be modified or removed.[25]

Under SYSC Rules the term 'senior personnel' is ambiguous here, because on initial analysis it is unclear if that means all senior managers. Second, it is unclear if the term refers only to senior managers subject to the FCA SMR. Third, it is unclear whether the term refers to a broader category of all senior managers and other senior employees.

---

[24] FCA SYSC 8.1.4R.

[25] FCA SYSC 8.1.6R.

The answer is complex, because it depends on the type of regulated firm. Based on guidance linked to the words senior personnel, the category covers board directors or anyone who is a member of a management committee. However, note for a UCITS management company,[26] it encompasses the senior managers conducting portfolio management.[27] Further, 'senior management' means the person or persons who effectively conduct the business of a management company.[28] The quickest route to clarity is gained by glancing at the Tree function offered on the FCA website linked to the words 'senior personnel'.

Most regulated firms will retain some key operations in-house. For example, in hedge funds many strategies and associated data sets are proprietary in nature. However, as detailed in Chapter 12 of this book, machine learning is increasing cloud computing use. There are increasing competitive advantages from commercial Big Data combined with machine learning which infer more cloud service provider use or at least an expanding hybrid model. Indeed an in-depth World Economic Forum study on AI highlights that cloud computing plays a pivotal role in providing both data storage and processing power for AI solutions.[29]

3.4   Cloud contract documentation

Contractual issues concerning cloud architecture frequently start when in-house legal counsel or instructed law firm counsel receive an email requesting that attached cloud computing contracts, typically a Terms of Service Agreement (ToS) and a Service Level Agreement (SLA), have to be promptly agreed. Subsequently there needs to be some re-drafting and negotiating on a wide range of issues with the cloud computing service provider.[30]

---

[26] Article 2(1)(b) UCITS IV Directive, 2009/65.

[27] Article 3(4) UCITS IV Directive, 2009/65.

[28] Article 7(1)(b) UCITS IV Directive, 2009/65.

[29] McWaters, R et al. (2018) *The New Physics of Financial Services* (World Economic Forum).

[30] A potentially overlooked regulatory requirement for cloud service providers is the P2B Regulation (EU 2019/1150) (the 'P2B Reg') which has been in force since 12 July 2020 and was transposed into UK law. Under the P2B Reg 'online intermediation services', a category of provider that may include cloud services, requires a contract clauses that provide, among other things, at least 30 days' notice of contract termination. An authoritative, succinct article explaining the significance of the P2B Reg in the context of cloud computing providers is: Hon, K (2020) 'Cloud/Hosting Providers Beware?

In my view, an overlooked aspect of legal counsel due diligence is the value of a pre-contractual demonstration of the proposed cloud computing service. Having a systems demonstration from each of the short-listed providers can provide insightful legal risk management angles. For example, the in-house procurement function or externally instructed experts may be conflicted for opaque reasons or biased judgement. They may ignore or diminish the priority on weightings and costs by communicating preference for a provider that is not the clear metrics-based choice. They might overlook a provider's security history, because of an especially attractive total cost of service.

The short-, medium- and long-term risk mind-set of a lawyer can often reveal these scenarios. In the context of international asset managers and investment banks, the costs and risks of some technology systems can be pivotal to growth and reputation. In sum, pre-contractual due diligence by a lawyer independent of procurement function decision making can be extremely valuable. Further, SYSC Rules require that a regulated firm has exit arrangements that ensure any contract termination is managed 'without detriment to the continuity and quality' of client services.[31] That task includes robust contract drafting that logically rests on the foundations of pre-contractual due diligence.[32]

At the contract drafting and negotiation phases, there is a need for regulated firms to draft financial regulation obligations as addenda to any general cloud services provider agreement. This may provide some extra comfort that the cloud service provider accepts the extra responsibilities attached to providing its technology in the financial services sector. The FCA's Cyber Coordination Groups has specifically mentioned that such an addendum provides extra assurance.[33]

Once a contract is formed, there is also a need for on-going due diligence to establish if there is a risk gap between what the regulated firm needs and what is being delivered. This lifecycle approach to looking at cloud

---

An Unintended Consequence of the P2B Regulation', *Society for Computers and Law*, www.scl.org/articles/10853-cloud-hosting-providers-beware-an-unintended-consequence-of-the-p2b-regulation.

[31]   FCA SYSC 8.1.8R at 7.

[32]   As covered earlier in this chapter, Principle 5 of the ESMA Cloud Computing Guidelines mirror FCA SYSC 8.1.8R(7).

[33]   FCA (2021) Insights from the 2020 Cyber Coordination Groups, at 6.

computing legal risks is memorably illustrated in Figure 3.1, which has been adapted from a cloud computing legal risks article published by the Royal Society. This requires a clear renegotiation rights clause. Further, there needs to be scheduled quarterly meetings with the Chief Operations Officer and the Chief Technology Officer to determine where service delivery or other issues raise evolving risks. There is a growing risk of over-concentration on one cloud provider, so that alone requires on-going due diligence.

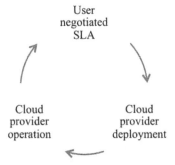

Source: Djemame, K et al. (2012) 'Legal Issues in Clouds: Towards a Risk Inventory', *Philosophical Transactions of the Royal Society A* (28 January 2013), at 4.

Figure 3.1   *Legal issues and the cloud life cycle*

3.5   Common risk themes

Each regulated firm, whether primarily complying with the Alternative Investment Fund Managers Directive (AIFMD), MiFID II or UCITS legislation relevant to their subsector, needs to factor in the specific out-sourcing rules. In support of this requirement both the EBA and ESMA have produced cloud computing guidelines that include specific contrac-tual terms to agree with providers. The EBA guidance[34] applies to all types of outsourcing. The cloud-specific ESMA guidance[35] not only absorbs the earlier EBA guidance, but also provides greater detail on, among

---

[34]   EBA/REC/2017/03, applicable from 1 July 2018.

[35]   ESMA 50/157/2403.

other things, information security. For instance, the need to integrate cloud services with the firm's systems to ensure security of application programming interfaces (APIs).[36]

Increasingly an SLA is not a new service used by the regulated firm, but concentration risk concerns result in a new priority to gain more feedback on the volumes of valuable data entrusted to each service provider. Legal issues are often mixed in with commercial discussions on what a specific service does or does not offer compared with direct competitors. The risk categories can be analysed thematically based on access, change, concentration, data, latency and shared infrastructure. There is some overlap with these risk themes given a weakness in one area can lead to vulnerabilities in another. For example, change in IT personnel at a cloud data centre because of a merger of two cloud providers may be the catalyst for creating gaps in computer security.[37]

3.5.1   Data loss

Data can be lost because of spontaneous technical hardware failure without sufficient time to make a back-up, or through erroneous corruption or deletion. Alternatively, or as a contributing factor to technical failure, there may be human error. Data loss can also cover the scenario of loss of confidentiality, because of an external attack or internal unauthorised disclosure.[38] Current technical reliability levels mean that there is a low probability of permanent data loss. This is because cloud computing systems are based on redundancy, by which is meant the duplication of storage devices to function as a back-up measure.[39] This is especially so if procurement decisions involve contracts with the largest cloud providers that have made multi-billion dollar infrastructure investment. With the exception of the largest asset managers and banks, it is likely that their safeguarding mechanisms are superior to any in-house storage system.

Nevertheless, legal counsel can contribute an independent evidential mind-set to this issue. There has to be a balance between the cost of due

---

[36]   ESMA 50/157/2403, p.33.

[37]   Note there is cloud computing subject matter overlap with other chapters in this book, especially Chapter 5 Cyber security and Chapter 6 Data protection.

[38]   The loss of data confidentiality is covered in the Chapter 5 Cyber security.

[39]   *Oxford Dictionary of Computer Science* (2016) (Oxford University Press).

diligence and time available, but given cloud architecture is becoming so vital to financial services operations, it is imprudent to delegate all due diligence solely to an in-house information technology (IP/IT) or outsourcing lawyer or both. Regulated firms will vary in their reliance on cloud services from a storage viewpoint, but seeking documentary proof from the cloud service provider on the following aspects is the bare minimum:

- the Cloud provider's own track record on availability and security of service, including any breaches registered with its national data protection regulator;
- compliance with ISO 27001 (information security management) or with ISO 27017 (cloud-specific information security controls) or both;[40]
- compliance with the GDPR and the Data Protection Act 2018;
- locations where the data will be stored and confirmation in writing of these specific locations;
- the cloud services provider's use or planned use of sub-outsourcing;[41]
- penetration testing results by the cloud services provider of the cloud to confirm the results match the scope of the specific service model, namely IaaS, PaaS or SaaS. A cloud services provider may inadvertently treat a component as out of scope when it is in scope;[42]
- penetration testing evidence to indicate there is a process of regular testing to satisfy relevant UK and EU laws;[43]
- any code of conduct produced by the cloud service provider, as encouraged under relevant UK and EU laws.[44] The lawyer is looking for gaps between any stated penetration testing policy and what the cloud service provider does in practice;
- penetration testing results by other financial services businesses that revealed vulnerabilities. The results can be provided anonymously, only confirming the type of financial services business;

---

[40] Renzo Marchini, a privacy, security and information partner at the international law firm Fieldfisher, makes the important distinction between a cloud provider confirming its compliance with ISO 27001 compared with actual ISO 27001 certification. Proof of certification is more robust evidence. See Marchini, R (2015) *Cloud Computing: A Practical Introduction to the Legal Issues*, 2nd edn. (British Standards Institute), at 3.6.1.

[41] ESMA regulated firms must include in the main cloud service provider's contract the conditions under which sub-outsourcing takes place, and all the specific obligations and rights.

[42] For example, the operating system of a PaaS may have been missed.

[43] Article 32(1)(d) GDPR.

[44] Article 40 GDPR.

- local laws in the jurisdiction of the cloud services that need to be complied with for the regulated firm to conduct penetration testing;
- encryption standards and policies; and
- contact details of an existing financial services customer that transitioned its in-house data for storage.

3.5.2   Change and migration risk

In Chapter 2 covering Accountability, detailed reference was made to an independent review commissioned by TSB, a post-mortem of its calamitous decision to have a single event IT system migration. That decision by the TSB board ultimately resulted in a migration failure and costs exceeding £330 million. Cloud computing is increasingly a significant or complete migration solution, so both Chapter 2 and the TSB review are valuable reading time investments.[45]

3.5.3   Concentration risk

The concentration of risks manifests itself in three ways. First, a concentration of the regulated firm's data stored with one cloud service provider. To do so is irrational, no matter how distributed its redundancy infrastructure is across multiple jurisdictions. An insider attack at one data centre at the right access level could cause disruptions to data retrieval with damage to the regulated firm's reputation for failing to maintain a diversified cloud storage strategy. Therefore, lawyers need to know the pie chart distribution of the regulated firm's data storage, including the categories of data stored with each cloud service provider.

Second, there is the risk of any regulated firm allowing too many critical functions to be trusted with a limited range of cloud service providers. Part of that challenge is something that on first analysis is incongruent with the general propensity of procurement functions to rely on a too narrow range of suppliers. In a UK Parliament Treasury Committee report concerning technology failures in the financial services sector, an expert from Barclays observed 'banks operate within an ecosystem of connected entities, many of which are suppliers or organisations that supply

---

[45]   Slaughter and May (2019) An Independent Review following TSB's Migration onto a New IT Platform in April 2018. See www.tsb.co.uk/news-releases/slaughter-and-may/.

services directly or indirectly to the financial services sector'.[46] In this same UK Parliament report, a director from TSB recalled that an outage incident affecting outsourced functions caused disruption to not only its operations for several hours, but also to a number of other financial services businesses all relying on the same third-party provider. Therefore, there is a need for the procurement function to audit, broaden and change the pool of cloud providers. In turn, legal counsel can have a role to play in auditing the list of existing and planned cloud service provider contracts.

Third, there is the systemic risk from a concentration of cloud service providers within the financial services sector, causing disruption that challenges the whole system. Technically, this may seem a far-fetched scenario, because of the competence and financial resources of the main cloud service providers. Yet it is also a highly complex topic, which means it cannot be simply ignored and put into the 'too hard' category of issues to mitigate.[47] The UK Parliament report concluded 'the cloud service provider market stood out as a source of concentration risk during this enquiry ... This market is already highly concentrated and there is probably nothing the Government or Regulators can do to reduce this concentration in the short or medium term.'[48]

Further, in my view, financial services businesses will increasingly seek to maximise the value of data sets which will require an increase in cloud services. The strategic importance of quality data sets will increase the importance of sharing data in clean rooms. The concept of data clean rooms originally referred to the maintenance of large reliable data sets by Amazon, Facebook and Google. However, the building of in-house clean rooms is a likely trend for the largest asset managers and banks. Therefore, concentration risk concerning cloud services has many evolving aspects. Consequently, regular audit and input by lawyers are important responsibilities.

There are on-going regulator and international efforts to manage systemic cloud concentration risk. Regulated firms as an ecosystem of mutual interests can certainly attempt to mitigate the risks. My own advice forming part of a Financial Stability Board (FSB) consultation on outsourcing

---

[46]   House of Commons Treasury Committee (2019) IT Failures in the Financial Services Sector, at 31.

[47]   IEEE (2016), Systemic Risks in the Cloud Computing Model: Complex Systems Perspective.

[48]   House of Commons Treasury Committee (2019) IT Failures in the Financial Services Sector, at 35.

and third-party relationships, focused on global systemically important banks (G-SIBs). Relevant to cloud computing Chief Operations Officers and Chief Technology Officers need to follow an agreed rule of thumb to mitigate systemic risks. The use of cloud computing requires contractual relationships based on:

- one-third (33.3 per cent) of total annual expenditure is made with companies in the jurisdiction in which the headquarters of the regulated firm is located;
- one-third (33.3 per cent) of total annual expenditure is made based on intra-group outsourcing which can be in the same jurisdiction as the headquarters of the regulated firm or distributed globally; and
- one-third (33.3 per cent) of total annual expenditure is made with companies globally excluding the jurisdiction in which the headquarters of the regulated firm is located.

Clearly this rule of thumb is most appropriate for G-SIBs – global businesses with huge resources. However, it is important to highlight that regulator expectations on operational resilience make the need for proportionate focus and investment by all sizes of asset managers, investment banks, platforms and FinTech SMEs. Each regulated firm must plan, implement and record how it mitigates systemic risk. Diversification of cloud service providers based on location of data centres is an essential part of any plan.

3.6   Data protection

Under the GDPR[49] personal data must be protected and kept confidential with responsibility placed on both controllers and processors. The majority of investment bank clients are corporate entities, which may at first glance make the GDPR largely out of scope. However, for many asset managers, platforms and FinTech SMEs, large numbers of clients can be individuals, so that requires compliance with the GDPR.

Chapter 6 of this book concentrates on data protection, where readers can find many detailed angles and issues concerning the GDPR. In the narrow context of cloud computing there are three thematic categories of

---

[49]   GDPR, 2016/679.

compliance. First, there is compliance with GDPR rules. Second, the need to apply authoritative GDPR-related case law relevant to cloud computing. Third, the sensible incorporation of EDPB guidance relevant to cloud service providers.

3.6.1 GDPR Rules

First, under the GDPR there are numerous rules governing cloud service providers in their capacity as a 'data processor'. A processor must only process personal data based on the written instructions from the controller.[50] The processor must be committed to a duty of confidentiality or subject to a statutory duty of confidence.[51] A processor cannot sub-outsource the cloud services to another processor without prior written authorisation from the regulated firm. In the event that the cloud service provider wanted to make such a sub-outsource decision, it would need to wait for the regulated firm to send written authorisation.[52] Further, the processor must take all appropriate measures concerning data security. There are many details to data security,[53] including confidentiality, integrity and resilience under an over-arching practical sense of proportionality. Methods of encryption and pseudonymisation are key aspect to meeting data security risks.

The processor must assist the regulated firm in various other ways, including assistance in providing subject access. In the case of data transferred outside of the EEA, for example data transferred into the UK, a data subject has a right to be informed of the various safeguards that mean the transfer outside of the EEA is deemed of comparable robustness to EU GDPR standards.[54] There are also requirements for the deletion of data as part of each data subject's 'right to be forgotten',[55] and the need for the processor to submit to audits and inspections.[56]

---

[50] Article 28(3)(a) GDPR.
[51] Article 28(3)(b) GDPR.
[52] Article 28(2) GDPR.
[53] Article 32 GDPR.
[54] Articles 15(2) and 46 GDPR.
[55] Article 17 GDPR.
[56] Article 28(3)(h) GDPR.

3.6.2   Data protection case law

Second, case law of the Court of Justice of the European Union (CJEU) steers the evolution of the GDPR. Since the UK left the EU there are no UK Supreme Court decisions that require factoring into data protection legal risk mitigation, but that can rapidly change so there is a need to continually check UK precedent. The most significant CJEU decision to date is *Schrems II*.[57] It is unnecessary to summarise the facts of *Schrems II* here as it is covered in Chapter 6. The decision of the CJEU in *Schrems II* resulted in the removal of the Privacy Shield that existed between the EU and the US. This Privacy Shield meant that cloud service providers in the US could receive personal data transmitted out of the EEA area based on a framework of adequacy between the standards of data protection in the EU compared with the US.[58]

The *Schrems II* decision invalidated the Privacy Shield, the consequence of which is that the continued transfer of data from the EEA to the US has to be subject to established standard contractual clauses (SCCs).[59] For ease of reference, the detailed content required in SCCs between an EEA controller and a non-EEA processor such as a US-based cloud service provider, are published as part of EU law.[60] Specifically, the 12 detailed SCCs are set out in an EC published Annex.[61] Simultaneously the CJEU stated that the laws of the non-EEA controller or processor have to be checked to ensure they do not override the SCCs. Further, the CJEU as part of its judgment signposted that important supplementary measures would be provided by the EDPB necessary to protect EEA personal data.

3.6.3   EDPB guidance

Third, the EDPB is an extremely authoritative arm of the EU given it has substantial experience juggling the data protection laws of EU Member States, as well as the laws of Norway, Iceland and Lichtenstein. The CJEU has also placed considerable confidence in the EDPB to provide vital guidance. The *Schrems II* decision is a perfect example of that, because

---

[57]   *Data Protection Commissioner v Facebook Ireland Ltd, Maximilian Schrems* and intervening parties ('*Schrems II*') Case C-311/18.

[58]   Article 45 GDPR.

[59]   Article 46(3)(a) GDPR.

[60]   EU Decision C(2010) 593.

[61]   Ibid., Annex.

Table 3.3   *The EDPB's six key steps*

	Step	Description
1	Exporters must know their transfers	Data exporters must know their transfers.[1] This requires a full mapping exercise to determine where all data is being transferred. The EDPB point out the efficiencies gained from building on existing data records created by obligations to keep records of processing activities,[2] and requirements to inform data subjects about automated decision making[3] and the movement of data outside the EEA.[4] It is important to bear in mind that data storage in a cloud infrastructure outside the EEA is a transfer.
2	Safeguards	Verify the appropriate safeguards your transfer relies on from those listed under Chapter V GDPR.[5] Check if the EC has made an adequacy decision.[6] Ensure the adequacy decision remains valid. If there is no adequacy decision, rely on the listed safeguards.[7] In limited scenarios there is the option of relying on derogations.[8]
3	Third country assessment	Assess the third country law to understand if it alters the effectiveness of the chosen appropriate safeguards.[9] Refer to the EDPB European Essential Guarantees[10] recommendations, especially when the legislation governing the access to data by public authorities is ambiguous or not publicly available.
4	Third country supplementary measures	If the third country law alters the effectiveness of the GDPR transfer tool,[11] apply appropriate supplementary measures. Annex 2 of the EDPB guidance provides examples of contractual, organisational and technical measures.[12] There may be a need to apply several supplementary measures. If you fail to find a suitable measure, do not initiate or terminate the data transfer. Further, all due diligence and decision making needs to be documented.

	Step	Description
5	Procedural steps for supplementary measures	Apply all procedural steps relevant to the planned supplementary measures.[13] The EDPB recommendations detail these formalities. You may also need to gain approval from your competent supervisory authority on some of them. For example, if SCCs are modified or a supplementary measure directly or indirectly contradicts the SCCs.
6	Periodic checks	Perform periodic checks on the appropriate level of data protection provided to the data in the relevant third countries.

Notes: [1] EDPB Recommendations 02/2020, Annex 1. [2] Article 30 GDPR. [3] Article 13(1)(f) GDPR. [4] Article 14(1)(f) GDPR. [5] Articles 44-49 GDPR. [6] Article 45 GDPR. Earlier decisions may have been made under the EU Directive 1995/46. [7] Article 46 GDPR. [8] Article 49 GDPR. [9] Article 46 GDPR. [10] EDPB (2020) European Essential Guarantees, Recommendations. [11] Article 46 GDPR. [12] EDPB Recommendations 02/2020, Annex 2. [13] Article 46 GDPR.

it was in effect only half a decision that required data processors to wait for subsequent EDPB guidance. The EDPB guidance was provided a few months later in the form of a detailed 38 page summary. The EDPB's essential supplementary guidance is set out in six key steps (Table 3.3).

It is notable that financial services firms often rely on various codes of conduct in the governance of their boards and more generally for staff. The EDPB's Step 2 includes reference to safeguards as a way to potentially transfer data in compliance with the GDPR. That list includes drafting an approved code of conduct.[62] For larger asset managers, banks or platforms a code of conduct would be a practical investment. The drafting of a data protection code of conduct may be a task for in-house counsel, external lawyers or indeed a collective sector choice from a chamber of commerce or other financial services sector body. However, if an in-house solution is chosen, it is important to allocate legal function resources to ensure the code of conduct remains up-to-date. If the code of conduct becomes dated, that is potentially damning evidence about the compliance culture of the business. English courts like consistent codes of conduct with proof of implementation.

---

[62]   Article 40 GDPR.

3.7   English High Court cases

The High Court in *Kingsway Hall Hotel v Redsky IT (Hounslow)* provides some perspective on risk management with large service technology providers that may not be prepared to change clauses in their standard contracts, including liability in the event of a malfunctioning IT system. This decision did not specifically concern cloud computing services, but it has general application. In *Kingsway Hall Hotel v Redsky IT (Hounslow)* the High Court held that an IT services standard terms contract between an IT provider and a business were unfair and unenforceable.[63] The plaintiff was a 170-bed four star Covent Garden hotel, so it had lower bargaining power compared with the majority of established financial services businesses. Nevertheless, growing regulated firms, for example FinTech start-ups, may take confidence from this High Court decision.

The judgment was based first on section 14 of the Sale of Goods Act 1979. Under this section a term is to be implied into the contract that the IT system would be fit for the purpose for which it was sold. The judge concluded the defendant's IT system was not. Second, under the Supply of Goods and Services Act 1982, s. 4, a term is to be implied into the contract that the goods are of satisfactory quality. The judge determined that the defendant's IT system did not meet the standard that a reasonable person would regard as satisfactory, based on its description, price and all other circumstances, to satisfy the Supply of Goods and Services Act 1982, s. 4.

Turning to another High Court case of potential significance, it concerns contractual agreements between software providers and their agents. It has resulted in an appeal to the Supreme Court who in turn referred interpretation of the matter to the CJEU. In *Computer Associates (UK) Ltd v The Software Incubator Ltd*, the Court of Appeal had to decide if release automation software used by among other businesses, large financial services firms, electronically supplied to such customers qualified as 'goods' under Article 2(1) of regulations relevant to commercial agents ('the Regulations').[64] If the software was classified as goods that meant that breaches of contract allowed for compensation under the Regulations. If classified as a service then no compensation was allowed.

---

[63]   *Kingsway Hall Hotel v Redsky IT (Hounslow)* [2010] EWHC 965 (TCC), (2010) 26 Const LJ 542.

[64]   Article 2(1) of the Commercial Agents (Council Directive) Regulations, 1993/3053. Available at www.legislation.gov.uk/uksi/1993/3053/contents/made.

The Court of Appeal[65] applied an existing High Court authority, namely that if no hardware is supplied then the Regulations do not apply to the supply of software because it is IP. Consequently, there is no sale of 'goods' within the meaning of Article 2(1) of the Regulations.[66] The CJEU, applying its established case law, based their interpretation on two aspects. First, the term 'goods' means products which can be (a) valued in money, and (b) are capable of forming the subject of a commercial transaction. Second, the term 'goods' can cover software supplied by any medium. So whether software is supplied on a CD-ROM or over the Internet both are 'goods'. The CJEU decision is potentially of general interest to cloud computing SaaS providers and regulated firm users, because it should be a current assessment of an arguably artificial and dated contractual treatment of software.

3.8   ESG disclosures

Finally, the EU Disclosure Regulation on sustainability concerning ESG, as set out in the Sustainable Finance Disclosure Regulation (SFDR), needs to be factored into regulated firm decision making on cloud computing. This is required on several levels, but especially corporate reputation and product offerings. In broad terms 'financial market participants, taking due account of their size, the nature and scale of their activities and the types of financial products they make available ... should integrate in their processes, including in their due diligence processes, the procedures for considering the principal adverse impacts alongside the relevant financial risks and relevant sustainability risks'.[67]

The SFDR affects not only EU entities, but also UK regulated firms that have EU subsidiaries or provide financial services in the EU. The FCA

---

[65]   *Computer Associates UK Ltd v The Software Incubator Ltd* [2018] EWCA Civ 518.

[66]   *Accentuate Ltd v Asigra Inc* (a company incorporated in Canada) [2009] EWHC 2655 (QB) per Tugendhut J, at 55. Available at www.bailii.org/ew/cases/EWHC/QB/2009/2655.html. See CJEU, Case C-410/19, *The Software Incubator Ltd v Computer Associates (UK) Ltd*, 16 September 2021, at 26–39.

[67]   SFDR (2021), 2019/2088, EU Regulation on sustainability-related disclosures in the financial services sector. The SFDR was brought into force on 10 March 2021. Further, from 2 August 2022, MiFID II rules require investment firms to assess internal sustainability risks, client sustainability preferences, and sustainability factors at the design phase of product development. See EU Delegated Regulation 2021/1253.

will produce further rules, and has already published a 'Dear Chair' letter that includes an annex of guiding principles.[68] Any new FCA rules in 2022 will be influenced by the UK government's Roadmap to Sustainability and the FCA's consultation feedback from its Discussion Paper (DP 21/4) on UK Sustainability Disclosure Requirements and Investment Labels.[69] However, given the international nature of the financial services sector future FCA rules are unlikely to deviate far from the SFDR. The SFDR apply to, among other businesses, asset managers, banks, some financial advisers and investment firms. The impact is quite wide, including communicating in pre-contractual disclosures, website information and product marketing. The SFDR also applies to policy document assessment details on adverse sustainability impacts based on quantitative metrics.

Under the final Regulatory Technical Standard that provides detail to supplement the SFDR, there are rules requiring the reporting of the sustainability impact of energy performance by investee companies. This includes expressing the weighted average of the energy consumption intensity per million euros revenue of investee companies measured in gigawatt-hours (GWh).[70] The SFDR GWh metric needs extra monitoring in the context of cloud computing providers. Technology, especially computer systems that include cloud service providers, is increasingly relied on, with sustainability risks associated with the significant use of electricity. This is especially so with machine learning.[71] For example, an asset manager or investment bank could analyse the financial performance benefits of a specific listed cloud computing provider as part of a portfolio, but the ratio of energy use expressed in GWh to revenue may place the investee company out of acceptable ESG parameters.

3.9   Competition risk and quantum computing

Finally, Chapter 13 of this book is dedicated to the subject of quantum computing. Leading cloud providers, such as Amazon and Microsoft,

---

[68] FCA (2021) Authorised ESG and Sustainable Investment Funds: Improving Quality and Clarity.

[69] See HM Government (2021) Greening Finance: A Roadmap to Sustainable Investing; and FCA (2021) DP 21/4, Sustainability Disclosure Requirements and Investment Labels.

[70] Joint Committee of European Supervisory Authorities (2021) Final Report on RTS under FSDR, at 61, Section 6.

[71] Chapter 12 Machine learning considers the detail.

have the financial resources to run, maintain and constantly monitor quantum hardware. These lead cloud providers will have an oligopoly on renting time on quantum systems, and as quantum computing advances commercial fees may radically increase. To illustrate the significance of this oligopolistic threat, it is predicted by QC Ware – a firm of Silicon Valley commercial quantum computing pioneers all with at least one PhD in physics or another highly quantitative discipline – that applications such as portfolio optimisation and Monte Carlo simulations will be solved 1 million times faster compared with classical algorithms.

There is uncertainty when widespread application of quantum computing to finance applications will occur. For legal and compliance functions there is a balance to strike between thinking there is no imminent change to commercial fees for cloud computing linked to quantum machine use, versus scaremongering about an imminent increase in costs. Regulated firms need to currently ensure they have appropriate renegotiation clauses within the ToS and SLAs, plus in the future to schedule, then conduct, annual quantum computing assessments of their cloud service providers.[72]

---

[72] Bouland, A et al. (2020) *Prospects and Challenges of Quantum Finance* (Cornell University arXiv), at 49.

4. Cryptoassets

The introductory chapter of this book made reference to the constant gap between human adaptability and technological advancement. By which is meant that to varying degrees our grasp of technology is always behind the progress of technology. This gap is often quite wide in the context of cryptoassets.

4.1 Introduction

Given the technical nature of how bitcoin works, it is necessary to first briefly summarise its key features. Only minimal reference is made early on in this chapter to products that compete against the bitcoin offering, because mentioning alternatives in an introduction obfuscates under-standing.[1] In my view, anchoring the mind on how bitcoin functions is a wise investment in effort and time. Further, the commercial reality is that the total combined market capitalisation of all alternatives is smaller than bitcoin.[2]

After a description of bitcoin, it is then timely to refresh memories on the three functions of money, providing a clear reference model to compare with cryptoassets. Thereafter legal analysis will dovetail with the reality that bitcoin is not money, but nevertheless a novel asset, and for some a lucrative one. In my view, it is easier to read these first two sections before digesting the subsequent black letter sections.

---

[1] For an in-depth comparative analysis of Bitcoin and established competitors, including Ethereum and Ripple, see Rauchs, M et al. (2018) *Distributed Ledger Technology Systems – A Conceptual Framework* (Cambridge Centre for Alternative Finance).

[2] www.cryptocoincharts.info.

4.2   Distributed ledger technology

The vital discipline of a lawyer's pedantry finds a kindred spirit in computer engineers. Technical descriptions of distributed ledger technology (DLT) matter. The term blockchain can be used interchangeably with DLT, but in fact blockchains are just one type of DLT.[3] A Royal Society paper explains succinctly that 'blockchains may be seen as instances of such DLT solutions where the data and its change history are presented in a linear chain of blocks that are cryptographically linked to make them resilient against unintentional or malicious manipulation'.[4]

Created in 2008, bitcoin trades via blockchains.[5] Protected by encryption, this type of DLT is an immutable ledger, a transactional database whose application and rules are agreed between members by consensus. The network is 'permissionless', by which is meant anyone can join to update the ledger. There is not one owner or party controlling the database, and all parties have equal access to the same information. Further, trust in the accuracy of the database (or ledger) does not require confirmation from an intermediary.

Compared with traditional electronic financial transaction processing that is ordinarily administered by a trusted third-party actor, typically a bank or clearing house, how blockchain transactions are processed is initially perplexing and unintuitive. The essential actors, elements and technology concerning bitcoin are listed in Table 4.1. Instead of a trusted third-party authorising or clearing a transaction, by means of DLT each provisional, unconfirmed transaction (or Candidate Block) enters a pool where all provisional transactions are visible for processing. A Candidate Block is selected by payment processors (or Miners). On average, one Candidate Block is added every second to the bitcoin system. However, it takes on average of 10 minutes for the Candidate Block to become a completed transaction – a Block.

There has been concern that bitcoin is the 21st century equivalent of the South Sea Company. Yet it has already weathered several potential

---

[3]   The different types of DLT are covered in UK Government Office for Science (2016) Distributed Ledger: Beyond Blockchain.

[4]   Royal Society (2020) An Overview of Blockchain Science and Engineering, at 1.

[5]   Nakamoto, S (2018) Bitcoin: A Peer-to-Peer Electronic Cash System (www.bitcoin.org).

Table 4.1   *Bitcoin actors, elements and technology*

Terminology	Description
Block	An accepted transaction on a blockchain. One Block represents the storage of data in a distinct structure. Each Block is time stamped and therefore chronologically linked to the Block before it. Hence the concept of a blockchain.
Candidate Block	A provisional payment that is waiting to be added as a Block to the blockchain.
DLT	Oversight of the blockchain is based on a DLT that creates a transparent record on a peer-to-peer network. All users (or nodes) in the network hold precisely the same information. There is no central administrator. Trust principally derives from the simultaneous updating of information that all users view.
Financial intermediaries	Brokers, exchanges and platforms that facilitate bitcoin trading.
Immutability	Once a Candidate Block becomes a Block, no network participant can change that ledger entry on the DLT.
Miners	Transaction processors who select a Candidate Block and attempt to add it the blockchain by successfully solving a cryptographic puzzle. If successful, Miners are rewarded with transaction fees and 6.25 bitcoins. Given it takes approximately 10 minutes to mine a new Block, based on the current reward system there are on average 900 new bitcoin produced each day. The bitcoin DLT system is based on a cap of 21 million bitcoins. Analogous to a physical coal or gold mine, when that limit is reached there is no new supply of bitcoins.
Private key	The means by which someone can decrypt an encrypted public key message or provide a signature request sent by a public key. A private key is how an owner of bitcoins can transfer or spend them. A private key is generated by a cryptographic algorithm. It is a secret and only known to the private key holder. The analogy of a password is often used.

Terminology	Description
Proof of work	The method agreed between DLT participants on how to reach consensus that a Candidate Block can change to a Block. Currently, the agreed method involves Miners competing to solve a puzzle based on a cryptographic puzzle. Each competition typically takes 10 minutes. The Miner that solves the puzzle is rewarded with 6.25 new bitcoins. If two Miners happen to solve the puzzle at exactly the same time, the 'longest chain rule' applies.
Public key	A unique number that is mathematically generated from a private key. The analogy of a traditional bank account number is often used.
Smart contracts	Blockchain-based code that automatically executes functions triggered by pre-specified events. For example, if FTSE 100 Index is greater than 6,000 points next Friday at noon, then pay X £1,000,000.

crashes. Some view bitcoin as a 'type of "digital gold" that provides investors with guaranteed scarcity and high mobility, as well as low correlation with other asset classes'.[6] Currently, its evolution is too early to know its true character. As with all new asset classes, legal counsel and compliance officers need to invest extra time to cautiously monitor how bitcoin functions and prospers.

This form of DLT and variants of it have great potential for other forms of cryptoassets by providing an immutable trusted record of clearing, collateral or settlement transactions at lower cost, and without the involvement of a third-party.[7] However, DLT has complex conflict of laws issues,[8] evolving vulnerabilities and poor ESG credentials.[9] For example, blockchains have already been hacked with the loss of cryptoassets worth

---

[6] Ferguson, N (2019) *The Ascent of Money – A Financial History of the World* (Penguin), at 440.

[7] Sheridan, I (2017) 'Mifid II in the Context of Financial Technology and Regulatory Technology', *Capital Markets Law Journal*, Volume 12, Issue 4, at Section 6.

[8] Financial Markets Law Committee (2018) Distributed Ledger Technology and Governing Law: Issues of Legal Uncertainty, provides a detailed analysis of these legal issues and proposed reform.

[9] The current bitcoin Proof of Work mechanism can use huge amounts of electricity, because for Miners to solve the cryptographic puzzle requires processing vast amounts of random numbers. This ESG issue is covered later in the chapter.

many millions of US dollars. Cyber security risks associated with DLT are covered in Chapter 5 of this book.

4.3   The functions of money

English law governing money is very well established.[10] In England, for more than 300 years hundred years, the Bank of England has issued bank notes. From 1855, on each printed bank note there has been a 'promise to pay the bearer on demand' the specified sum.[11] Money, whether printed by the Bank of England or in accounts, provides three functions. It is (a) a store of value; (b) a medium of exchange; and (c) a unit of account.[12] The meaning of a medium of exchange and a store of value are self-explanatory. However, to refresh memories from perhaps distant Economics 101 classes, a unit of account refers to a stable, measurable unit that allows meaningful comparison of everything in an economy, for example assets, goods, liabilities and services. A unit of account is pivotal to meaningful financial accounting.

A memorable way of encapsulating the hierarchical importance of these three functions is illustrated in Figure 4.1. It is an adaptation of a diagram forming part of a presentation by a former Governor of the Bank of England, Mark Carney.

Based on this analysis, bitcoin is not a unit of account. Second, bitcoin acts as a very limited medium of exchange given it is not accepted by the vast majority of businesses to buy goods and services. Third, bitcoin has been an extremely volatile store of value. For example, my own research on the volatility of bitcoin between 2017–2018 revealed a 400 per cent decrease in the value of one bitcoin. Over that same 12 months the Argentine peso depreciated by 100 per cent.

In 2020 bitcoin rose 300 per cent. In Q4 2020 the FCA published rules banning the sale to retail consumers of derivatives referencing certain

---

[10] Bank of England Act 1694.

[11] The Bank Charter Act 1844 formalised the Bank of England's note issuance responsibilities, and this same statute started the phasing out of the rights of other private banks to issue their own notes in England and Wales.

[12] Smith, A (1776) *The Wealth of Nations* (W Strahan and T Cadell).

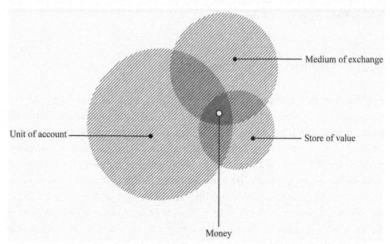

Medium of exchange

Unit of account

Store of value

Money

Source: Carney, M (2018) https://www.bankofengland.co.uk/speech/2018/
mark-carney-speech-to-the-inaugural-scottish-economics-conference/.

Figure 4.1   *The three functions of money*

cryptoassets.[13] In early 2021, bitcoin increased by 30 per cent in one week. Subsequently, it fell by 25 per cent the next week, resulting in the FCA publishing a general warning notice to consumers about the risks associated with investing in cryptoassets. In the first half of 2021, bitcoin climbed from below $30,000 to above $60,000, then fell back to $37,000. In sum, it is naïve to classify bitcoin as a stable asset until a track record of its long-term volatility is established.

4.4   Common law analysis

A detailed explanation of the impact of DLT is found in a Bank of England, FCA and HM Treasury 'Cryptoassets Taskforce Final Report' (the 'UK Cryptoassets Report').[14] Subsequent to the UK Cryptoassets Report, an authoritative committee of mainly legal experts was formed called the UK Jurisdiction Taskforce (UKJT). Contributors to the UKJT

---

[13]   FCA (2020) FCA Bans the Sale of Crypto-Derivatives to Retail Consumers, 6 October 2020.
[14]   UKFT (2018) Cryptoassets Taskforce – Final Report.

work included judges, lawyers, cryptographers and an FCA director. The UKJT committee published a 'Legal Statement on Cryptoassets and Smart Contracts' (the 'UKJT Legal Statement'), which focuses on, among other things, cryptoassets.[15] Combined, these documents provide important direction on this dynamic area of financial services.

If there is any doubt that the UKJT Legal Statement has influenced the judiciary, it was dispelled in less than one month after its publication in a High Court judgment.[16] Stated briefly, a Canadian insurance company became a victim of a ransomware cyber security attack. Hackers managed to breach the plaintiff's firewall and install malware that encrypted all of the insurance company's records. Blackmailers then used the insurance company's computer system to communicate ransom demands.

The plaintiff was an English insurance company with whom the Canadian company had taken out cyber-crime attack insurance. The plaintiff instructed an Incident Response Company (IRC) to negotiate with the blackmailers, namely the first defendants designated as 'persons unknown who demanded bitcoins'. The initial demand by the first defendant was for US$1.2 million to be paid in bitcoins. Thereafter, a reduced ransom sum of US$950,000 was paid to the first defendant. Consequently, the first unknown defendant sent a tool that enabled the Canadian company to decrypt its files.

Investigators were able to track the transfer of the ransom bitcoins to a specified address linked to the Bitfinex exchange. The third and fourth defendants jointly ran Bitfinex. However, the investigators were unable to identify the specific address where the ransom bitcoins were transferred (the second defendant). Based on Know Your Customer (KYC) anti-money laundering (AML) requirements, both the owners of Bitfinex were joined as third and fourth defendants because they were the parties able to identify the second defendant.

The plaintiff's applications were threefold: (a) an application for an injunctive order for the third and fourth defendants to provide information about the cryptocurrency account held by the second defendant; (b)

---

[15] UKJT (2019) Legal Statement on Cryptoassets and Smart Contracts.
[16] *AA v Persons Unknown & Ors, Re Bitcoin* [2019] EWHC 3556 (Comm) per HHJ Bryan, at 57. This judgment was released from reporting restrictions on 17 January 2020.

a proprietary injunction application on the bitcoins held at the account of the fourth defendant; and (c) a freezing injunctive order (Mareva injunction) to prevent the bitcoins held at the specified account with the third and fourth defendants from being dissipated.[17]

On initial analysis, the legal barrier for the High Court judge was that for any injunction to be granted, bitcoins have to be classified as a form of property. English law divides property into two categories, namely choses in action and choses in possession.[18] There is no third category.

If cryptoassets qualify as property, that determines their treatment in bankruptcy, insolvency, fraud, succession or theft. In the UKJT Legal Statement there is an important section entitled 'What is property, and why does it matter?'. One paragraph encapsulates the general importance and varying form of property in this way:

> Strictly, the term property does not describe a thing itself but a legal relationship with a thing: it is a way of describing a power recognised in law as permissibly exercised over the thing. The fundamental proprietary relationship is ownership ... Proprietary rights are of particular importance in an insolvency, where they generally have priority over claims by creditors, and when someone seeks to recover something that has been lost, stolen or unlawfully taken. They are also relevant to the questions of whether there can be a security interest in a cryptoasset and whether a cryptoasset can be held on trust.[19]

However, the judge was influenced by the detailed legal analysis of the UKJT. He remarked:

> the [UKJT] Legal Statement is not in fact a statement of the law. Nevertheless, in my judgment, it is relevant to consider the analysis in that [UKJT] Legal Statement as to the proprietary status of crypto currencies because it is a detailed and careful consideration and, as I shall come on to, I consider that that analysis as to the proprietary status of crypto currencies is compelling and for the reasons identified therein should be adopted by this court.[20]

---

[17] A succinct single paragraph explanation of the difference between proprietary and Mareva injunctions is provided by the Hong Kong High Court in *Zimmer Sweden AB v KPN Hong Kong Ltd and Brand Trading Limited* HCA 2264/2013. The Judge in that case cited *Falcon Private Bank Ltd v Borry Bernard Edouard Charles Limited*, unreported, HCA 1943/2011/.

[18] *Colonial Bank v Whinney*, [1885] 30 ChD, per Fry LJ at 261.

[19] UKJT (2019) Legal Statement on Cryptoassets and Smart Contracts, at 11.

[20] *AA v Persons Unknown & Ors, Re Bitcoin* [2019] EWHC 3556 (Comm) per HHJ Bryan, at 57.

The essence of the decision to treat cryptoassets as a third type of property[21] was justified by applying an authoritative four-limbed qualification test.[22] The four criteria for determining if something qualifies as property are that it is (a) definable; (b) identifiable by third-parties; (c) capable of assumption by third-parties; and (d) has some degree of permanence. First, definable means that through the allocation and use of a public key, the data stored in that unique public key is distinct from all other data. Each public key is linked to a cryptoasset holder.

Second, identifiable by third-parties means a cryptoasset can be compared logically with established legal property, for instance a traditional bank account balance record or a freehold title to a house. A key aspect of identifiability in property law is the degree of control that a person has over the asset. In particular, the power to exclude others is important. The bitcoin DLT provides such power of exclusion by allocating a private key to the bitcoin owner after each transfer. Any third-party has no access to that unique bitcoin.

Third, being 'capable in its nature of assumption by third-parties' is the type of criterion that makes non-lawyers suspicious of the law, and legal counsel and compliance officers seek out a cold towel to wrap around their heads in a quiet study. In short, it means that third-parties respect the rights of the owner and place some value in the property, in the sense there is a buy/sell market in it. English property laws have established ways to deal with scenarios where a third-party asserts ownership over property owned by another. For example, in England and Wales the HM Land Registry[23] allows third-parties to search, then obtain notice, of many different types of real property ownership, such as freehold and leasehold titles. The DLT for bitcoin provides a comparable practical role, albeit to date, under English law, it is not an official register of title.

Fourth, to qualify as property requires some degree of permanence. Bitcoins achieve permanence because they are controlled by the owner and cannot be cancelled by anyone. The only possible ways that bitcoins

---

[21] In *Armstrong v Winnington* [2013] Ch 156, EU carbon emission allowances were treated as a third type of property so the treatment of cryptoassets in this way is not unique.

[22] *National Provincial Bank v Ainsworth* [1965] AC 1175.

[23] www.gov.uk/search-property-information-land-registry.

can unlawfully disappear would be by an unauthorised person obtaining the private key or by hacking.

Applying these four limbs, the judge in the Canadian insurance company case concluded:

> as elaborated upon in the [UKJT] Legal Statement, which I consider to be an accurate statement as to the position under English law, I am satisfied for the purpose of granting an interim injunction ... that crypto currencies are a form of property capable of being the subject of a proprietary injunction.[24]

The UKJT legal analysis that illuminates the four stage test as the means of categorising cryptoassets as property is not English law. Yet the fact it has been quickly applied by the English High Court makes it more likely that UK judiciary will treat cryptoassets in this way. It is also notable that other common law jurisdictions have already followed suit. For instance, the Singapore High Court has held that bitcoins qualified as property applying the same English High Court test.[25] The New Zealand High Court has also judged that bitcoins and equivalent assets meet the four criteria to qualify as property.[26] The New Zealand High Court also makes extensive reference to the detailed analysis in the UKJT Legal Statement.

More recently, in an ex parte interim application, the English High Court has endorsed that there is at least a serious issue to be tried that cryptoassets qualify as property.[27] This application was also notable for two other legal points of specific relevance to cryptoassets. First, that the choice of law to apply when a conflict exists could be determined by the location that the company or person who owns the cryptoassets is domiciled.[28] Second, that a Bankers Trust order for an injunction could be

---

[24] *AA v Persons Unknown & Ors, Re Bitcoin* [2019] EWHC 3556 (Comm) per HHJ Bryan, at 61.

[25] *B2C2 Ltd v Quoine Pte Ltd* [2019] SGHC(I)03.

[26] *Ruscoe v Cryptopia Limited* (in liquidation) [2020] NZHC 728.

[27] *Ion Science Ltd v Persons Unknown* (unreported, 21 December 2020).

[28] The Latin legal term used for this jurisdictional law to determine the location of property that is subject to litigation is the *lex situs*. The judge in *Ion Science Ltd v Persons Unknown* (unreported, 21 December 2020) had no case law to rely on, but referred to authoritative academic analysis by Professor Andrew Dickinson found in Fox, D, and Green, S (2019) *Cryptocurrencies in Public and Private Law* (Oxford University Press).

made to compel out of jurisdiction cryptocurrency exchanges to disclose information concerning cryptoassets.[29]

4.5 Financial regulation

Whether including DLT or not, cryptoassets are constantly evolving. A regulated firm with global business investments and trades will have to grasp the varying international classifications of cryptoassets by leading economies.[30] However, as with the earlier analysis anchored intentionally on bitcoins, in my view it is vital to know in detail how the FCA categorises different cryptoassets. To make this memorable, bitcoin will continue, where relevant, to be the sole example. Further, there is a need for legal counsel and compliance officers to devote on-going monitoring of UK regulator assessments of what is or is not within the FCA's regulatory perimeter.

4.5.1 Exchange, security and utility tokens

The UK Cryptoassets Report divides cryptoassets into three broad types of token, namely exchange tokens, security tokens and utility tokens.[31] Each of these is dealt with in turn. Figure 4.2 captures the functions common to (a) all three types of token; (b) two types of token; and (c) where use is solely relevant to one of them.

Exchange tokens function as a medium of exchange, but are a very limited medium compared to fiat money (government-backed) such as the British pound or euro. To elaborate, an exchange token cannot pay for many different things in one jurisdiction, such as clothes, supermarket food, fuel or hotel accommodation. The stark purchasing options contrast is between government-issued and guaranteed fiat money and bitcoin.[32] However, exchange tokens are also purchased as an investment, just as

---

[29] *Bankers Trust Co v Shapira* [1980] 1 WLR 1274 (4 June 1980). The court also relied on *MacKinnon v Donaldson, Lufkin and Jenrette Securities* [1986] Ch 482 for the principle that in exceptional circumstances a Bankers Trust Order can be served out of the jurisdiction.

[30] A comprehensive multi-jurisdictional comparative taxonomy has been published by the Cambridge Centre for Alternative Finance. See Allen, J et al. (2020), Legal and Regulatory Considerations for Digital Assets (University of Cambridge Judge Business School).

[31] UKFT (2018) Cryptoassets Taskforce – Final Report.

[32] It is notable that bitcoin has over 8,000 competitors. See https://coinmarketcap.com/.

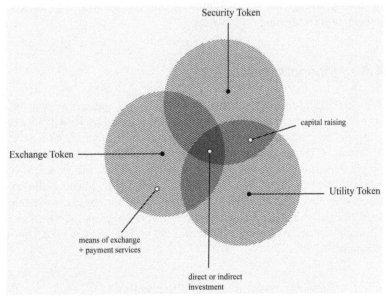

Source: Adaptation of data from a chart in UKFT (2018) Cryptoassets Taskforce – Final Report, at 13.

Figure 4.2   *Exchange, security and utility token functions*

an investor may choose to buy equities or fixed income products. The vast majority of bitcoins serve this function as either direct or indirect investments.

Further, some exchange tokens may meet the definition of e-money under the Second Electronic Money Directive (EMD2). Under the EMD2 'electronic money means electronically, including magnetically, stored monetary value as represented by a claim on the issuer which is issued on receipt of funds for the purpose of making payment transactions … and which is accepted by a natural or legal person other than the electronic money issuer'.[33] For example, a prepaid card with a specific cryptoasset value may qualify with the private key providing the equivalent of a PIN code as used with a credit or debit card.

---

[33]   Article 2(2) EU Directive 2009/110.

The Payment Services Regulations 2017 does not apply to exchange tokens. The scope of the Payment Services Regulations is 'funds' in the form of bank notes, coins and e-money. On initial analysis, cryptoassets fall outside of the perimeter.[34] However, FCA guidance indicates that cryptoassets are governed by the Payment Services Regulations when they are used to facilitate regulated payment services. In the FCA guidance on this issue,[35] the example of 'money remittance' is given.[36] To illustrate, a payer in one jurisdiction may transfer British pounds to an intermediary that converts them into bitcoins. The intermediary charges a low cost per transaction. The bitcoins are then converted into Singaporean dollars, which are in turn transferred to a payee in Singapore. The cryptoassets are facilitating the service.

Turning to security tokens, these generally have rights of ownership and include some entitlement to the repayment of a specific sum or a percentage of future profits. Security tokens are regulated under the FSMA Regulated Activities Order 2001.[37] Under Part III covering Specified Investments of the Regulated Activities Order, there are numerous categories of investment that may apply to security tokens, which means they are regulated activities.[38] For instance, many security tokens have common traits compared with shares, such as rights of ownership, voting rights, and access to dividends or equivalent profits based on the number or value of shares owned.[39] There are many other investments in the Regulated Activities Order that may result in a security token being treated as a regulated activity.[40] For example, certificates representing certain securities,[41] collective investment scheme units,[42] debt instruments,[43] and warrants.[44] A valuable section in the FCA Guidance

---

[34] Article 2 PSR (2017).

[35] FCA PS 19/22 (2019), Guidance on Cryptoassets, paragraphs 57–61.

[36] Schedule 1 at paragraph 1(f) PSR (2017).

[37] FSMA (Regulated Activities) Order 2001, SI 2001/544.

[38] Note there is a difference between digital securities and dematerialised securities. The latter are governed by the Uncertified Securities Regulation 2001, SI 2001/3755.

[39] Article 76 RAO.

[40] FCA PERG 2.6.

[41] Article 80 RAO.

[42] Article 81 RAO.

[43] Article 77 RAO.

[44] Article 79 RAO.

on Cryptoassets on this point is entitled 'How do I know if my token is a specified investment?'.[45]

Under MiFID II, security tokens may also be treated as transferable securities, defined as 'those classes of securities which are negotiable on the capital market, with the exception of instruments of payment'.[46] The MiFID II definition is broad, and includes bonds, depository receipts and shares, and 'any other securities giving the right to acquire or sell any such transferable securities or giving rise to a cash settlement determined by reference to transferable securities, currencies, interest rates or yields, commodities or other indices or measures'.[47]

Focusing attention on utility tokens, these provide entitlement to a specific good or service. Under FSMA and FCA regulation, utility tokens are unregulated. For example, when you purchase a good you may receive a voucher entitling you to a discount on a future purchase. Under FSMA and FCA regulation, exchange tokens are unregulated.

4.6   Legal risk management

Whether the legal categorisation of a cryptoasset is one of an exchange token, security token or utility token, what are the core risk issues? The answer to that question will vary depending on whether the client is an asset manager, bank or platform provider, but the following are recurring common denominator themes.

4.6.1   AML

A dominant issue is the link between money laundering or terrorist financing and the use of all three types of token. The key risk lies in the pseudo-anonymous nature of bitcoin and its competitors or variants. By which is meant when someone trades to buy or sell a bitcoin their specific identity is not known, because the ownership is determined by the private key and the bitcoin account.

---

[45]   FCA (2019) PS 19/22, Guidance on Cryptoassets, at 30.

[46]   Article 4(44) MiFID/2014/65.

[47]   Article 4(44)(c) MiFID/2014/65.

As reported by the Financial Action Task Force (FATF) increased use of bitcoin and equivalents for money laundering and other criminal purposes has been occurring for a number of years.[48] Consequently, the 5th Money Laundering Directive (AMLD5) was introduced partly to more robustly manage the trend by requiring cryptocurrency exchange providers and custodian wallet providers to comply with AML regulations. Most importantly, both these service providers, often collectively called Virtual Asset Service Providers (VASPs), have to carry out and record KYC verification. So bitcoin and equivalent transactions cannot be anonymous to either type of provider.

The definition of cryptoasset is important from not only a regulatory compliance perspective, but also serves as a valuable component for consistent, unambiguous drafting in contracts and policy documents: 'A cryptoasset is a cryptographically secured digital representation of value or contractual rights that uses a form of DLT and can be transferred, stored or traded electronically ... [and] includes a right to, or interest in, the cryptoasset'.[49]

The detail on AML regulations in the context of cryptoassets can be digested by referring to the guidance of the Joint Money Laundering Steering Group.[50] AML regulations cannot be overlooked. A leading cryptoassets intelligence company, CipherTrace, monitors more than 800 globally traded products. In a multi-jurisdiction risk report it concluded that 'notwithstanding the AMLD5, our researchers have discovered that Europe has the highest count of VASPs with deficient KYC procedures. Sixty per cent of European VASPs have weak or porous KYC.'[51]

AML requirements are increasing for firms dealing in cryptoassets. Since the beginning of 2021, cryptoasset firms must register with the FCA before commencing business. This is because the FCA acts as the AML and counter-terrorist financing supervisor of UK cryptoasset businesses.[52]

---

[48]   FATF (2018) FATF Report to G20 Finance Ministers and Central Bank Governors.

[49]   Regulation 14A(13)(a) and (c) Money Laundering and Terrorist Financing (Amendment) Regulations 2019, SI 2019/1511.

[50]   JMLSG Part II (2020), Prevention of Money Laundering and Combating Terrorist Financing, at 252–263. Note that any regulated firm must also refer to JMLSG Part I (2020).

[51]   CipherTrace (2020) Geographic Risk Report: VASP KYC by Jurisdiction.

[52]   Section 56 Money Laundering, Terrorist Financing and Transfer of Funds (Information on the Payer) Regulations 2017, SI 2017/692, as amended.

The documents required by the cryptoasset registrant firm are extensive. The most significant documents include:

- AML and counter-terrorist finance framework and risk assessment: highlighting specific risks and mitigation plans;
- AML and counter-terrorist finance staff training material;
- budget forecasts and financials for the first three financial years;
- business plan, including financial resources and the number and type of clients;
- cryptoasset public keys and wallet addresses;
- customer on-boarding agreements and processes;
- details on the programme of operations, setting out the specific cryptoasset activities for the business;
- marketing plan, including a description of customers and distribution channels;
- money laundering reporting Individual forms for all directors, executives and officers;
- record-keeping and recording procedures;
- structural organisation, including a corporate structure chart and any outsourcing arrangements; and
- systems and controls, including details of the key IT systems and security policies.[53]

As cryptoassets become of greater interest to asset managers, banks and platform providers there are reputational risks associated with offering products that derive their value from the value of such assets. For instance, Bloomberg and Galaxy Digital Capital Management have launched the Bloomberg Galaxy Crypto Index (BGCI) whose constituents include bitcoin and four similar products.[54] Referencing derivatives against the BGCI offers clients a new investment that can diversify a portfolio, but from a reputational risk viewpoint the provenance of the underlying cryptoasset owners requires due diligence and on-going monitoring.

4.6.2 Retail customers and cryptoasset derivatives

Product volatility risk is also prevalent in the context of cryptoassets. ESMA, the Basel Committee on Banking Supervision and the International

---

[53] FCA (2021) Cryptoassets: AML/CTF regime: Register with the FCA.
[54] See www.bloomberg.com/professional/product/indices/bloomberg-galaxy-crypto-index/.

Organization of Securities Commissions (IOSCO) have all expressed concerns on consumer protection surrounding cryptoassets. The FSB has also noted that the IOSCO's Committee on Secondary Markets has already begun to examine Internet-based platforms, including cryptoasset platforms. The FSB has identified a number of key issues to consider including custody, cyber security, settlement, systems integrity, trading and transparency.[55]

Since January 2021, the FCA has banned the marketing, distribution and sale of any derivatives products referenced to cryptoassets for retail customers. This ban covers all types of contracts for difference, futures and options. These rules affect, among other regulated firms, creators of such products, issuers, distributors as well as operators of trading venues and platforms.[56]

4.7   Law reform

In terms of influential ideas on law reform affecting the treatment of cryptoassets, the Financial Markets Law Committee (FMLC) produced an incisive report entitled 'Distributed Ledger Technology and Governing Law: Issues of Legal Uncertainty'.[57] The focus is on the complex conflict of laws issues that arise from the treatment of cryptoassets as legal property on DLT systems. The FMLC incisive advice is that 'any solution is promulgated by a body such as the *Hague Convention, UNIDROIT* or *ISDA*, in order to ensure that it is adhered to on an international basis'.[58]

Second, under the FMSA, exchange tokens are currently unregulated. However, the UK Government proposed to add 'qualifying cryptoassets' to be covered by the general prohibition on their marketing unless the person doing so is authorised or exempt.[59] The proposed new defined term to add to the Financial Promotions Order (FPO)[60] covers 'any cryptographically secured digital representation of value or contractual rights

---

[55] FSB (2018) Crypto-assets Report to the G20 on Work by the FSB and Standard-setting Bodies, at 6.

[56] FCA PS 20/10 (2020).

[57] FMLC (2018) Distributed Ledger Technology and Governing Law: Issues of Legal Uncertainty.

[58] Ibid., at 23.

[59] Section 19 FSMA 2000.

[60] Schedule 1, Part II, FPO, SI 2005/1529.

that uses a form of distributed ledger technology' on a DLT that: (a) is fungible; (b) is transferable or confers rights or is promoted in either of those ways; (c) is not already classified in Schedule 1, Part II of the FPO; (d) is not e-money under the Electronic Money Regulations (EMR); and (e) is not fiat money.[61] However, as the earlier mentioned FMLC feedback pointed out the long-term goal is to have consistent regulation. There are questions over the wisdom of having too many cryptoasset definitions that create contradictions.[62]

4.8   ESG disclosure regulation

Finally, the current bitcoin Proof of Work mechanism uses a huge amount of electricity. This is because for Miners to solve the cryptographic puzzle requires processing random numbers through a hash function on very powerful energy-hungry computers. In short, Proof of Work energy consumption is counter to mitigating climate change. The EU Disclosure Regulation on sustainability (ESG) disclosures in the financial services sector is relevant to cryptoasset production just as a physical coal or gold mine has environmental costs.[63] Regulated firms investing in cryptoassets will need to report on the related power consumption linked to the running of the bitcoin or competitor DLT, disclosing the weighted average of the energy consumption intensity per million of revenue in GWh. In the future, it is likely that climate-related disclosures will be required as part of cryptoassets Proof of Work activity. Evidentially, the main objective way to address this issue is, in my view, to require that Proof of Work activity is substantially carried out with auditable renewable energy sources.

Based on a 2019 survey conducted at Cambridge University, renewable energy sources are estimated to contribute less than half of the total energy consumption for Proof of Work activities. Further, several leading economies still have a considerable dependency on coal mining so there is a double harm from the viewpoint that coal mining is used to produce

---

[61]   HM Treasury (2020) Cryptoassets Promotion Consultation, at 4.17.

[62]   FMLC (2020) Reply to HM Treasury Consultation, at 3.

[63]   EU Regulation 2019/2088.

Table 4.2   *Bitcoin renewable energy use*

Region	Average share of renewables (%)	Weighted share of renewables in bitcoin Proof of Work (%)
Africa and Middle East	N/A	N/A
APAC	26	20
Europe	30	4
North America	63	5
South America and Caribbean	20	0
Global total		29

electricity that is then used to power the digital mining administration processes that make bitcoin and equivalent cryptoassets function.[64]

As Table 4.2 shows, the total global share of renewables used to power bitcoin mining could be as low as 29 per cent.[65] This figure is accurate as of 2020 and is based on a sophisticated methodological approach. Beyond that figure there is the issue of what types of renewable energy sources are used. What is clear is that the use of any coal is in contradiction to a forward looking use of technology to both evolve business and simultaneously manage climate change. Expect UK regulation to continue to pioneer and attempt to be congruent with emerging regulations in major APAC, European and North American jurisdictions.

4.9   Central bank digital currency initiatives

The development of cryptoassets presents potential innovation for growth and simultaneously needs increasing legal and regulatory attention. The Basel Committee has already started to consult on how capital requirement rules may have to change to account for all the different categories

---

[64]   Blandin, A et al. (2020) Cambridge Centre for Alternative Finance, 3rd Global Cryptoasset Benchmarking Study, at 26.

[65]   Ibid., at 28.

of cryptoasset exposures.[66] The UK is at the point where assessing the correct, detailed regulatory approach is in its infancy but gaining momentum. The Q1 2021 Kalifa Review proposed the introduction of a Central Bank Digital Currency (CBDC), perhaps introducing a wholesale CBDC first, followed by a retail CBDC.[67] By Q2 2021, HM Treasury and the Bank of England had established a CBDC taskforce.[68] By Q4 2021 a joint statement by HM Treasury and the Bank of England projected that after development phases the earliest launch of a CBDC would be the second half of the decade.[69]

Given CBDC pilot schemes are already underway in China, Singapore and Sweden, to name just three ambitious FinTech economies, the likelihood of an imminent CBDC from at least one of these jurisdictions is high.[70] Equally, the international regulatory consensus that provides long-term acceptance and trust of CBDCs will be an on-going focus for legal and compliance functions.

---

[66] BIS (2021) Basel Committee on Banking Supervision Consultative Document Prudential Treatment of Cryptoasset Exposures, Table 1, at 3.

[67] Kalifa, R (2021) Kalifa Review of UK FinTech, at 29.

[68] Bank of England (2021) Bank of England Statement on Central Bank Digital Currency.

[69] Bank of England and HM Treasury (2021) Statement on Central Bank Digital Currency – Next Steps.

[70] In the USA, pilot schemes have already been planned by The Digital Dollar Project. See https://digitaldollarproject.org/.

5. Cyber security

Annually, the UK National Cyber Security Centre (NCSC) produces a detailed report summarising its activities.[1] Each year, the overall impression left is that cyber risk occurs on an increasing scale that mirrors the risk gap between technology and human understanding of it. The scale and sophistication of criminal attacks and espionage operations are not overstated.[2] For example, in December 2020 the SolarWinds breach to its Orion monitoring platform affected more than 18,000 customers, including the US Commerce Department and the US Defense Department.[3] Further, the Sword of Damocles swings markedly over financial services, given IBM Security has repeatedly measured it to be the most attacked sector.[4]

For FCA regulated seniors managers the stakes could not be higher. At an AI conference my question put to the Chief Executive Officer of the NCSC, Lindy Cameron, was how can corporate boards do more? She replied '[c]yber security is as important as financial risk, and is made up of legal, operational and reputational risk. You do not hear CEOs saying I do not understand finance.'[5] Further, at a Chatham House Cyber conference Cameron expanded the parallel commenting that 'a CEO would never say

---

[1] Since 2020, an additional increase in the volume of cyber attacks is technically more likely given the global Covid-19 pandemic forced a massive jump in home working activity. While the total number of employees involved in home working subsided in 2021, it is likely to remain at a higher level compared with before the pandemic. See NCSC Annual Review 2021.

[2] CogX Artificial Intelligence Conference (2021) SolarWinds, Russia and the New Cold War seminar, 14 June 2021. The different terminology for state and non-state actor cyber activity, namely 'intelligence operation' and 'attack' was illuminated in a seminar by Lauren Zabierek, fellow at Harvard University and a former US Air Force intelligence officer. If the cyber perpetrators are only spying and not degrading or disrupting technology systems, based on international norms that are tolerated behaviours and given that US intelligence services would also engage in cyber intelligence.

[3] Joint Statement by the Federal Bureau of Investigation (FBI), the Cybersecurity and Infrastructure Security Agency (CISA), The Office of the Director of National Intelligence (ODNI), and the National Security Agency (NSA), published 5 January 2021.

[4] IBM Security (2021) X-Force Threat Intelligence Index Report 2021, at 34.

[5] CogX Artificial Intelligence Conference (2021) Leadership in Cyber Security seminar, 16 June 2021.

they don't need to understand legal risk just because they have a General Counsel. This is a board-level issue.'[6]

5.1   Introduction

It is fundamental to any analysis of English law, FCA rules or transposed EU regulations relevant to financial services cyber security to know what is really being analysed. What is cyberspace and what are its boundaries? Past information attacks were based on the physical domains of air, land, sea and space.[7] The introduction of cyberspace is a fifth man-made domain that moves across all the other four domains. To many engineers that complexity is well understood, but it is less common to think of it in the context of financial services transactions, governed by a contract, as travelling between these four domains via multiple nodes. The more nodes and changes from one domain to another, the more potential points of attack. Complexity and vulnerability are on an exponential scale.

5.2   The role of legal counsel and compliance officers

How can legal counsel and compliance officers advising an asset manager, an investment bank, a platform or a FinTech firm contribute to avoiding and mitigating cyber attacks? That question is the stem of a number of leaf questions that determine how legal risks are managed in written financial regulation advice, contract drafting, M&A due diligence, dispute resolution, policies and standard operating procedures. The FCA has produced a helpful infographic that captures the key questions to answer. These are paraphrased below along with any specific accreditation or scheme promoted by the FCA's cyber security professionals.

- Is the information you hold classified?
- Do you review who has access to your most sensitive data?
- Do you understand your vulnerabilities?
- Do you know if you are able to restore services in the event of an

---

[6]   Chatham House Cyber Conference (2021), Key Note Speech, 11 October 2021.

[7]   Bank of England (2016) CBEST Intelligence-Led Testing Version 2 – Understanding Cyber Threat Intelligence Operations, at 8.

attack?

- Do you make sure your computer network is configured to prevent unauthorised access?
- Do you use encryption software to protect your critical information from unauthorised access?
- Do you align your firm to a recognised cyber scheme, such as Cyber Essentials or an equivalent accreditation?
- Do you use two-factor authentication where the confidentiality of the data is most crucial?
- Do you educate your staff on cyber security risks?
- Are you a member of any information sharing arrangements, such as CiSP or an equivalent network?[8]

5.3   Threat classification

The range of potential unauthorised access, alteration, control over or deletion of data evolve, but Table 5.1 sets out the STRIDE acronym model developed by Microsoft and widely applied by computer professionals working inside financial services firms and regulators.

5.4   Risk management frameworks

5.4.1   G7 Cyber Security Guidelines

The Group of Seven (G7) has consulted on and then published its Fundamental Elements of Cybersecurity for the Financial Sector guidelines (the 'G7 Guidelines').[9] The G7 Guidelines are aimed at assisting financial services sector businesses to build and implement a suitable cyber security strategy and operational framework. Further, given all seven constituent regulators worked on the G7 Guidelines, they have

---

[8]   FCA (2017) Good Cyber Security – The Foundations. See www.fca.org.uk/publication/documents/cyber-security-infographic.pdf.

[9]   As a reminder, the G7 is an intergovernmental organisation comprising of Canada, France, Germany, Italy, Japan, UK and the US. So an influential group in terms of their collective GDP as a percentage of the global total.

Table 5.1   *Main types of cyber attacks*

STRIDE threat category	Description
Spoofing identity	Illegal access and use of another's authentication information. For example, username and password.
Tampering with data	The malicious modification of data. For example, unauthorised changes to data held in a database, and the alteration of data as it flows between two computers over an open network.
Repudiation	Threats associated with users who deny performing an action and other parties cannot prove the illegality. For example, a user performs an illegal operation in a system that lacks the ability to trace the prohibited actions.
Information disclosure	Threats to expose information to individuals who have no rights to access it. For example, the ability of users to read a file that they were not granted access to, or the ability of an intruder to read data flowing between two computers.
Denial of service	Attacks denying service to valid users. For example, by making a Web server temporarily unavailable or unusable. Denial of Service is often abbreviated to DoS.
Elevation of privilege	When an unprivileged user gains privileged access sufficient to compromise or destroy the entire system. Elevation of privilege threats include those situations in which an attacker has effectively penetrated all system defences and become part of the trusted system.

Source: Microsoft (2009) The STRIDE Threat Model.

a drafting quality that can be applied to any regulated firm in any jurisdiction. The eight elements are set out below.

- *Cyber security Strategy and Framework*: Building and maintaining a cyber security strategy and framework.
- *Governance*: Defining and facilitating performance of roles and responsibilities.
- *Risk and Control Assessment*: Identifying activities, functions, products and services, including dependencies, interconnections and third parties.
- *Monitoring*: Establishing monitoring processes that can quickly detect

cyber incidents. The key aspect of this element is the need to conduct penetration testing, and then auditing the results so that these can be compared with other results.

- *Response*: Quickly assessing the impact of the incident, then mitigating its impact. Notifying all internal and external stakeholders, including clients, law enforcement actors and regulators.
- *Recovery*: Restarting operations in a responsible manner. Establishing and testing contingency plans for essential activities and key processes.
- *Information Sharing*: Sharing reliable cyber security information with internal and external stakeholders.
- *Continuous Learning*: Regularly reviewing the cyber security strategy and framework, so analysing and implementing improvements.[10]

A pivotal element of the G7 Guidelines is the establishment of a Cyber security Strategy and Framework, with the aim of specifying the most robust ways of identifying and reducing risks that integrate on the bases of the complexity, culture, nature, risk profile and scale of the business.[11] Beyond these high-level themes, other elements of the G7 Guidelines cover detailed technical aspects.

Further, each business should be 'informed by the cyber threat and vulnerability landscape, a jurisdiction can also establish sector-wide cyber security strategies and frameworks that outline how cooperation occurs between entities and public authorities in the financial sector, with sectors upon which the financial sector depends, and with other relevant jurisdictions'.[12]

5.4.2   Financial Stability Board

The Group of Twenty (G20) governed FSB[13] has also produced an authoritative report entitled 'Effective Practices for Cyber Incident Response and

---

[10] G7 (2016) G7 Fundamental Elements of Cyber security for the Financial Services Sector. See https://assets.publishing.service.gov.uk/government/uploads/system/uploads/attachment_data/file/559186/G7_Fundamental_Elements_Oct_2016.pdf.

[11] Ibid.

[12] Ibid.

[13] The FSB includes all G20 countries with a remit focused on the global financial system. See www.fsb.org/about/.

Recovery'.[14] It is important to note that the FSB has been influenced by the US NIST. Specifically, the NIST definitions of respond and recover are applied.[15] First, respond is defined as the function to 'develop and implement the appropriate activities to take action regarding a detected cyber security event'.[16] Second, recover refers to the function to 'develop and implement the appropriate activities to maintain plans for resilience and to restore any capabilities or services that were impaired due to a cyber security event'.[17]

There are other G20 initiatives that may influence a regulated firm's cyber security framework and related contracts. For instance, The Osaka Declaration on the Digital Economy (the 'Osaka Track'), a G20 led framework for promoting data flows with better, consistent protection, including cyber security, may play a long-term role in harmonising laws. This is especially so given it is led by a range of both liberal market and state-controlled economies, including China, France, Germany, Japan, Russia, Saudi Arabia, Singapore, the UK and the US.[18]

5.4.3   European Union agency for cyber security

Originally established in 2004 as the European Network Information Security Agency[19] and renamed the European Union Agency for Cyber security and retaining the abbreviation ENISA,[20] it functions as the EU's agency focused on cyber security, including the objective of fostering cooperation with Members States and all relevant private and public stakeholders.[21]

---

[14]   FSB (2020) Effective Practices for Cyber Incident Response and Recovery – Final Report. See www.fsb.org/2020/04/effective-practices-for-cyber-incident-response-and-recovery-consultative-document/.

[15]   See https://csrc.nist.gov/glossary See https://nvlpubs.nist.gov/nistpubs/ir/2019/NIST.IR.7298r3.pdf.

[16]   See https://csrc.nist.gov/glossary/term/respond_CSF.

[17]   See https://csrc.nist.gov/glossary/term/recover_CSF.

[18]   See www.wto.org/english/news_e/news19_e/osaka_declration_on_digital_economy_e.pdf.

[19]   EC Regulation No. 460/2004, establishing the European Network and Information Security Agency. See https://eur-lex.europa.eu/LexUriServ/LexUriServ.do?uri=CELEX:32004R0460:EN:HTML.

[20]   See www.enisa.europa.eu/about-enisa.

[21]   Article 4(4) EU Regulation 2019/881. See https://eur-lex.europa.eu/legal-content/EN/TXT/PDF/?uri=CELEX:32019R0881&from=EN.

5.4.4   FCA cyber coordination groups

Given the complexity of cyber security, a rational part of any regulated firm cyber security strategy is collaboration. Legal counsel and compliance officers collaborating across the financial services sector form part of such processes. With whom should a regulated firm collaborate? That is going to depend in part on the specific business areas of focus, resources and scale.

Since 2017, the FCA has coordinated the collaboration of over 175 regulated firms in information sharing on cyber attacks and cyber security best practices by the Cyber Coordination Groups (CCG).[22] Each CCG represents a specific subsector. Originally, the CCG were fund management, investment management, insurance, retail banking and lending. This later expanded to brokers, principal trading firms, trading venues and benchmark administrators. The CCG has evolved to cover diverse regulated firms, including many small businesses. Further, an organisation with similar objectives, the Investment Banking Information Security Special Interest Group (IBSIG) performed a similar function and cooperated with the FCA.[23]

A significant by-product of the CCG is the publication of its annual insights. By which is meant the FCA combines insights from subsector discussion with themes that are published for anyone to read. For example, a past publication focused on, among other things, malicious emails, third parties and supply chain, and cloud security.[24] More recently, the CCG published annual insights on good practice on cyber risks posed by fourth-party suppliers. By which is meant when a regulated firm's suppliers outsource aspects of their own operations.

To mitigate this often low visibility risk, the CCG good practice recommendation is for greater due diligence at the contractual stage with a third-party supplier. Specifically for lawyers, good practice could include establishing a full picture of a potential third-party's supply chain. Further, for the agreement with third-party suppliers to include contractual obligations on them to update the regulated firm about any

[22]   FCA (2021) Insights from the Cyber Coordination Groups.
[23]   FCA (2019) Cyber Security Industry Insights, at 3.
[24]   FCA (2021) Insights from the 2020 Cyber Coordination Groups.

supply chain changes.[25] For many regulated firms' lawyers, this CCG good practice already forms part of pre-contractual due diligence and contract clause drafting. Nevertheless, this CCG focus on what is already good legal practice does provide all regulated firms with a diplomatic justification for thoroughness when involved in third-party supplied due diligence and contract negotiation.

5.4.5   Cyber Security Information Sharing Partnership

A major initiative of the NCSC is its Cyber Security Information Sharing Partnership (CiSP). The CiSP allows cyber security professionals in registered businesses to share free confidential information across a network about other's mistakes as well as earlier warning on some cyber threats. Further, certain enhanced technical guidance is available to CiSP members.[26]

5.4.6   Financial Sector Cyber Collaboration Centre

An emerging option for all regulated firms is contributing to the Financial Sector Cyber Collaboration Centre (FSCCC), a private/public partnership set up to coordinate responses to cyber attacks in the financial services sector. The FSCCC is the brainchild of UK Finance, a financial services sector trade association representing over 250 regulated firms.[27]

The FSCCC seeks to 'identify threats and disseminate information to the sector so that financial institutions of all sizes are able to act on that information and harden their security posture. In some cases, the information will be specific to a particular subsector or size of organisation ... Consistent in this will be the NCSC's CiSP platform so that all firms can have access to the outputs.'[28]

The power of the FSCCC lies in its ability to blend the deep technical expertise from GCHQ and the NCSC with multiple interactions with a wide range of companies. Collaborative working between NCSC and

---

[25]   Ibid., at 6.

[26]   To send the NCSC a specific query about CiSP email cisp@ncsc.gov.uk.

[27]   See www.ukfinance.org.uk/about-us.

[28]   See www.ukfinance.org.uk/news-and-insight/blogs/collaboration-key-response-cyber-security-threats.

businesses is achieved by the Industry 100 initiative, which to date has included contributions from Bank of America, Lloyds Banking Group, MasterCard, RBS and Tesco Bank.[29]

The FSCCC also collaborates with the Financial Services Information Sharing and Analysis Center (FS-ISAC) analysing cyber threats.[30] The FS-ISAC is a non-profit consortium with more than 6,000 financial services firms as members.[31] So the FS-ISAC also contributes immense depth in understanding the specific cyber risks.

5.5 Cyber security best practices

Turning to specific best practices, these are numerous and there is no single best, established answer, because the nature and sophistication of cyber attacks evolve so quickly. However, all of the following are recurring, respected choices.

5.5.1 FCA recommendations on cyber resilience

In 2013, the Bank of England's Financial Policy Committee recommended that the UK financial services regulators and other relevant authorities cooperate to test and improve the financial services sector vulnerabilities against cyber attacks.[32] Consequently, the Bank of England, FCA and HM Treasury began consulting with regulated firms and professional penetration testing companies with the aim of developing a robust cyber attack testing framework. Called CBEST, this framework allows regulated firms to conduct realistic simulated cyber attacks to improve on-going avoidance, response and recovery linked to actual cyber attacks.[33]

The risks to business disruption for any regulated firm intentionally exposing their IT systems to a simulated cyber attack has historically meant that investment in penetration testing exercises varied.[34] CBEST

---

[29] See www.ncsc.gov.uk/information/industry-100.

[30] NCSC (2020) Annual Review 2020 at 55.

[31] See www.fsisac.com.

[32] Bank of England (2013) Financial Stability Report, Issue No. 33, at 64.

[33] See www.bankofengland.co.uk/glossary.

[34] See www.bankofengland.co.uk/financial-stability/financial-sector-continuity.

has sought to increase confidence by, among other things, providing trusted lists of qualified penetration testers and cyber threat intelligence analysts, and promoting regular vulnerability testing.[35]

The FCA has subsequently provided its own broad range cyber resilience advice. Its recommendations include applying standards from the NIST Cyber security framework, applying ISO27001/2, SANS CIS, NCSC's '10 Steps to Cyber Security' and the NCSC's 'NIS Directive Cyber Assessment Framework'.[36] So it is important to briefly summarise what each of these potentially contribute. However, from an analysis and planning perspective cyber resilience also forms part of general operational resilience for regulated firms, so that has to be factored into legal advice.

Complementing its specific cyber resilience advice, in March 2021 the FCA published its final rules on general operational resilience ('the final FCA operational resilience rules').[37] General operational resilience is far broader, concerning the protection of consumers, and the financial stability of financial subsectors and the whole UK financial system.[38] Nevertheless, for cyber security in this context, impact tolerances will have to be established and reviewed annually for each business service of a regulated firm.[39] In my view, Equation 5.1 is a memorable way of capturing FCA expectations that include evidence of contingency planning and resource commitment and expenditure.

Operational Resilience = Impact Tolerances + Contingency Planning + Resources   (5.1)

The FCA final operational resilience rules require that a regulated firm 'must carry out scenario testing of its ability to remain within its impact tolerance for each of its important business services in the event of

---

[35]   Dual-regulated firms can communicate with the Bank of England Sector Cyber Team to answer questions on the CBEST process. Send any queries to cbest@bankofengland.co.uk.

[36]   FCA (2019) Cyber Security – Industry Insights, at 6.

[37]   FCA (2021) Feedback to CP19/32 and Final Rules.

[38]   Deadlines for compliance with the final FCA operational resilience rules are (a) by 31 March 2022 to identify critical business services and set impact tolerances, and (b) before 1 April 2025 to complete mapping and testing with the aim of remaining within impact tolerances, including making investment so the firm operates within its chosen tolerance levels.

[39]   FCA (2021) Feedback to CP19/32 and Final Rules.

a severe but plausible disruption of its operations'.[40] Further, of specific relevance to cyber security, the final FCA operational resilience rules include guidance that the scenario testing takes into consideration:

- corruption, deletion or manipulation of data critical to the delivery of its important business services;[41]
- unavailability of third-party services which are critical to the delivery of its important business services; and[42]
- loss or reduced provision of technology underpinning the delivery of important business services.[43]

Determining impact tolerances requires establishing the length of time that a specific service can be affected by disruption, then adjusting by thorough scenario testing the final set impact tolerances. So the forensic due diligence and evidence required are of a different order of magnitude compared with established risk tolerances any regulated firm sets based on its own risk appetite affecting profits and reputation.

To highlight how pivotal operational resilience is for asset managers, investment banks and platforms, the example of the SolarWinds espionage operation discovered in December 2020 deserves a reference. SolarWinds provides IT monitoring solutions to over 300,000 clients. A computer security breach to its Orion monitoring platform affected more than 18,000 customers, including the US Commerce Department, the US Department for Home and Security (DHS) and the US Defense Department. This was an espionage operation of unprecedented scale and sophistication, which by some estimates involved over 1,000 state-sponsored engineers.[44] Added to this sophistication is the complexity of actor attribution, which creates legal redress uncertainties. The Russian government denied its involvement and in the context of cyber activity it is very challenging to identify the precise antagonists.[45]

---

[40] FCA SYSC 15A.5.3R.

[41] FCA 15A.5.6 G(1).

[42] FCA 15A.5.6 G(3). Arguably, the pivotal third party service is cloud computing, but that presumption needs careful due diligence.

[43] FCA 15A.5.6 G(5).

[44] Joint Statement by the Federal Bureau of Investigation (FBI), the Cybersecurity and Infrastructure Security Agency (CISA), The Office of the Director of National Intelligence (ODNI), and the National Security Agency (NSA), published 5 January 2021.

[45] This challenge of attribution was highlighted in a seminar in a contribution by Steve Pifer, Fellow at Stanford University and former ambassador to the Ukraine. Source: CogX (2021) SolarWinds, Russia and the New Cold War seminar, 14 June 2021.

In its Emergency Directive, the US DHS Cybersecurity and Infrastructure Security Agency (CISA) summarised the impact and uncertain prognosis in the following way:

> The adversary enjoyed longstanding, covert access to the build process that *SolarWinds* uses for *Orion*, including to the code underlying the *Orion* platform. While the immediate known consequence of this access was the insertion of the malicious code into the affected versions of *SolarWinds Orion*, there may be other unknown consequences as well. Consequently, it is likely that the adversary is in a strong position to identify any potential (and as yet unknown) vulnerabilities in the *SolarWinds Orion* code that are unrelated to the inserted malicious code and may therefore survive its removal. This adversary has demonstrated the capability and willingness to exploit *SolarWinds Orion* to compromise US government agencies, critical infrastructure entities, and private organizations.[46]

5.5.2   NIST Cyber Security Framework

First, the NIST Cyber Security Framework for critical infrastructure provides a robust model that can be communicated across all the functions of a regulated firm. Designed with the electricity, health, nuclear and rail industries in mind, it has also been applied in the financial services sector.[47] The five core aspects are: Identify, Protect, Detect, Respond and Recover.[48] The detail applied is not prescriptive, but outcome-driven to the needs of each business. However, the NIST framework is also formidably well thought out. For example, it provides 108 subcategories for improving a cyber security framework.[49]

5.5.3   ISO 27001

An in-depth, globally respected information security framework is provided by the International Organization for Standardization – ISO 27001.[50] Applicable to all sizes and types of organisation, ISO 27001 specifies requirements for building, implementing and maintaining an

---

[46]   US Cyber DHS (2020) Emergency Directive 21-01, Mitigate SolarWinds Orion Code Compromise, 13 December 2020.

[47]   Royal Academy of Engineering (2019) Cyber Safety and Resilience, at 19.

[48]   See https://www.nist.gov/cyberframework/online-learning/components-framework.

[49]   NIST (2018) Framework for Improving Critical Infrastructure Cyber Security, at 23–44.

[50]   ISO/IEC 27001 (2013), Information Technology – Security Techniques – Information Security Management Systems – Requirements. See www.iso.org/isoiec-27001-information-security.html.

Table 5.2   *SANS CIS 20 best practice controls*

	Recommended controls
1	Inventory and control of Hardware Assets
2	Inventory and control of Software Assets
3	Continuous Vulnerability Assessment and Remediation
4	Controlled Use of Administrative Privileges
5	Secure Configurations for Hardware and Software on Mobile Devices, Laptops, Workstations, and Servers
6	Maintenance, Monitoring, and Analysis of Audit Logs
7	Email and Web Browser Protections
8	Malware Defences
9	Limitation and Control of Network Ports, Protocols, and Services
10	Data Recovery Capabilities
11	Secure Configurations for Network Devices such as Firewalls, Routers, and Switches
12	Boundary Defence
13	Data Protection
14	Controlled Access Based on the Need to Know
15	Wireless Access Control
16	Account Monitoring and Control
17	Implement a Security Awareness and Training Program
18	Application Software Security
19	Incident Response and Management
20	Penetration Tests and Red Team Exercises

information security management system. There is an emphasis on continuous improvement, and the provision of 114 security controls revolving around people, processes and technology. A potential source of confusion can occur when reading references to ISO 27002, which is in fact Annex A of ISO 27001, which contains the 114 security controls.[51]

---

[51] See www.iso.org/standard/54533.html.

5.5.4   SANS Centre for Internet Security

The SANS Centre for Internet Security (CIS) is a non-profit organisation with over 20 years' experience.[52] As set out in Table 5.2, the current version of its 20 best practice controls forms an important framework for many US businesses.[53] The development of the 20 defensive controls has included contributions and feedback from many technology experts. This has included input from leading commercial forensics teams, leading commercial penetration testing teams, the US Department of Defense Cyber Crime Center, the FBI, the NSA, and the US Army Research Laboratory. The SANS CIS philosophy can be encapsulated as a shared problem based on shared technology.

5.5.5   NCSC's 10 Steps to Cyber Security

Developed in 2012, the NCSC's 10 Steps to Cyber Security are used by most FTSE 300 companies.[54] Brevity has impact in any business but often more so in regulated firms that deal with ever-increasing regulatory and technological complexity. The 10 technical advice topics are:

- Risk Management Regime
- Secure Configuration
- Home and mobile working
- Incident management (Resilience)
- Malware prevention
- Managing user privileges
- Monitoring
- Network security
- Removable media controls, and
- User education and awareness.

A memorable global point of advice is provided as part of the NCSC 10 steps guidance. They advise 'assess the risks to your organisation's data and systems with the same vigour you would for legal, regulatory, financial or operational risks' achieved by embedding the Risk Management Regime (Step 1) across your firm with the support of the board and senior

---

[52]   See www.cisecurity.org/.
[53]   SANS CIS Version 7.1, released 4 April 2019.
[54]   See www.ncsc.gov.uk/collection/10-steps-to-cyber-security/the-10-steps.

managers.[55] Indeed, a failure by directors to do so raises the risk of breaching statutory duties.[56] However, an experienced legal counsel knows all too well that using just the 'stick' of legal consequences does not always maximise influence. A 'carrot' of cyber security is to view it as a strategic asset, a competitive advantage with which to advance because competitors have failed to do so.[57]

5.5.6   NCSC Cyber Essentials

As a natural development from the 10 steps regime, the NCSC has developed two accreditation schemes.[58] The first scheme, Cyber Essentials, provides any business with simple risk framework based on proving your regulated firm has the following five technical controls in place:[59]

- Boundary firewalls and Internet gateways
- Secure configuration
- User access control
- Malware protection, and
- Patch management.

To gain the Cyber Essentials certification requires following a three-stage process of:

- establishing the boundary of scope for your firm, and determining what is in scope within this boundary;
- review each of the five technical control areas; and
- ensure your firm meets every requirement, throughout the scope.

Evidence will be required to show consistency in the determined scope and five review areas, such as a board member signing that all assessment answers are correct. Subsequently, an independent qualified assessor must check through the sign-off assessment answers. If successful, the

---

[55] See NCSC (2020) 10 Steps to Cyber Security Infographic, 1. See www.ncsc.gov.uk/collection/10-steps -to-cyber-security.

[56] Section 174 Companies Act 2006 requires directors to perform their duties with reasonable care, diligence and skill.

[57] Powell, T, and Hepfer, M (2020) 'Make Cyber Security a Strategic Asset', *MIT Sloan Management Review*, 8 September 2020.

[58] See www.ncsc.gov.uk/cyberessentials/overview.

[59] See www.ncsc.gov.uk/files/Cyber-Essentials-Requirements-for-IT-infrastructure-2-1.pdf.

Cyber Essentials certification is awarded for a period of 12 months to be renewed annually.[60] In short, it is a verified self-assessment scheme.

The second scheme, Cyber Essentials Plus, is based on the same process of providing evidence concerning the same five technical controls. The key difference is that analogous to accounting the veracity of the audit is checked by an independent cyber security assessor running vulnerability tests.

Both Cyber Essentials and Cyber Essentials Plus provide regulated firms, and also their advisers and third-party suppliers, with not only protection against basic cyber attacks, but also the opportunity to signal via certification logo on a website home page that the firm has robust cyber security in place. Additionally, the NCSC's Board Toolkit provides board-level senior managers with a valuable framework based around questions for (a) individual board members, (b) the whole board, and (c) subject matter experts.[61]

5.6   Network and Information Systems Directive I

The EU implemented the Network and Information Security Directive ('NIS I') in 2016.[62] NIS I is also replicated under English statute.[63] Over time the UK law in this area may diverge from NIS I, but subsequent EU changes will still be important to the UK financial services sector given its cross-border nature. Broadly put, NIS I seeks to achieve a number of ambitious goals. These include requiring each Member State to join cooperative forums, put in place a cyber security strategy, and establish computer security incident response teams (CSIRTs).

Of specific relevance to the financial services sector, NIS I requires 'essential service providers' and 'digital service providers' not only to apply cyber security measures, but also report serious incidents to the national regulator.

---

[60] NCSC (2020) 10 Steps to Cyber Security Infographic, 1.

[61] NCSC (2019) Cyber Security Toolkit for Boards.

[62] EU 2016/1148.

[63] Ibid.

So how can regulated firms quickly identify 'essential service providers'? NIS I provides that this requires applying the criteria in the definition of that term and simultaneously checking in Annex II of NIS I to discover the relevant subsectors covered. The term 'essential service providers' includes entities identified by each Member State that meet the criteria of (a) providing a service essential for 'the maintenance of critical societal and/or economic activities'; (b) the service is dependent on 'network and information systems'; and (c) an event would cause 'significant disruption' to the service.[64] Importantly, Annex II includes three financial services subsectors, namely central counter-parties,[65] credit institutions[66] and operators of trading venues.[67]

Turning to the term 'digital service providers', the relevant types of businesses are set out in Annex III of NIS I. These are cloud computing services, online market places and online search engines.[68] While identifying a cloud service provider is self-evident, if in any doubt about a specific provider the way to decide requires reference to the definition of 'service' in another EU directive.[69]

In sum, regulated firms' due diligence processes need to include determining if both types of provider are complying with NIS I. Further, service provider contracts need to be drafted to record these obligations.

5.6.1   Network and Information Systems Directive II

The implementation of NIS I is inconsistent across the EU. The reasons appear to be mixed, including the fact that technology has evolved in importance across all sectors and a lack of clarity on the scope for operators of essential services and the national regulator competence over digital service providers. Consequently, there are already detailed propos-

---

[64]   Article 5(2) EU 2016/1148.
[65]   Article 2(4) EU Regulations 2012/648, defines trading venues.
[66]   Article 4(1) EU Directive 2013/575, defines credit institutions.
[67]   Article 4(24) EU Directive 2014/65 defines the trading venues as an MTF or an OTF.
[68]   EU 2016/1148, concerning measures for a high common level of security of network and information systems. Ibid., at Annex III.
[69]   Article 1(1)(b) EU 2015/1535.

als to repeal NIS I and replace it with a NIS II that addresses the current deficiencies.[70]

5.7   FCA cyber resilience survey

Cyber security has been on the FCA agenda for some time. When even the most powerful financial and technology-savvy businesses are victims of cyber attacks, for example JP Morgan and Yahoo!, this is unsurprising. The FCA conducted a cyber resilience survey that yielded a number of important insights based on answers to 46 questions aligned with the NIST framework.[71] The FCA results were based on 256 regulated firms from all subsectors, including asset management, wholesale banking and wholesale financial markets.

Perhaps the most significant point from the FCA survey was that while most regulated firms review hardware and software to check what needs to be updated, many do not have a continuous accurate understanding. The FCA concluded '[t]here is a significant risk that vulnerabilities of unsupported assets are not identified and fixed in a timely way. This is a regular route for attackers. We are concerned that firms are not addressing the more obvious risks presented to their business and customers by their technology estate.'[72] More recently, the FCA's Head of Technology, Resilience and Cyber again highlighted the risk of failing to update hardware and software.[73]

A second important point concerned the emerging picture of smaller regulated firms reporting several weaknesses in their cyber security management. Ownership of cyber risk was missing at board level, with no or inadequately implemented cyber security strategy.[74]

---

[70] EC COM 2020/823, Proposal for a Directive on Measures for a High Common Level of Cyber Security across the Union Repealing Directive (EU) 2016/1148.

[71] The five core NIST aspects are Identify, Protect, Detect, Respond and Recover.

[72] FCA (2018) Cyber and Technology Resilience – Themes from Cross-sector Survey 2017–18, at 7.

[73] Inside FCA Podcast (2020): What Does Cyber Security and Resilience Mean for Firms? See www.fca .org.uk/multimedia/inside-fca-podcast-what-does-cyber-security-and-resilience-mean-firms.

[74] FCA (2018) Cyber and Technology Resilience – Themes from Cross-sector Survey 2017–18, at 6.

Clearly cyber resilience challenges are constantly changing, so this requires dedicated, regular checks with the FCA and other authoritative regulators to search for the latest surveys that capture issues emanating from emerging threats.

5.8   Asset management and wholesale banks review

Following on from the cyber resilience survey, the FCA then conducted another survey, this time focusing on only the asset management and wholesale bank subsectors.[75] The FCA found that the 'firms which appeared to be more "cyber mature" were better able to talk about cyber risk versus other risks. They were also better informed about the potential interdependencies of these risks and the detailed commercial and operational impact they could have on their firm, if and when they crystallised and how their firm could recover.'[76]

Another FCA finding fits into a regulated firm's SMF. The FCA observed that almost all the board members and non-IT senior management communicated that they struggled to understand and summarise specific cyber risks. The FCA concluded that board members and senior managers need more training so that cyber security can be treated as a global risk and not confined to the IT function.[77]

5.9   Specific cyber security opportunities and threats

In 2001, when practising at Allen & Overy, I published an article entitled 'Prosecuting Fraud over the Internet'. The article's principal aim was to serve as a primer for judges. Part of my research was based on interviews with technology experts from IBM and the FCA's predecessor.[78]

---

[75] FCA (2018), Wholesale Banks and Asset Management Cyber Multi-firm Review Findings.

[76] Ibid.

[77] Ibid.

[78] At that time the UK financial services regulator was called the Financial Services Authority (FSA). On 3 April 2013 the FSA changed its name to the FCA.

However, the most revealing aspects of my research derived from US cyber attacks made in the mid-1990s. In the US, hackers had already been sentenced for unauthorised access to companies over the Internet via mobile phones. These US cyber attack insights underlined that hackers are often at the cutting-edge of technology.[79] These cyber attacks were made when not only was the commercial Internet in its infancy, but also the use of mobile phones. In effect hackers were exploiting 3G technology, so small mobile computer plus mobile phone, five years before it was commercially available.

In the next sections, cutting-edge technologies are briefly explained, because in the short, medium and long term all represent a cyber security threat. Consequently, each has to be factored into legal function risk management. The technologies are AI, Ransomware, DLT, 5G and quantum computing.

5.10 AI

There is a whole chapter in this book dedicated to machine learning, given that it is the most popularly applied form of AI in the financial services sector. In the context of cyber security it is evident that machine learning, and other forms of AI, can be both a threat and an opportunity. An ENISA AI report has identified 74 discrete threats related to AI use.[80] By which is meant their analysis breaks down all possible threats linked to the use of AI, including indicating if the potential impact is one or more of (a) availability; (b) confidentiality; or (c) integrity.

Given the potential ambiguity with the ordinary meaning of integrity, in cyber security this means accuracy and completeness.[81] Further, they indicate for each threat the affected hardware or software assets. The affected assets are varied, but are mainly data, the model itself or a process. [82] The ENISA eight high-level threat categories are set out in

---

[79] See www.justice.gov/archive/opa/pr/Pre_96/February95/89.txt.html.

[80] ENISA (2020) AI Cyber security Challenges – Threat Landscape for Artificial Intelligence.

[81] ISO/IEC 27000:2018.

[82] ENISA (2020) AI Cyber security Challenges – Threat Landscape for Artificial Intelligence, at Annex B, 43–57.

Table 5.3   ENISA main threat categories

Main AI threat category	Definition or description
Disaster	'A sudden accident or a natural catastrophe that causes great damage or loss of life.'
Eavesdropping/ interception/hijacking	'Actions aiming to listen, interrupt, or seize control of a third-party communication without consent.'
Failures	'Partial or full insufficient functioning of an asset (hardware or software).'
Legal	'Legal actions of third parties (contracting or otherwise), in order to prohibit actions or compensate for loss based on applicable law.'
Nefarious activity/abuse	'Intended actions that target ICT systems, infrastructure, and networks by means of malicious acts with the aim to alter, destroy or steal a specified target.'
Outages	'Unexpected disruptions of service or decrease in quality falling below a required level.'
Physical attacks	'Actions which aim to destroy, expose, alter, disable, steal or gain unauthorised access to physical assets such as infrastructure, hardware, or interconnection.'
Unintentional damage	Unintentional actions causing 'destruction, harm, or injury of property or persons and results in a failure or reduction in usefulness.'

Source: ENISA (2020) AI Cyber security Challenges – Threat Landscape for Artificial Intelligence, at 27.

Table 5.3. This language may form a part of contract drafting and the consistent communication with senior managers about types of threats.

The ENISA analysis pin-points a number of nefarious threats specific to machine learning based approaches which are valuable information in terms of establishing the likely recurring risks these will present for any financial services business. These include backdoor attacks on training data sets, compromising the accuracy of algorithms, manipulation of labelled data, and compromising the integrity of a validation data set.[83]

Turning to legal threats, there is a significant risk to personal information across all stages of the AI lifecycle.[84] The ENISA report focuses on the likely need to conduct a Data Protection Impact Assessment (DPIA) at the design phase.[85] There is a whole chapter in this book dedicated to data protection, including detail on the criteria for determining if a DPIA is required, and if so the necessary format.

As so often is the case with financial services and technology issues, the complete answers is a mix of legal, regulatory and technical expertise. On the technical level it cannot be forgotten that 'an engineering axiom for security professionals is that you cannot bolt "security" onto a system design as an afterthought'.[86] From a legal risk angle, what cannot be omitted, in my view, is the involvement of lawyers as early as possible in the plain English language design summary of core IT systems to audit and verify the presence of security.

A related threat is inadequate data protection compliance by third-party data suppliers. For example, a key aspect of achieving effective machine learning models is the need for a sufficiently large volume of training data. That may only be accomplished by relying on third-party data providers. The same point can be made about the reliance on third-party providers of libraries and models.[87]

Further, there is a risk to the corruption of data indexes. The term data indexes refer to the way that a user retrieves data from a database by looking for items with the same values. Availability of data or data integrity loss is the potential impact. Examples include corruption caused by an attack, loss of network connectivity or the crashing of the system.[88]

---

[83] Ibid., at 43–44.

[84] Ibid., at 52.

[85] Article 35 GDPR.

[86] Royal Academy of Engineering and The Institution of Engineering and Technology (2015) Connecting Data Driving Productivity and Innovation, at 35.

[87] ENISA (2020) AI Cyber security Challenges – Threat Landscape for Artificial Intelligence, at 55.

[88] Ibid., at 52.

While it is clear there are a number of legal threats there is also great potential to lever AI to avoid, deter and mitigate a variety of scenarios. For instance, IBM's computer security division offers a range of preventative measures, including real-time alerts communicated to in-house technology function professionals sourced from IBM's Watson Group. In short, AI can enhance awareness of potential cyber attacks and vulnerabilities.[89]

5.11 Ransomware

Compared with other targeted sectors, financial services is the most common target of ransomware criminals.[90] Specifically, the trend appears to be a surge in the number of financially motivated attacks, rather than attempts by one nation state to undermine another. Specifically, IBM calculate that across all sectors in 2019 there was a 67 per cent increase in ransomware attacks, with a further increase of 20 per cent in 2020.[91]

The key standard operating procedure concerning a ransomware attack is to resist any payment. Legal and compliance functions play an important supporting role to any external or in-house view that no ransom should be paid. This logic is based on the significant experience of the UK National Crime Agency (NCA), whose guidance is updated online.[92] The FCA provides helpful, succinct guidance on essential steps to take and questions to ask.[93]

From a technical viewpoint, a former strategy director at Qinetiq and current professor of cyber security at Oxford University has advised that the critical task is to understand 'the control flow of how an attack works, then you can start to establish the plan to deal with it'.[94] Further, getting the right level of independent technical expertise is very likely to require

---

[89] IBM (2020) IBM Security MaaS360 with Watson – A Guide to How MaaS360 Establishes Effective Device and User Security.

[90] IBM Security (2021) X-Force Threat Intelligence Index Report 2021, at 34.

[91] IBM Security (2020) X-Force Threat Intelligence Index Report 2020, at 15, and IBM Security (2021) X-Force Threat Intelligence Index Report 2021, at 8.

[92] See www.nationalcrimeagency.gov.uk/what-we-do/crime-threats/cyber-crime?highlight=WyJyYW5zb213YXJlIl0. zb213YXJlIl0.

[93] See www.fca.org.uk/publication/documents/ransomware-infographic.pdf.

[94] Creese, S (2021) Cyber Security – The Ransomware Threat, Oxford University seminar to senior managers and professionals, 17 June 2021.

external cyber security consultants. Legal counsel, in conjunction with human resources, should have robust ways of vetting that the external experts have the precise technical expertise and integrity to be given access to the IT system.

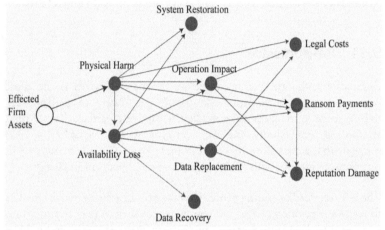

Source: Adaptation of a diagram by Creese, S (2021) 'Cyber Security – The Ransomware Threat', Oxford University seminar to senior managers and professionals, 17 June 2021.

Figure 5.1   Consequences of a ransomware attack

As captured in Figure 5.1, in these scenarios there are the potential additional costs of data recovery, data replacement, operational impacts, system restoration and permanent reputational damage. Ultimately, if the system has been infiltrated to the point that all or some control has been lost, even if the system was returned to the regulated firm's control it has been compromised. A new system may have to be built. For example, in May 2021 a US oil infrastructure company, Colonial Pipeline, was a victim of a ransomware attack. Within hours of the attack a multi-million dollar ransom, estimated to be just under $5 million, was paid for an encryption key that enabled the pipeline system to return to operations. No doubt subsequent IT system rebuilding costs will far exceed the initial ransom.[95]

---

[95]   ZDNet (2021) Colonial Pipeline Ransomware Attack: Everything You Need to Know. Available at www.zdnet.com/article/colonial-pipeline-ransomware-attack-everything-you-need-to-know/.

5.12 DLT

When thinking about DLT in the narrow context of cryptoassets and blockchain, it can appear to be a technology waiting to find an application. By which is meant cryptoassets could be traded over many established platforms owned by a single institution. In many applications other than cryptoassets, DLT has great potential as a disruptive strategy in the financial services sector across many activities.[96] However, it is not immune to the threat of hacking. For example, in August 2021, a crypto asset platform, Poly Network, sustained a cyber attack that initially resulted in the loss of more than USD $600 million of crypto tokens.[97]

From a technical cyber security viewpoint, DLT is superior to many centralised IT systems. As a UK Government Office for Science report on DLT observed 'distributed ledgers are inherently harder to attack because instead of a single database, there are multiple shared copies of the same database, so a cyber attack would have to attack all the copies simultaneously to be successful'.[98]

5.13 5G mobile networks technology

Based on the projected complexity and volume of use, 5G mobile networks ('5G') represent a greater cyber security risk compared with implemented 4G technologies. For instance, an independent expert has calculated the design targets for 5G include 1–100x peak data rate, 1,000x network capacity, 10x energy efficiency, and 10–30x lower latency.[99] Further, telecommunications experts assisting the UK government in its risk assessments have concluded 'the security design of 5G does not take into account the potential increased risk presented due to the increased capacity and capabilities of a 5G network on the user plane. The increased

---

[96] Sheridan, I (2017) 'MiFID II in the Context of Financial Technology and Regulatory Technology', *Capital Markets Law Journal*, Volume 12, Issue 4, Section 6 on scope of DLT applications, at 6.

[97] Stafford, P and Venkataramakrishnan, S (2021) 'Poly Network tries to persuade hacker to return stolen assets', *Financial Times*, 17 August 2021.

[98] UK Government Chief Scientific Adviser (2016), at 6. See https://assets.publishing.service.gov .uk/government/uploads/system/uploads/attachment_data/file/492972/gs-16-1-distributed-ledger -technology.pdf.

[99] Rodriguez, J et al. (2015) *Fundamentals of 5G Mobile Networks* (Wiley), at 34.

risk to the network for a rogue or malicious device is a lot larger due to the capacity and capabilities of a 5G network.'[100]

A detailed 2020 ENISA report, entitled 'Threat Landscape for 5G Networks', applies the Microsoft STRIDE risk framework outlined earlier in this chapter to structure all its information about threats. That choice of structure maybe an analytical point of efficiency for some regulated firms already using or planning to use STRIDE. The ENISA report also includes a detailed 5G networks threat terminology mind map made up of 17 main branches and over 50 sub-branches.[101]

From a legal threat viewpoint, the ENISA report pin-points three discrete risks, namely: (a) breach of legislation; (b) failure to meet contractual obligations; and (c) breaching SLAs.[102] Within the 5G stakeholder eco-system most financial services businesses will be customers of service providers. That means that service provider contracts will need to include detailed references to cyber security frameworks, especially in the context of asset management and wholesale capital market trading applications that will increasingly rely on 5G delivery.

5.14   Post-quantum computing cryptography

Chapter 13 of this book is dedicated to quantum computing (QC), so that is a valuable detailed cross-reference resource when its impact increases generally across the financial services sector. Put briefly, QC is not a simple concept to explain. Traditional computers are based on binary calculations, so processing revolves around either a 1 or 0 – classical mechanics. QC presents a radical alternative technology based on the different properties of quantum mechanics.

QC cannot be explained by reference to an existing understanding of classical mechanics, because it functions so differently. As two Silicon Valley QC experts have explained 'a quantum bit representing 0 or 1 can neither be viewed as "between" 0 and 1 nor can it be viewed as a hidden unknown

---

[100] House of Commons Defence Committee (2020) The Security of 5G – Written evidence submitted by techUK, at 3.

[101] ENISA (2020) ENISA Threat Landscape for 5G Networks, Figure 26 5G Threat Taxonomy.

[102] Ibid., at 128.

state that represents either 0 or 1 with a certain probability'.[103] In quantum mechanics this quality is called superposition.

QC has been researched for more than four decades. Compared with classical supercomputers the practical advantages of QC continue to be a source of debate. With some QC algorithms, multiple quantum bits, called qubits can be manipulated to interact, resulting in exponential speed of calculation.[104] In quantum mechanics this dynamic is called entanglement.

In the context of financial services, QC presents a specific threat of unknown timing. The UK Department for Business, Energy and & Industrial Strategy has concluded that 'quantum computers, when fully scalable machines do come, are expected to pose a significant threat to the cryptographic systems which underpin much of our existing cyber security'.[105]

The threat arises from the key strength of one QC algorithm, namely Shor's algorithm, which has the ability to find the factors of very large numbers. The current private key elements of public key cryptography, such as RSA,[106] rely on the difficulty of factoring the product of two large numbers. The technical risk is that a future QC system will be created with sufficient qubits to apply Shor's algorithm to break public key cryptography that is used to encrypt messages over the Internet, including bank transfers and trading data.[107]

From a practical legal risk viewpoint, lawyers and compliance officers need to know at least five years before independent QC experts predict a QC is able to decrypt RSA and similar public key cryptography schemes.

---

[103] Rieffel, E, and Polak, W (2000) 'An Introduction to Quantum Computing for Non-physicists', *ACM Computing Surveys*, Volume 32, Issue 3, 300–335, at 301.

[104] Ibid., at 301.

[105] UK Department for Business, Energy & Industrial Strategy (2021) National Security and Investment: Sectors in Scope of the Mandatory Regime Consultation on Secondary Legislation to Define the Sectors Subject to Mandatory Notification in the National Security and Investment Bill 2020, at 64.

[106] The RSA patent granted to MIT can be seen at https://patents.google.com/patent/US4405829. Although note GCHQ had in reality been applying its own classified public key algorithm before RSA. Unsurprisingly, NCSC, the cyber security dedicated arm of GCHQ, has already designed its first 'quantum safe' cryptographic algorithms. See NCSC 2021 Annual Report, at 59.

[107] Knight, P, and Walmsley, I (2019) UK National Quantum Technology Programme, Quantum Science Technology, 4 040502, at 4–6.

This is because the regulated firm will need sufficient time to upgrade hardware, firmware and software. In short the arrival of QC means potentially multiple projects for which the time to complete could be easily underestimated.

From a technical viewpoint, QC cannot reliably decrypt public key cryptography until error correction is achieved. By which is meant the QC architecture must have control over environmental noises (decoherence) to function.[108] Achieving error correction may take a decade or more to control. Conversely, the commercial self-interest of some businesses in the QC industry could easily produce a replication of some of the scaremongering surrounding the Y2K problem. As a reminder for some, the Y2K event turned out to be unfounded.[109] Although, the comparison is imperfect given Y2K was a specific date, and QC decrypting public key cryptography could occur in five, 10 or 20 years time. Whatever the progress of QC it deserves cautious monitoring. Unsurprisingly, NCSC, the cyber security dedicated arm of GCHQ, has already designed its first 'quantum safe' cryptographic algorithms.[110]

5.15 Reporting cyber security incidents

The FCA specifically requires regulated firms to report all material incidents.[111] By which is meant any event that results in a significant data loss, IT system availability or control issues affecting large numbers of customers and any unauthorised access or the presence of malware. In the event of a cyber attack, the FCA website provides a helpful list of email addresses and phone numbers relevant to your circumstances and UK regulators.[112] Most poignantly, consistent with the on-going importance of cross sector collaboration, the FCA proposes that each regulated firm

---

[108] Rieffel, E, and Polak, W (2000) 'An Introduction to Quantum Computing for Non-physicists', *ACM Computing Surveys*, Volume 32, Issue 3, 300–335, at 328.

[109] Anderson, R (1999) The Millienium Bug – Reasons Not to Panic. See www.cl.cam.ac.uk/~rja14/Papers/y2k.pdf.

[110] NCSC 2021 Annual Report, at 59.

[111] FCA Principle 11.

[112] See www.fca.org.uk/firms/cyber-resilience.

communicates its experience via the CiSP platform. Dual-regulated firms also need to contact the PRA.[113]

5.16 GDPR requirements

Chapter 6 of this book focuses on data protection. However, in the context of cyber security breaches there are specific duties that regulated firms must comply with, or risk in the event of a fine being imposed that aggravating factors are taken into account. The requirements are three-fold. First, there are 'by design and by default' requirements.[114] By which is meant the regulated firm is required, at the design phase of an IT system, to 'bake in' data protection.[115] In my view, while these requirements do not explicitly prescribe encryption, elsewhere the GDPR requires the implementation of appropriate technical and organisational measures.[116] Therefore, the encryption of personal data is an essential requirement of cyber security design.

Second, after becoming aware of a data breach, 'without undue delay' the Information Commissioner's Office (ICO) has to be informed within 72 hours. If notification is made after 72 hours have elapsed then reasons for the delay in informing have to be submitted.[117] Third, where there is a chance the breach presents a 'high risk to the rights and freedoms of natural persons' the affected data subject must be informed.[118] The potential detail required in the ICO notification, and the consequence of providing an inadequate notice, means lawyers play a valuable checking and drafting role before any notice is sent.[119]

---

[113] All dual-regulated firm reports can be sent to the PRA at pra.firmenquiries@bankofengland.co.uk.

[114] Articles 25(1) and 25(2) GDPR.

[115] ICO (2019) Guide to the GDPR, at 181.

[116] Article 32(1) GDPR.

[117] Article 33 GDPR.

[118] Article 34 GDPR.

[119] Article 33(3) GDPR.

5.17   Cyber insurance

There is also the issue of cyber attack insurance. Consequently, advising lawyers will have to invest time in scrutinising the fine detail of cyber attack insurance policies. Insurance contract obligations will also vary, but compensation after a cyber attack may be conditional on evidence of implementing specific cyber risk frameworks, for example the NCSC Cyber Essentials Plus, and sustaining competence by membership of prominent networks, such as CCG or FSCCC. For each regulated firm, the matrix of trusted security frameworks and cooperative networks will have many permutations given their diverse complexity, resources and scale.[120]

It is notable that Lloyd's of London already requires their own managing agents to obtain Cyber Essentials on an annual basis,[121] and to cooperate in cyber information sharing with peer companies and government actors.[122] Lawyers negotiating their client's specific choices into insurance clauses have scope to argue that the client choices are equivalent and should be drafted into the contract. The implementation of risk frameworks and verifiable commitment to cooperative networks should both be reflected in a discounted premium.

---

[120]   Celso de Azevedo, C (2019) Cyber Risks Insurance – Law and Practice (Sweet & Maxwell), is a practitioner book focused on all aspects of cyber insurance.

[121]   Lloyd's (2021) Minimum Standards MS11, Cyber Resilience and Data Management, at 7.

[122]   Ibid., at 11.

6. Data protection

The Royal Society produced a report on the governance of data in the UK. They observed that 'for some, data is the "new oil": the fuel for new industries and rapid economic growth. Others see more parallels with carbon emissions: individuals produce it, but the impacts are societal as well as individual. Data can also be seen as infrastructure: of public benefit and requiring management.'[1] In short, data is a complex commodity that might be profitable or harmful or of societal benefit, or possess all these characteristics at the same time.

6.1   Introduction

In the financial services sector, there are, in my view, three aspects of data that require special concentration. At the highest level of abstraction data is a source of (a) revenues; (b) costs; and (c) legal and compliance responsibilities. First, data is a source of revenues of potentially high value with unknown growth potential. Data has been described as the key raw material of the information age, its ownership as significant as the ownership of the factory during the industrial age.[2] Data's value can be growing but a challenge to accurately estimate because the contents of a data file or record can communicate multiple values and take the form of a strategy or structure or both.[3] A realistic way to analyse the value of data is to measure it as a unique asset class. To understand the unique financial value of data, observe how leading global technology groups, such as Ant Financial and Google, make multiple profitable uses from it.

Second, processing, storing and retrieving data is a significant cost for any regulated firm. Further, on occasion, locating and retrieving data

---

[1]   Royal Society (2020) The UK Data Governance Landscape.

[2]   Ross, A (2016) *The Industries of the Future* (Simon & Schuster), at 182.

[3]   Sheridan, I (2018) 'Financial Technology and Global Capital Markets – The Impact of Pro-enterprise Regulation and English law', *CMLJ*, Volume 13, Issue 4, at 591.

can be an unexpected expense. For instance, relocating a misplaced file with commercial agreements or compliance reports is a sunk cost. Time is money, and that wasted time cannot be recovered. Third, the use of data comes with legal and compliance responsibilities. For example, negligently allowing third-parties to access client data without client permission can ultimately lead to huge fines potentially calculated by reference to annual revenue.[4] Legal and compliance responsibilities are the focus of this chapter.

6.2   Senior manager responsibilities

Financial services businesses are increasingly liable for the flow, processing and storage of a data space that may be local or global or both. That includes personal data. Under the FSMA,[5] senior managers are ultimately responsible for risks that may have serious consequences for authorised persons,[6] clients, consumers, another business or other third-party interests.

As expanded upon in Chapter 2 covering Accountability, there are three pillars that require special attention by a senior manager responsible for technology. These are (a) to know the remit of the SMF responsible for technology; (b) to check the drafting as well as practical execution of the Statement of Responsibilities; and (c) to check the drafting of the Management Responsibilities Map as well as its practical implementation.

In support of the SMF, legal counsel and compliance officers need to explain with clarity what data needs to be assessed based on data protection regulation. Senior managers need to understand the key concepts, underlying logic and consequences. Therefore, it is on these essential aspects that this chapter focuses.[7] Further, to satisfy regulators, and potentially tribunals, it is essential to have a succinct record of what

---

4   Article 83 GDPR.
5   Section 59ZA FSMA 2000.
6   Under Section 31 FSMA 2000 'authorised persons' includes both individuals performing a specific regulated role under FSMA and any regulated firm.
7   ICO (2019) Guide to the GDPR.

aspects of data protection law and responsibilities have been explained to senior managers.[8]

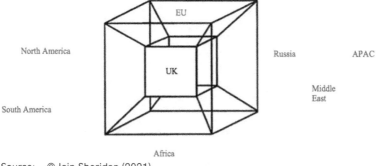

Source: © Iain Sheridan (2021).

Figure 6.1   *Data space of a UK regulated firm*

In Chapter 3 Cloud computing, the analogy of an air traffic control system was used. By way of background, the concept derived from training legal counsel and compliance officers from EU central banks and fund managers on data flows under MiFID II. They seemed to quickly absorb the comparison of financial markets data control with the unenviable task of managing air traffic control at Heathrow Airport. This is also, in my view, a memorable way of explaining the concepts of data protection law for any jurisdiction, which can otherwise easily appear to be a nebulous topic. Figure 6.1 will allow any senior manager to remember the complexity of the responsibility of data protection as something with nearly always more than one jurisdiction requiring regulatory compliance.

The comparison in Figure 6.1 is based on a 4-D cube of air space to manage aircraft applied to the movement of data. A 4-D cube is also often referred to as tesseract or a cubic prism. At the centre of the inner cube is the senior manager responsible for systems and controls over data in a defined data space.[9] For a UK regulated firm, the faces of the inner cube

---

[8]   FCA SYSC 9.1R.

[9]   It is important to note that among commercial software engineers, data space already has more than one precise meaning. Perhaps to avoid confusion always qualify in discussions and written communication with technology colleagues that your reference is to 'legal data space'.

are borders of UK data space, the area where certainly UK law and FCA regulation apply. Farther away from the manager, data is also flowing into the UK data space from the EU, represented by the larger cube. Outside of the larger cube are the data regulations of North America, Russia, and so forth – all other jurisdictions. Incoming data has travelled into the UK with other regulations applying to it. In some instances, those laws will still apply along with UK laws.[10]

6.3 The GDPR

In force across the EEA since May 2018, the GDPR[11] is of direct relevance to all financial services firms controlling or processing the personal data of EU data subjects, and data subjects in Norway, Iceland and Liechtenstein. The GDPR also applies to goods and services offered to data subjects in the EEA from third countries, and also data subjects' information transferred from the EEA to any third country. The UK's exit from the EU at the end of 2020 means it is a third country.

Collectively, the GDPR's 99 articles, its linked guidance from the EDPB, and decisions of the CJEU, have influenced data protection laws outside the EEA. For instance, the substance of the GDPR can be seen in equivalent data protection laws in many dynamic technology-focused jurisdictions, including California, China, India, Japan, South Korea and Singapore.

In the UK, the GDPR has been fully transposed, although the original text should be read alongside the Data Protection, Privacy and Electronic

---

[10] If some readers think that Figure 6.1 aids analysing or explaining UK, EU and global data flows, consider drawing or scanning it as a separate image, then adding specific footnotes, side comments and references.

[11] In 2021, as part of retained EU law following its exit from the EU, the UK applies the GDPR along with the Data Protection Act 2018. Under the European Union (Withdrawal) Act 2018, the ministers of the United Kingdom have the power to introduce secondary legislation, via statutory instruments, to make the necessary changes to retained EU regulations law, consequently adopting the Data Protection, Privacy and Electronic Communications (Amendments etc.) (EU Exit) Regulations 2019 ('DPPEC Regulations'). The DPPEC Regulations amend Regulation (EU) 2016/679 as brought into United Kingdom law through the European Union (Withdrawal) Act 2018, the DPA 2018, and other data protection legislation to fit the domestic context.

Communications (Amendments etc.) (EU Exit) Regulations 2019.[12] The term UK GDPR is used only when absolutely necessary to clarify some distinction from the EU GDPR. So when reading just the letters GDPR the analysis applies equally to the UK and the EU. No doubt over time there will be a divergence between the two GDPRs, but in this first edition of the book they are essentially the same in substance. Currently, the UK treats data transmitted from the EEA into the UK as equivalent. The EC also treats UK data transmitted from the UK into the EEA as equivalent, although this status has a 'sunshine' clause which expires on 27 June 2025.[13]

The interplay between the GDPR and UK financial regulation is not too challenging. Both the FCA and the ICO have recognised this, pointing out in a joint statement just before its implementation that 'the GDPR does not impose requirements which are incompatible with the rules in the FCA Handbook. Indeed, there are a number of requirements that are common to the GDPR and the financial regulatory regime detailed in the FCA Handbook.'[14]

Legal advice on data protection in any jurisdiction tends to become hard to digest for the non-expert in part because the terminology does not lend itself to logical parallels with financial services regulation. The key terminology needed to read an expert opinion on the GDPR as it applies to a regulated firm is set out in Table 6.1.[15]

Since Brexit there has been an English High Court case judgment concerning GDPR extra-territoriality.[16] The hearing took place in December 2020,[17] so the judge did not deal with UK GDPR, but if he had done so the analysis would have been almost identical albeit with some new nuance as outlined below. This judgment was helpful in showing how the EU GDPR is interpreted over extra-territoriality provisions. Specifically, GDPR,

---

[12] Part 2 Data Protection Act 2018. See www.legislation.gov.uk/ukpga/2018/12/part/2/enacted. Along with the Data Protection, Privacy and Electronic Communications (Amendments etc.) (EU Exit) Regulations 2019, SI 2019/419.

[13] EC (2021) Brussels, C(2021) Implementing Decision of 28 June 2021, Pursuant to Regulation (EU) 2016/679 on the Adequate Protection of Personal Data by the UK.

[14] FCA and ICO (2018) Update on the EU GDPR.

[15] Article 4 GDPR.

[16] *Soriano v Forensic News LLC & Ors* [2021] EWHC 56 (QB).

[17] The final Brexit date and time was 31 December 2020 at 23.00 GMT.

Table 6.1   *GDPR essential terminology*

Terminology	Meaning
Personal data	Any information directly or indirectly relating to an identifiable natural person ('data subject').
Processing	Any automatic or manual operation performed on personal data, including alteration, collection, disclosure by transmission, deletion and storage.
Processor	Entity of person processing personal data on behalf of the controller. For example, a Seattle-based cloud computing service company storing personal data for a UK hedge fund.
Controller	Entity or person determining the purpose and means of processing. For example, a UK hedge fund manager deciding to store client data with a cloud computing service company based in Seattle.
Pseudonymisation	How data can be processed so that it cannot be attributed to a specific data subject without additional information. The additional information must be kept separately in a technically secure way.

Article 3(1). To summarise the essential facts, a habitually resident UK citizen brought an action against a Californian-incorporated company called Forensic News, and five US resident journalists. He relied on a number of causes of action, including data protection, malicious falsehood, libel, harassment and misuse of private information. The claimant's case concerned 10 Internet publications and social media postings such as Facebook and Twitter.[18]

Article 3(1) states that the EU GDPR 'applies to the processing of personal data in the context of the activities of an establishment of a controller or a processor in the [EU], regardless of whether the processing takes place in the [EU] or not'.[19] Under established EU GDPR case law, the test for determining if a controller or processor is an establishment in the EU require 'any real and effective activity – even a minimal one – exercised

---

[18]   *Soriano v Forensic News LLC & Ors* [2021] EWHC 56 (QB).

[19]   Article 3(1) GDPR.

through stable arrangements'.[20] Notably, the absence of a branch or subsidiary is not determinative, and the presence of one employee may be sufficient to pass the 'stable arrangement' threshold if the processing was carried out by the EU-based employee.[21]

The English High Court concluded that the processing of personal data was outside of GDPR, Article 3(1). Crucially, the fact the publications existed over the Internet in English and that donations to Forensic News were solicited in euros and pounds sterling were insufficient factors to demonstrate 'stable arrangements' and therefore neither the Californian company nor the US-based journalists constituted an 'establishment'.

If today, a case with identical facts were brought before the English High Court, given that the UK GDPR is essentially the same, an identical approach would be applied, albeit the focus is 'the processing of personal data in the context of the activities of an establishment of a controller or processor in the United Kingdom, whether or not the processing takes place in the United Kingdom'.[22] However, it is notable that in this UK case the judge introduced the new term of 'core activities' to differentiate what an individual or organisation mainly did.[23] This characterisation is not part of the EU GDPR case law, and it may be further developed under future judicial interpretations of extra-territoriality under UK data protection regulations.

6.4 Data governance as a framework for data protection laws

The term data governance refers to the flexible framework to examine what the GDPR and all other UK data protection legislation seeks to achieve. The Royal Society is naturally biased towards sectors that are heavily science-based, such as medicine. But as they point out there are potential additional benefits from applying a sector-neutral framework: 'New ways of using data and the interconnected nature of digital systems

---

[20] *Weltimmo* (Judgment) [2015] EUECJ C-230/14, paragraph 31. This *Weltimmo* test was also applied in *Verein für Konsumenteninformation v Amazon EU Sàrl*, Case C-191/15.

[21] *Weltimmo* (Judgment) [2015] EUECJ C-230/14, at 28.

[22] Section 207(2) Data Protection Act 2018.

[23] *Weltimmo* (Judgment) [2015] EUECJ C-230/14, at 67.

mean that governance frameworks and mechanisms designed for one purpose or application may have implications for the use of data in another.'[24]

In my view, it is more practical to use themes provided under a data governance framework. The reason is that governance captures the broader range of responsibilities expected of legal counsel and compliance officers managing data in financial services, a multi-dimensional sector that is not revolving around data protection. Further, these data governance themes serve as long-term practical pegs for hanging not only specific GDPR articles, but also inevitable future changes to English law. For example, in the past the UK would solely look to the EDPB to provide detailed guidance on CJEU decisions concerning the GDPR. That is no longer the case and on-going UK-specific guidance has to be factored in as well.

6.5 Data ethics

The first data governance theme can be broadly described is ethics. In the context of machine learning, there are additional distinct ethical issues concerning data sets, for example algorithmic bias. These are covered in Chapter 12, which focuses on machine learning. Ethics encompasses a commitment to be accountable, to be honest with data subjects, not to mislead, and to stay within the compliance requirements of the regulations. Under the GDPR there are six principles of recurring application. These are paraphrased below and adjusted for financial services regulated firms.

- There is the fundamental principle that data must be 'processed lawfully, fairly and in a transparent manner';[25]
- *Limitation of purpose*: Data collected for an explicit, legitimate and specified purpose, must not be processed for other purposes;[26]
- *Data minimisation*: The processing of personal data must be relevant and limited to achieve the aim;[27]
- *Accuracy*: Data must be accurate and kept up to date, with effort

---

[24] Royal Society (2020) The UK Data Governance Landscape, at 17.
[25] Article 5(1)(a) GDPR.
[26] Article 5(1)(b) GDPR.
[27] Article 5(1)(c) GDPR.

expended on ensuring personal data is, where relevant, altered or deleted;[28]

- *Storage limitation*: Data should be stored in a form to enable identification of data subject for the length of time required to achieve the aim.[29]
- *Security*: Data should be kept secure from accidental damage, destruction or loss, so protected from unauthorised or unlawful processing.[30]

The six GDPR principles focus on the human responsibility to avoid the manipulation of hardware to misuse data. In GDPR terminology the 'controller' of data is responsible for demonstrating compliance with all these six principles.[31] The focus of the six principles is ethical principles, or at least all of them have ethical underpinnings. An eminent Oxford professor of computer ethics has provided an acute observation about data ethics when he remarked 'it is not a specific technology (computers, tablets, mobile phones, online platforms, cloud computing and so forth), but what any digital technology manipulates that represents the correct focus'.[32] This may seem a pedantic point, but when 'what is data?' remains a question without an internationally agreed definition, in my view, the GDPR principles provide a consistent consensus in the UK and across the EEA on what unethical data management encompasses. Further, the GDPR has already been influential in other non-EEA countries, so these ethical principles are increasingly the norms in other data spaces.

As a practical example, for regulated firms Big Data and machine learning analytics are of increasing importance. For either to succeed requires increasingly larger data sets and the ability to quickly gain competitive advantages by doing new things with existing data. In these scenarios it is all too tempting to use data collected for one purpose for multiple applications without the knowledge or consent of the data subjects – the second GDPR principle.[33]

---

[28]   Article 5(1)(d) GDPR.

[29]   Article 5(1)(e) GDPR.

[30]   Article 5(1)(f) GDPR.

[31]   Article 5(2) GDPR.

[32]   Floridi, L, and Taddeo, M (2016) What is Data Ethics?, *Philosophical Transactions of the Royal Society A*, at 374.

[33]   Article 6(1)(a) GDPR.

Another example is the transparency requirement under the first GDPR principle. Individual data subjects and the public have to be communicated to with clear, concise and plain language. Among other things, the purpose for which data is being processed has to be communicated in a clear and concise style so that existing, former and potential customers understand what is going on.[34] It is evident that institutional asset managers and investment banks have really mastered this transparency requirement on websites so that marketing continues to attract and inform, but also comply with the GDPR. That polish reflects 20 years of compliance and marketing cooperation. Many smaller regulated firms may still need to strike the right balance between attractive, succinct marketing and GDPR compliance.

6.6   Data privacy

The second theme, data privacy, encompasses consents required and compliance with related obligations. Further, it includes how data is shared with third-parties. Under the GDPR consent means 'clear affirmative action' based on informed and unambiguous confirmation that the data subject agrees to the processing of his or her personal data.[35] Data subjects are frequently asked for consent online in the form of affirming by ticking a box. All readers will have at some point come across a question requiring consent that required the de-selection of a box to in effect confirm consent is not given. This common scenario was referred by the German Federal Court of Justice to the CJEU concerning an online lottery company called Planet 49.[36] The important question posed was does a pre-checked checkbox, which the user must deselect to refuse his or her consent for the purposes of Article 5(3) of the EU e-Privacy Directive, a cookie consent requirement, meet the consent requirements under the GDPR?[37]

---

[34]   Article 13 GDPR.

[35]   Article 4(11) GDPR.

[36]   *Planet 49*, CJEU (2019) C-673/17.

[37]   Note also that the e-Privacy Directive, which is implemented in the UK, complements the GDPR regime by providing specific privacy rights on electronic communications. See The Privacy and Electronic Communications (EC Directive) Regulations 2003, SI 2003/2436.

The CJEU held that pre-ticked check-boxes authorising the use of cookies and similar technologies are invalid consent under the e-Privacy Directive, and that the consent required for cookies had to meet the GDPR standard of consent. The Planet 49 decision applies not just to cookies but to evolving technologies, such as device fingerprinting techniques that combine diverse information elements to uniquely identify a particular device. Examples of the information elements from which device fingerprinting can build inferences include, among many others, the use of any APIs. The decision also confirms the position on consent in the GDPR and reflects recent regulators' guidance in the UK and across the EEA.[38] The vast majority of regulated firms will have adjusted their website consent mechanisms and cookies notices, but it is an easy aspect to overlook.

Turning to privacy as a right associated with the storage of data, under the GDPR this is known as the right of erasure (the 'right to be forgotten').[39] This right creates an obligation on both controllers and processors. Of particular importance is the obligation to delete personal data that is no longer required for the purposes for which it was collected or processed.[40] There are many scenarios within asset managers, investment banks and platforms when established databases relating to previous clients may commercially not be a high priority to locate, check through and delete. Yet the fines for breaching the GDPR already point to the risks of neglecting to delete personal data.

For example, in the case of the German real estate company Deutsche Wohnen, the Berlin data protection regulator[41] imposed a €14.5 million fine for storing data for a substantially longer period than necessary in breach of the GDPR.[42] From an operational controls viewpoint, the case is also important because the core deficiency in data management was an archive system that was not designed to remove any personal data that was no longer required. The Deutsche Wohnen data concerned the financial

---

[38] ICO (2020) What are Cookies and Similar Technologies? Available at https://ico.org.uk/for -organisations/guide-to-pecr/guidance-on-the-use-of-cookies-and-similar-technologies/what-are -cookies-and-similar-technologies/.

[39] Article 17 GDPR.

[40] Article 17(1)(a) GDPR.

[41] See https://edpb.europa.eu/news/national-news/2019/berlin-commissioner-data-protection-imposes -fine-real-estate-company_en.

[42] Articles 5 and 25(1) GDPR.

and personal details of tenants, including bank statements, employment contract extracts, health insurance, salary and social security details. So the case has many parallels with the type of data held by regulated firms across the financial services sector.

6.7   Pseudonymisation

As set out earlier in the GDPR essential terminology (Table 6.1), there is a requirement for pseudonymisation.[43] To clarify, anonymisation and pseudonymisation are legally distinct. The GDPR does not apply to anonymised data, namely information in a format that makes the data subject unidentifiable.[44] Pseudonymisation refers to how data can be altered so that it cannot be attributed to a specific data subject without additional information. The additional information must be kept separately in a technically secure way. Pseudonymisation is important from technical and organisational viewpoints,[45] because it is how the key data protection principle of data minimisation is achieved.[46]

Further, in my view, financial services businesses will increasingly seek to maximise the value of the data sets they possess by collaborating with other businesses both in the financial services sector and outside of it, by sharing data in clean rooms. Data clean rooms originally referred to the maintenance of large reliable data sets by Amazon, Facebook and Google. However, other companies are also building their own in-house clean rooms. While the commercial potential is clear, there will be a need for legal counsel and compliance officers to check that the data does not result in GDPR breaches, given third parties will be accessing the data and subsequently making commercial decisions.

6.8   Data sharing

The third theme is data sharing. Data sharing can be intra-group or between unrelated organisations. It can also be based on routine or

---

[43] Article 4(5) GDPR.
[44] Recital 16 GDPR.
[45] Article 25 GDPR.
[46] Article 5(1)(c) GDPR.

one-off sharing practices. The ICO provides a detailed Data Sharing Code of Practice.[47] The following questions from the ICO Code provide a solid foundation for legal and compliance due diligence:

- What is the sharing meant to achieve?
- What information needs to be shared?
- Who requires access to the shared personal data?
- When should it be shared?
- How should it be shared?
- How can we check the sharing is achieving its objectives?
- What risk does the data sharing pose?
- Could the objective be achieved without sharing the data or by anonymising it?
- Do I need to update my notification?
- Will any of the data be transferred outside of the EEA?[48]

6.9   Data protection and security

The fourth theme is data protection and security. The processing of data under the GDPR requires a commitment to 'integrity and confidentiality', including accidental damage, destruction or loss, and also hacking and other forms of attack that cause unauthorised or unlawful processing.[49] The GDPR states that 'the controller and the processor shall implement appropriate technical and organisational measures to ensure a level of security appropriate to the risk'.[50] That specifically includes encryption.[51] Encryption can be defined as a 'mathematical function that encodes data' so that it is only readable with a key or passcode.[52]

Given the responsibility to encrypt data rests with the controller and processor, the legal function needs to scrutinise not only the technical in-house encryption policies, but also the contracts of all external service providers involved. Contractual obligations and liabilities need to be

---

[47] ICO (2011) Data Sharing Code of Practice. See https://ico.org.uk/for-organisations/data-sharing-a-code-of-practice. Note that this ICO Code has not been updated since 2011.

[48] Ibid., at 14–15.

[49] Article 5(1)(f) GDPR.

[50] Article 32(1) GDPR.

[51] Article 32(1)(a) GDPR.

[52] ICO (2019) Guide to the GDPR, at 227.

drafted precisely, so that the levels of encryption required are recorded and that the responsibility to upgrade technical standards is in line with recommended advice from the ICO, and the NCSC and other internationally respected organisations, such as the ISO[53] and the International Electrotechnical Commission (IEC)[54] It is also sensible to invest time in checking which organisations understand security risks specifically associated with financial services.

The ICO GDPR Guide includes basic encryption advice which highlights four important aspects when managing encryption risk. These are (a) the right decision making on the choice of the algorithm; (b) the key size; (c) the software; and (d) how to keep the key secure.[55] The ICO's GDPR and encryption guidance points out the need also to reference sector-specific guidance. Clearly, encryption is an essential element of preventing unauthorised viewing of data.[56]

When choosing encryption software there is a need to meet internationally recognised standards, namely the US Federal Information Processing Standard Publication (FIPS) 140-2 and FIPS 197.[57] Legal counsel and compliance officers should also get comfort from software engineers that apply encryption solutions recommended by the NCSC. It is important to note that effective from September 2019 there exists FIPS 140-3, which has an overlapping transition period with FIPS 140-2 from September 2021. The FIPS 140-3 update includes references to two joint international standards, namely ISO/IEC 19790:2012, 'Information technology – Security techniques – Security requirements for cryptographic modules'; and ISO/IEC 24759:2017, 'Information technology – Security techniques – Test requirements for cryptographic modules'.[58]

The FCA recommends applying standards from the NIST Cybersecurity framework, ISO27001/2, SANS CIS, NCSC's '10 Steps to Cyber Security' and the NCSC's 'NIS Directive Cyber Assessment Framework'.[59]

---

[53] www.iso.org.

[54] www.iec.ch.

[55] ICO (2019) Guide to the GDPR, at 236.

[56] See also Chapter 5 Cyber security.

[57] National Institute of Standards and Technology (2002) Security Requirements for Cryptographic Modules.

[58] NIST (2019) NIST/ITL Cyber Security Annual Report, at 16.

[59] FCA (2019) Cyber Security – Industry Insights, at 6.

6.10   The *Schrems II* decision

The *Schrems II* case concerned an individual challenging the transfer of his personal data to the US.[60] In *Schrems II*, the CJEU invalidated the Privacy Shield that existed between the EU and the US. This Privacy Shield meant that cloud service providers in the US could receive personal data transmitted out of the EEA area based on a framework of adequacy between the standards of data protection in the EU compared with the US.[61] In sum, the *Schrems II* decision has implications for all controllers and processors responsible for data transferring out of the EEA.

The consequence of the CJEU removing the Privacy Shield is that the continued transfer of data from the EEA to the US has to be subject to SCCs.[62] For ease of reference, the detailed content required in SCCs between an EEA controller and a non-EEA processor, such as a US-based cloud service provider, are published as part of EU law.[63] For example, these SCCs apply to a French company (controller) transferring its personal data out of the *EEA* to a cloud computing service provider (processor) based in the US. Simultaneously the CJEU stated that the laws of the non-EEA controller or processor have to be checked to ensure they do not override the SCCs. Further, the CJEU as part of its judgment signposted that important supplementary measures would be provided by the EDPB necessary to protect EEA personal data. This additional EDPB guidance is also summarised in this chapter.

An important point of differentiation here between EU GDPR and UK GDPR it that while the *Schrems II* assessment applies to a regulated UK firm transferring data to a third country with inadequate data privacy laws, in such a scenario SCCs are no longer mandatory.[64] In their place, before the end of 2022 the UK is very likely to have finalised its own version of SCCs. Drafted by the ICO, the UK equivalent to the SCCs is

---

[60]   EU Case C-311/18 – *Data Protection Commissioner v Facebook Ireland Ltd and Maximillian Schrems.*

[61]   Article 45 GDPR.

[62]   Article 46(3)(a) GDPR. Importantly, the EU has revised the content on technical and organisational measures that need to be described. See EU Implementing Decisions 2021/915 at Annex III.

[63]   EU Decision C(2010) 593.

[64]   The CJEU *Schrems II* decision applies to the UK given it was made pre-Brexit in 2020. However, from 27 September 2021 new EU SCCs, published on 4 June 2021, do not apply in the UK.

called an International Data Transfer Agreement (IDTA).[65] As the IDTA title suggests, the UK approach is a template contract framework rather than following the modular SCC format.[66]

An important aside here is to highlight that since 27 September 2021 only the new SCCs can be applied, in the context of new contracts subject to the EU GDPR.[67] There is also a 15 month transitional period to update existing contracts concluded before 27 September 2021.[68] The new SCCs are not only a consolidating modernisation of the three previous versions, but also reflect the *Schrems II* judgment. The liability clause deserves extra scrutiny. When one party is held liable in the context of joint liability, it is entitled to claim back compensation or damages from the other party based on proportionate liability. For instance, in the common scenario of data flowing intra-group between two financial services subsidiaries, the level of damages for liability of a French subsidiary exporting the data could be measured differently from a US subsidiary importing the data.[69]

6.10.1 EDPB guidelines supplementing *Schrems II*

The EDPB has produced a succinct summary of all the implications of *Schrems II*.[70] The EDPB guidance was provided a few months later, a detailed 38 page summary of what is expected of data controllers and processors.[71] The EDPB's essential supplementary guidance six key steps are summarised in Table 6.2.

---

[65] ICO (2021) Draft International Data Transfer Agreement. See EC Implementing Decision (EU) 2021/914.

[66] Ibid, at 12–55, the draft IDTA is made up of four elements, namely Tables, Extra Protection Clauses, Commercial Clauses and Mandatory Clauses.

[67] Article 4 EU Implementing Decision 2021/914.

[68] Ibid, at Article 4(4), so all relevant contracts have to be updated by 27 December 2022.

[69] The exception when safeguards are unnecessary is when an adequacy decision, as covered as a separate topic later in this chapter, is made in favour of the country to which data is being transferred from the EEA. See Article 45(3) GDPR.

[70] See https://edpb.europa.eu/sites/edpb/files/files/file1/20200724_edpb_faqoncjeuc31118_en.pdf.

[71] See https://edpb.europa.eu/our-work-tools/public-consultations-art-704/2020/recommendations-01 2020-measures-supplement-transfer_en.

Table 6.2   *Six recommendations*

Step	Substance
Know your transfers	Due diligence on where your data goes, and also verify the data transferred meets GDPR principles, such as data minimisation.[1]
Check the transfer tool relied on	For regular and repetitive transfers a listed GDPR transfer tool has to be checked and applied.[2] The two main exceptions are when relying on an adequacy decision[3] or a derogation.[4] Adequacy decisions can apply to specific sectors, so check that financial services data is included.[5]
Assess the law or practice in the third country	Relevant to the chosen transfer tool, check third country law on data transfer and governmental access to data for the purpose of surveillance.[6] Analyse by reference to the following four recommendations: • processing should be based on clear, precise and accessible rules; • necessity and proportionality with regard to the legitimate objectives pursued need to be demonstrated; • an independent oversight mechanism should exist; and • effective remedies need to be available to the individual. Document all due diligence completed on the above four aspects.[7]
Identify and adopt supplementary measures	If the third country law affects the effectiveness of the transfer tool relied on, the EDPB provides a non-exhaustive list of examples of supplementary measures.[8]

Step	Substance
Take any formal procedural steps	Where necessary, consult with regulators concerning transfer tool relied on.
Check for any changes	Self-explanatory. Note an adequacy decision can be altered or withdrawn.[9]

Notes: [1] Article 5(1)(c) GDPR. [2] Article 46 GDPR. [3] Article 45 GDPR. [4] Article 49 GDPR. [5] Article 45(3) GDPR. [6] EDPB (2020) Recommendations on 01/2020 on Measures that Supplement Transfer Tools to Ensure Compliance with the EU Level of Protection of Personal Data, Annex 3, at 38, provides a non-exhaustive list of possible third country legal sources. [7] EDPB (2020) Recommendations on 01/2020 on Measures that Supplement Transfer Tools to Ensure Compliance with the EU Level of Protection of Personal Data, at 8–19. [8] EDPB (2020) Recommendations on 01/2020 on Measures that Supplement Transfer Tools to Ensure Compliance with the EU Level of Protection of Personal Data, at 21. [9] Article 45(5) GDPR.

Source: EDPG (2020) https://edpb.europa.eu/sites/default/files/consultation/edpb _recommendations_202001_supplementarymeasurestransferstools_en.pdf.

6.11 Adequacy decisions

Transfers on the basis of an adequacy decision to a third country can only occur when the EC has decided that the third country has a comparable level data protection.[72] Current adequacy decisions by the EC include. Andorra, Argentina, Canada, Faroe Islands, Guernsey, Israel, Isle of Man, Japan, Jersey, New Zealand, South Korea,[73] Switzerland, the UK and Uruguay.

The EC assessment is based primarily on the following factors: (a) the relevant legislation including case law and rules concerning the onward transfer of data; (b) the rule of law; (c) respect for human rights; (d) public authority access to personal data; and (e) data subject administrative and judicial redress relating to data being transferred.[74]

Further, the assessment is based on the existence and competence of a data protection authority with adequate enforcement powers and its

---

[72] Article 45 GDPR.

[73] In September 2021, the EDPB produced its opinion on the EC's draft adequacy decision covering South Korea. That EDPB opinion requested the EC to clarify certain aspects. Confirmed adequacy decisions are published at https://ec.europa.eu/info/law/law-topic/data-protection/international -dimension-data-protection/adequacy-decisions_en.

[74] Article 45(2)(a) GDPR.

willingness to cooperate with EU member states. Finally, evidence of the international commitments by the third country to international conventions or instruments and multilateral systems is required, especially in the context of personal data protection.[75]

6.12 Automated decision making

The GDPR deals with the specific protection of individuals from decisions made solely by an automated process.[76] However, the UK government may legislate to diverge from Article 22 GDPR. It has already sought evidence and opinion from UK industry. The main context is the likely future significant increase in automated decision making by machine learning makes a human review impracticable.[77] This type of automated decision making is especially common in machine learning and other AI methods linked to financial services advice, so-called robo-advice. For example, an asset manager may provide advice to an existing or potential retail customer in the form of computer driven decisions on the percentages of money to spread amongst a portfolio of equity, fixed income and other assets based on their age and circumstances.

Under the GDPR, automated decisions can only be made when it is (a) necessary for entering into or performing a contract; (b) authorised by domestic law; or (c) based on the data subject's explicit consent.

An additional challenge for automated decision making is the requirement at the time when the personal data are obtained to provide data subjects with 'meaningful information about the logic involved, as well as the significance and the envisaged consequences of such processing for the data subject'.[78] The ICO has also advised that human reviewers must check that a system's recommendations are meaningful. Further, human reviewers must have the authority to go against the computer's recommendations.[79]

---

[75] Article 45(2)(b)–(c) GDPR.

[76] Article 22 GDPR.

[77] See UK Government, DDCMS (2021) Data: A New Direction, at 38–40.

[78] Article 13(2)(f) GDPR. See https://eur-lex.europa.eu/legal-content/EN/TXT/PDF/?uri=CELEX:02016R0679-20160504&from=EN.

[79] ICO and Alan Turing Institute (2020) Explaining Decisions Made with AI.

6.13 Data protection impact assessments

Before implementing new technologies for contract management, portfolio management and trading, the crucial tasks are often algorithm validation and model testing. Does the computer system work as planned? What is it doing that is unexpected? When is personal data involved? The GDPR requires that a DPIA is carried out prior to the live processing of data.[80] For AI initiatives, often in the form of machine learning used in the financial services sector, a DPIA may be required.

A DPIA must be carried out if the new technology 'is likely to result in a high risk to the rights and freedoms of natural persons'. As an exception, if a DPIA has already been completed on a similar system that had similar high risks, then a second DPIA is unnecessary.[81]

Three types of processing will always require a DPIA,[82] namely: (a) systematic and extensive profiling with significant effects; (b) large-scale use of sensitive data; and (c) large-scale public monitoring. To assisted decision making on what processing operations may require a DPIA, each regulator must publish a list of factors that might, individually or in combination, indicate likely high risk.[83] The ICO has relied on nine criteria originating from a working party of EU data protection authorities (the 'WP 248').[84] A DPIA is required if two or more of the following criteria apply:

- automated decision making with legal or similar significant effect;
- data concerning vulnerable data subjects;
- data processed on a large scale;
- evaluation or scoring;
- innovative use or applying new technological or organisational solutions;
- matching or combining data sets;
- preventing data subjects from exercising a right or using a service or

---

[80] Article 35 GDPR.
[81] Ibid.
[82] Article 35(3) GDPR.
[83] Article 35(4) GDPR.
[84] EC (2017) Guidelines on Data Protection Impact Assessment (DPIA) and Determining whether Processing is 'Likely to Result in a High Risk' for the Purposes of Regulation 2016/679.

contract;
- sensitive data or data of a highly personal nature; or
- systematic monitoring.

The WP248 provides guidance on these nine factors, including detailed reasoning for the high-risk indicators, and also examples of processing likely to result in high risk. In addition, the ICO has published 10 additional criteria. Some of these types of processing will automatically require a DPIA, and some when they exist in combination with another of the 10 or any of the nine WP248 criteria. Of the 10 criteria, in my opinion the following four are most relevant to financial services firms.

- *Data matching*: By which is meant combining, comparing or matching personal data obtained from multiple sources;
- *Denial of service*: Decisions about an individual's access to a product, service, opportunity or benefit that is based to any extent on automated decision making (including profiling) or involves processing special category data;
- *Innovative technology*: Processing involving the use of innovative technologies, or the novel application of existing technologies, including AI;
- *Large-scale profiling*: Any profiling of individuals on a large scale.[85]

The GDPR also permits regulators to provide a list of processing operations that do not require a DPIA.[86] The ICO has yet to do so. Given machine learning is increasingly applied by financial services firms and the models and techniques are well known, it would, in my view, be valuable to have a list of the models that do not require a DPIA. The minimum DPIA contents requirements are (a) a description of the envisaged operations; (b) a necessity and proportionality assessment; (c) a risk assessment concerning the rights and freedoms of data subjects; and (d) a planned risk management measures and mechanisms.[87] In the event the conclusion is the new technology is not high risk, it is essential to document the reasoning for not conducting a DPIA.

Finally, in most scenarios the data protection regulator does not need to be sent the DPIA. However, there is a requirement for prior consultation

---

[85]   ICO (2021) Guide to Data Protection Impact Assessments.
[86]   Article 35(5) GDPR.
[87]   Article 35(7) GDPR.

where the DPIA indicates that the processing would be high risk without risk mitigation measures applied by the controller.[88]

6.14   GDPR breaches

Under the GDPR, the ICO has wide powers, including the right to impose fines,[89] which must be effective, proportionate and dissuasive.[90] The scale of the fine depends upon the specific GDPR principle or article breached. The two fining scales are (a) the higher of £8.7 million or 2 per cent of worldwide annual turnover for the last financial year;[91] and (b) the higher of £17.5 million or 4 per cent of worldwide annual turnover for the last financial year.[92] For example, if a regulated firm was found to have breached one of the fundamental ethical principles of the GDPR, such as failing to ensure that data is 'processed lawfully, fairly and in a transparent manner', the higher £17.5 million or 4 per cent scale would apply. A notable example is the penalty notice[93] concerning a £20 million fine imposed on British Airways for failing to prevent a cyber attack on the personal and financial data of 244,000 customers.[94] The data included names, addresses, Card Verification Value (CVV) numbers and payment card numbers.

Based on the mitigating acts of British Airways in the aftermath of the cyber attack, the ICO's proposed fine of £30 million was reduced by 20 per cent to £24 million. The fine was finally reduced by another £4 million because of the impact of Covid-19 on British Airways. Mitigating aspects included the fact that British Airways had contacted and cooperated with the FCA and other relevant bodies, such as the NCSC. Given the annual worldwide turnover of British Airways for the relevant year was £12.26 billion, the ceiling of the fine applying the 4 per cent rule would have been just over £489 million. It pays to cooperate.

---

[88]   Article 36(1) GDPR.

[89]   Article 58(1)(i) GDPR.

[90]   Article 83(1) GDPR.

[91]   Article 83(4) GDPR.

[92]   Article 83(5) GDPR.

[93]   Section 155 and Schedule 16 Data Protection Act 2018.

[94]   Articles 5(1)(f) and 32 GDPR.

6.15   Remote working patterns and privately owned devices

Increased reliance on home working as part of how employees and contractors communicate, invest and trade requires on-going adjustment in the context of GDPR and other data protection rules compliance. FCA expectations are that regulated firms have:

> updated their policies, refreshed their training and put in place rigorous oversight … particularly regarding the risk of use of privately owned devices. These policies should be demonstrable to us and to your audit teams. It should go without saying that policies should prevent the use of privately owned devices for relevant activities where recording is not possible. New communication mechanisms, before they are used, should have controls in place where required and their use should be approved by firm management. The regulatory obligations have not changed. How compliance is achieved may be changing, but the substance remains the same.[95]

6.16   AI

Finally, in the context of the development of AI and data protection, the UK House of Lords committee in a report entitled 'AI in the UK: No Room for Complacency', has already proposed that the ICO develops training courses for use by regulators, such as the FCA, to provide its staff with the necessary understanding of ethical uses of data and AI systems.

The House of Lords analysis and conclusions included the following: 'Sector-specific regulators are better placed to identify gaps in regulation, and to learn about AI and how it applies to their sectors. The CDEI [Centre for Data Ethics and Innovation] and the Office for AI can play a cross-cutting role, along with the ICO, to provide that understanding of risk and the necessary training and up-skilling for sector specific regulators.'[96] Only time will tell if the FCA keeps pace with the CDEI, ICO and the Office of AI.

---

[95] FCA (2020) Market Abuse in a Time of Coronavirus, speech by Julia Hoggett, Director, Market Oversight, FCA. See www.fca.org.uk/news/speeches/market-abuse-coronavirus.

[96] UK House of Lords Liaison Committee (2020), 7th Report of Session 2019–21, AI in the UK: No Room for Complacency, at 19.

6.17 Final points

When thinking about the most dynamic financial services firms levering technology, it is the disruptive innovative use of data that is often at the heart of their business models. The greatest challenge is often the asynchronous nature of compliance, a common characteristic of FinTech that can be defined as 'business strategies and operations that are moving at markedly different speeds compared with financial services regulation. Asynchronous compliance creates uncertainty that dynamic business initiatives meet regulatory requirements.'[97] The protection of personal data is no exception.

While acknowledging this asynchronous nature, the EU has adapted and evolved its data protection laws at an admirable pace. The GDPR, and accompanying EDPB guidance, keeps pace with technology and other changes. This reflects the depth of EU data protection law. The GDPR is the product of decades of development and adjustment to keep up with and anticipate technology. Currently, UK regulated firms have clarity and details to comply with and document compliance. Only time will tell if the UK law diverges from the coordinated pace of the EU.

---

[97] Sheridan, I (2017) 'MiFID II in the Context of Financial Technology and Regulatory Technology', *Capital Markets Law Journal*, Volume 12, Issue 4, at 419.

7. Sandbox

Making a profit in the financial services sector from a genuinely innovative product or service is a formidable challenge. New ideas are often treated with scepticism, not only internally within a business, but also by clients. If an idea has ran an internal socialising gauntlet to reach the point of project approval, there are often two significant risk factors. First, there is the issue of how to defend robustly the innovation from competitors copying it. That largely involves IP protection.[1] The second issue is whether or not the new initiative is within the FCA perimeter.[2] The General Counsel and head of compliance will both ask the question: Is this project regulated under the Financial Services and Markets Act 2000 (Regulated Activities) Order or not?[3] This chapter answers that question and other related ones that are of vital importance to innovative growth.

7.1   Introduction

Regulated firms and unauthorised firms with financial technology (FinTech) initiatives need to determine if their proposed project is subject to UK financial services regulation. Any firm that plans to start a regulated activity in the UK is required to first obtain authorisation from either the FCA or the PRA. If in any doubt, it is vital to seek legal advice in each instance given that specific facts make this a complex area, especially so if cutting-edge technologies are part of the new product or venture. Before analysing how the UK Sandbox and some other programmes functions, it is necessary to cover the issues of 'dual-regulated' firms and the FCA Perimeter Guidance.

---

[1] Considered in Chapter 9 Innovation protection.
[2] See www.handbook.fca.org.uk/handbook/PERG.pdf.
[3] The Financial Services and Markets Act 2000 (Regulated Activities) Order 2001, SI 2001/544.

7.1.1 Dual-regulated status

Readers from outside the UK may be justifiably puzzled about situations where firms are referred to orally or in writing as 'dual-regulated'. This term means the firm is both authorised and regulated by the PRA; and regulated by the FCA. When a firm is dual-regulated, for example Nationwide Building Society[4] a memorable way to grasp what is occurring is to think about the underlying reasoning for two different types of compliance that avoids duplication of effort by these regulators. That involves applying a two-limbed test.[5] The FCA acts for firms who collectively determine the integrity of the financial system with the key aim of protecting consumers. That is why for the vast majority of scenarios the FCA is the key regulator for firms operating in subsectors where there are greater risks for consumers and therefore overall market integrity.

The PRA is the prudential regulator for a small number of dual-regulated firms. In this scenario the FCA acts as each dual-regulated firm's conduct regulator.[6] Of most importance to the PRA are fewer than 20 large financial services groups, called systemically important institutions (SIIs) all headquartered in the UK with capital levels that position them as core risks to the UK financial system. By which is meant the financial instability of any could cause a financial crisis.[7]

---

[4] See www.nationwide.co.uk/.

[5] The FCA Handbook sets out the two-limbed prudential context test as follows:

  (1) For the FCA, in relation to activities carried on by a *firm*, the context in which the activities have, or might reasonably be regarded as likely to have, a negative effect on:

    (a) the integrity of the *UK financial system*; or

    (b) the ability of the *firm* to meet either:

      (i) the 'fit and proper' test in *threshold condition* 2E and 3D (Suitability); or

      (ii) the applicable requirements and standards under the *regulatory system* relating to the *firm's* financial resources.

  (2) For the PRA, in relation to activities carried on by a firm, the context in which the activities have, or might reasonably be regarded as likely to have, a negative effect on:

    (a) the safety and soundness of PRA-*authorised persons*; or

    (b) the ability of the *firm* to meet either:

      (i) the 'fit and proper' test in *threshold condition* 5 (Suitability); or

      (ii) the applicable requirements and standards under the *regulatory system* relating to the *firm's* financial resources'.

[6] The Financial Services and Markets Act 2000 (PRA-regulated Activities) Order 2013, SI 2013/556.

[7] The systemically important institutions (SIIs) are determined annually by the PRA. In 2021 these included: Barclays Plc, Citigroup Global Markets Limited, Credit Suisse International, Credit Suisse Investments (UK), Goldman Sachs Group UK Limited, HSBC Holdings Plc, JP Morgan

Beyond these very large groups, PRA-regulated activities include deposit taking,[8] insurers,[9] and dealing in investment as principal. Further, approximately 40 or so building societies are also prudentially regulated by the PRA.[10] Another PRA-regulated subsector group is mutual insurance societies that hold significant pension funds, for example the National Farmers Union Mutual Insurance Society.[11]

7.1.2 The FCA regulatory perimeter

The FCA Perimeter Guidance (the 'Perimeter Guide') needs to be assessed as part of any planning exercise for a FinTech project, whether to determine if there is a need to seek authorisation or to extend existing authorisation. The Perimeter Guide applies generally to a person, meaning a business entity or a human.[12] To elaborate it is relevant to any person who is:

- planning to carrying on activities in the UK which may fall within the scope of the FSMA and seeking guidance on whether authorisation is required;
- seeking to become an authorised person under the FSMA and applying, or considering applying, for permission to carry on regulated activities in the UK;[13]
- seeking guidance on whether any communication he may be seeking to make or cause to be made will be a financial promotion and subject to the restriction under the FSMA.[14]

Capital Holdings Limited, Lloyds Banking Group Plc, Merrill Lynch International, Morgan Stanley International Limited, Nationwide Building Society, Nomura Europe Holdings Plc, The Royal Bank of Scotland Group Plc, Santander UK Group Holdings Plc, and Standard Chartered Plc. Looking back at the SII lists for previous years, this collection is fairly static. UBS is absent from 2018.

[8] Article 5 Regulated Activities Order, SI 2001/544. Note that it is also amended by SI 2002/682.

[9] Article 10 Regulated Activities Order, SI 2001/544.

[10] It is important to note there is not a complete logic of differentiation between FCA and PRA supervision of building societies, because the FCA is responsible for many building society subsidiaries. A more accurate way to describe this situation is the sharing of responsibilities based on the PRA as an organ of the Bank of England focused on systemic risks. Indeed, the creation of the PRA was in response to the perceived poor systemic risk supervision by the FSA, the FCA's predecessor, before and during the Global Financial Crisis 2007–2008.

[11] See www.nfumutual.co.uk.

[12] Schedule 1 of the Interpretation Act 1978, 'person' includes a body of persons corporate or unincorporate.

[13] Part IV FSMA 2000.

[14] Section 21 FSMA 2000.

It is timely to mention that any FCA guidance, whether in the Perimeter Guide or read in the FCA Handbook or other PRA rule-based publications, do not bind UK courts, but given the UK regulators have consulted with industry participants and deliberated over the contents, it is persuasive evidence at any level of court or tribunal.[15] Importantly, failure to follow guidance does not bind the courts in the context of enforcing contracts because of breaches of other sections of the FSMA.[16] The FCA view is that regulated firms that follow its guidance create a presumption of compliance.[17] The FCA's attitude is that it 'will proceed on the same footing that the person has complied with the aspects of the requirement to which the guidance relates'.[18] In short, FCA guidance is neither compulsory nor optional, but logical corroboration for any regulated firm.

7.2   UK Sandbox

Globally, the concept of a regulatory sandbox was a UK brainwave. Conceived in 2014, and live from 2016, the FCA's regulatory sandbox (the 'UK Sandbox') provides a ring-fenced environment in which currently regulated firms, and other firms applying for authorisation, can test new technologies immune from the potential consequences of engaging in FCA unauthorised activity. Over more than five years, UK Sandbox has contributed to growing numbers of FinTech companies gravitating around London, Cambridge and Edinburgh.[19]

The focus of the UK Sandbox, and any other sandbox programme, is financial technology ('FinTech') products and services. FinTech is a challenge to define precisely,[20] but its key characteristics tend to include three aspects, namely: (a) disruptive innovation occurring; (b) free from

---

[15] Section 139A FSMA 2000.

[16] The FCA Guidance (2021) uses the examples of Section 19 FSMA 2000 (the general prohibition), Section 21 FSMA 2000 (restrictions on financial promotions) and sections 26-30 FSMA (enforceability of agreements), and Section 138D FSMA 2000 (actions for damages).

[17] FCA Guidance (2021), at 1.3.1G.

[18] FCA PERG 1.3.1.

[19] See www.fca.org.uk/firms/innovation/regulatory-sandbox.

[20] The *Oxford Dictionary* definition refers to 'computer programs and other technology used to support or enable banking and financial services'. While helpful that definition has limitations, given it would cover the Society of Worldwide Interbank Financial Telecommunications (SWIFT), which was established in the early 1970s.

legacy technology systems; and with (c) asynchronous compliance.[21] First, disruptive innovation may be either a significant change or improvement. This is an old wine in a new bottle concept, which can be traced to Joseph Schumpeter, a Vienna law student turned Harvard economist.[22] His concept of 'creative destruction'[23] captures the evolutionary nature of free-markets, where established ways of doing things are replaced by new ones – disruptive innovation. In essence, new entrants to existing markets tend to succeed when introducing significant improvements.[24] In the context of FinTech significant changes or improvements are achieved with technology, principally machine learning, DLT networks and Big Data analytics or a combination of one or more of these specialisms.

Second, legacy-free technology systems is a well understood term. Established asset managers and investment banks tend to have extensive legacy IT systems that cannot be ignored when any new technology projects is implemented. That can create costs, delay and inefficiency absent from a project implemented from scratch. This presents a significant competitive advantage for small- and medium-sized FinTech firms, but it cannot be presumed that even the largest global incumbents will not choose to 'start up' a new FinTech venture autonomous from its group IT systems. Already a number of the global banks have done so as either collaborative or solo participants in the UK Sandbox. Three examples are ABN AMRO, Citigroup and Société Générale.

Third, the term asynchronous compliance characterises the recurring challenge that FinTech companies face of business strategies and operations that are developing at markedly different speeds compared with financial services regulation. Figure 7.1 captures the interplay.[25]

---

[21] Sheridan, I (2017) 'MiFID II in the Context of Financial Technology and Regulatory Technology', *Capital Markets Law Journal*, Volume 12, Issue 4, 1 October 2017, at 417–427. This article sets out in detail the boundaries of FinTech.

[22] See www.econ.univie.ac.at/de/institut/geschichte-des-instituts; and www.iss-evec.de/info.

[23] A direct translation from the German *Schöpferische Zerstörung*.

[24] See Mueller, D (2000), *Capitalism and Socialism in the 21st Century* (Springer Publishing), at 2; also at www.iss-evec.de/info.

[25] Sheridan, I (2018) 'FinTech and Global Capital Markets – The Impact of Pro-Enterprise Regulation and English Law', *Capital Markets Law Journal* Volume 13, Issue 4, at 587–599, available at https://doi .org/10.1093/cmlj/kmy027.

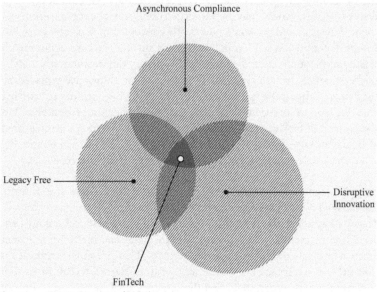

Asynchronous Compliance

Legacy Free

Disruptive
Innovation

FinTech

Source: © Iain Sheridan (2021).

Figure 7.1   The challenge and opportunity of FinTech

7.2.1   Legal basis for UK Sandbox

On initial fast legal thinking,[26] it is counter-intuitive that a regulator such as the FCA is also a catalyst for innovation. Regulators make rules, offer guidance and punish when it all goes awry. Yet in the UK, perhaps uniquely so, the financial services statute includes innovation as part of the FCA's mandate. Under the FSMA, a formal promotion of competition enables change to happen. The matters that the FCA may factor in when considering the effectiveness of competition in the market for any services include:

- the needs of different consumers, existing or potential, including their desire for information that enables them to make informed choices;

---

[26]   As first mentioned in the introductory chapter of this book, fast thinking is a term coined by the psychologist Daniel Kahneman, a Nobel Prize winner in Economic Sciences. In his best-selling book Thinking, Fast and Slow (2011) (Penguin), Kahneman characterises 'fast thinking' as frequent, instinctive or unconscious thoughts. A memorable example is that we use fast thinking to solve 2+2=?.

- how consumers, existing or potential, may access and use those services, including consumers in deprived socio-economic areas;
- how consumers who obtain those services can change their existing
  service provider;
- the ease with which new entrants can enter the market; and
- how far competition is encouraging innovation.[27]

Clearly, the last aspect, namely encouraging innovation, is the key statutory element, but as will become clear in later sections of this chapter
the first four points deceptively encompass different forms of innovative
services.

In a past financial regulation articles focused on FinTech, my thought
was that regression analysis of a statistical sample of the top 40 ranked
innovative countries may reveal positive correlations between innovative
countries and innovative regulators.[28] Put another way, FinTech may be
confirmation that a dynamic financial regulator, such as the FCA and
equivalent regulators in other top ranked innovative economies, are not
only protecting investors and managing financial stability, but also contributing to long-term economic growth. More recently, from a narrower
business start-up viewpoint, a regression analysis has revealed a very
positive influence between sandbox activity and investment in FinTech
firms.[29]

7.2.2   UK Sandbox qualifying criteria

Consistent with the FSMA requirement for the FCA to promote innovation, the UK Sandbox aims to provide authorised and unauthorised firms
with:

- the ability to test products and services in a controlled environment;
- reduced time-to-market at potentially lower cost;
- support in identifying appropriate consumer safeguards as compo-

---

[27] Section 6(1) E Financial Services Act 2012. Note the Section 6(1) E statutory requirements apply
equally to the PRA.

[28] Sheridan, I (2017) 'MiFID II in the Context of Financial Technology and Regulatory Technology',
Capital Markets Law Journal, Volume 12, Issue 4, at 7–8.

[29] Goo, J, and Heo, J-Y (2020) 'The Impact of the Regulatory Sandbox on the Fintech Industry, with
a Discussion on the Relation between Regulatory Sandboxes and Open Innovation', *J. Open Innov.
Technol*, Volume 6, Issue 2, at 43.

nents of new products and services; and
- improved access to finance.[30]

It makes sense to clarify the context in which UK Sandbox applicants can be unauthorised. If an unauthorised firm is accepted into a UK Sandbox cohort, they will need to apply for a tailored authorisation that will enable the participant to test their ideas for the duration of the testing programme. The FCA terms this procedure a restricted authorisation.[31] Eligibility criteria and application processes are set out succinctly on the FCA website.[32] The risk of the UK Sandbox and equivalent programmes for any growing FinTech company, often a start-up, is that it may not succeed in gaining FCA authorisation to extend beyond the programme. Yet it cannot be overlooked that entrepreneurial projects are inherently risky and often evolve to match market demand and accommodate technological constraints. By analogy, the FinTech aeroplane that trundles down the start-up runway often has different shaped wings and a changed destination on take-off.[33]

An example of a UK Sandbox participant is Pyctor, a project led by ING Bank in collaboration with ABN AMRO, BNP Paribas Securities Services, Citibank, Invesco, Société Générale, State Street, UBS and others. This project involved testing a DLT network that aims to provide digital asset safekeeping and transaction services, with a focus on regulated security tokens issued either on a private or public blockchain.[34]

Up to 2021, 140 firms have had the opportunity to test their initiatives in the UK Sandbox, with another 13 firms joining the programme in 2021. The geographical spread of the participants' UK bases includes Belfast, Birmingham and London. Participants also have parent company origins from diverse countries across the world, including Iran and the US. The fact each FCA Cohort has been subject to periodic application deadlines seems to have closed off opportunities for support for regulated firms and unregulated firms. Conversely, that application policy, at least in the pioneering years, may reflect the organised success of the scheme

---

[30] See www.fca.org.uk/firms/innovation/regulatory-sandbox.
[31] Ibid.
[32] See www.fca.org.uk/firms/innovation/regulatory-sandbox-prepare-application.
[33] Sheridan, I (2018) 'FinTech and Global Capital Markets – The Impact of Pro-Enterprise Regulation and English Law', *Capital Markets Law Journal* Volume 13, Issue 4, at 595, 587–599.
[34] See www.fca.org.uk/firms/regulatory-sandbox/regulatory-sandbox-cohort-6; and www.pyctor.com.

and should not be an absolute impediment to progress any initiative not inside the UK Sandbox. In the spirit of critical thinking the FCA has also made considerable efforts to analyse how UK Sandbox can be improved and learn from mistakes.[35] Consequently, from August 2021 the FCA has accepted Sandbox applications on a rolling basis.[36]

7.2.3   DLT initiatives under the UK Sandbox regime

It is notable that the FCA's UK Sandbox has attracted many DLT projects. Indeed, in some past cohorts up to one-third of all cohort firms were testing DLT-based products and services. With this depth of experience, there is a good chance, albeit unquantifiable, that the UK government will be able to implement new financial regulation that attempts to keep pace with the opportunities and risks of DLT.

As just one example, a project that was part of a past UK Sandbox cohort concerned the development of a DLT network to facilitate the issuance of short-term debt. The planned activities fell within the FCA custody rules.[37] The DLT platform issued debt to investors and maintained records of client assets and client money. It allows reconciliation on an intra-day basis.[38] This project performed above the existing standard guidance to FCA rules, because it can potentially allow the issuer to view each investor's holdings and reconcile more frequently than on a daily basis.[39] This example illustrates the gap between human understanding and technology being narrowed by the positive role of a sandbox programme. There is no reason to think this short-term debt project, and other initiatives, cannot be valuably applied in capital markets.

7.3   Alternatives to UK Sandbox

A logical question is what other support is available from the FCA or other influential organisations? There are currently three alternatives

---

[35] FCA (2017) Regulatory Sandbox Lessons Learned, www.fca.org.uk/publication/research-and-data/regulatory-sandbox-lessons-learned-report.pdf.

[36] See www.fca.org.uk/firms/innovation/regulatory-sandbox-prepare-application.

[37] FCA CASS Handbook.

[38] FCA (2017) DP 17/3, Discussion Paper on Distributed Ledger Technology, at 18.

[39] FCA CASS 6.6.39G applied to FCA CASS 6.6.37R(1).

sources of support for innovative projects, two directly with the FCA and a third in the form of a City of London Corporation Digital Sandbox.

7.3.1 FCA Direct Support

The first alternative is the FCA Direct Support service ('Direct Support'). Both authorised firms considering varying existing permissions and unauthorised firms assessing whether to apply for authorisation can apply. Ultimately, the Direct Support service is an opportunity for a FinTech initiative to have the benefit of understanding applicable regulations.[40] In contrast to the UK Sandbox, Direct Support applications can be made at any point in time. However, this service receives a high number of continuous applications. Based on my communications with Direct Support personnel at the FCA on behalf of clients, there are months when no new applications can be considered. However, requests are typically responded to within seven days of receipt to avoid any uncertainty.

Eligibility for Direct Support is based on:

- persuasion that the project is innovative based on evidence that it is 'significantly different';[41]
- a good prospect of identifiable benefit to consumers, either directly or through greater competition;
- sufficient background research in understanding the regulations in the context of the firm's own position; and
- genuine need for support, based on the key factors of lack of in-house compliance support and an initiative that does not easily fit into existing regulations.[42]

The substance of the Direct Support service is divided into four or five phases depending on circumstances. First, a request is made to the Direct Support service. Second, the FCA provides a response. Third, where applicable, assistance is provided by a dedicated Direct Support case officer in preparing an authorisation. This third phase applies equally to regulated firms that need a variation of permission. Fourth, support is

---

[40] See www.fca.org.uk/firms/innovation/direct-support.

[41] Note this test is not a rigid patent law type test involving 'state of the art' proof.

[42] See www.fca.org.uk/firms/project-innovate-innovation-hub/eligibility.

provided by the FCA to a firm applying for authorisation.[43] Fifth, the FCA provides on-going support.

One of the most valuable aspects of the Direct Support service is the second phase, because it includes explanations of relevant financial services regulation based on, where applicable, the Direct Support case officer's internal communication with colleagues throughout the FCA. It is vital to note that any feedback provided by the FCA in the second phase response, including on financial regulation, qualifies as an informal steer. The legal implications of this feedback include the following:

- a restatement of existing FCA rules that a firm must not expressly or by implication communicate in any public statement or to a client that the innovation has the approval of the FCA or any other competent authority;[44]
- if the premises upon which individual guidance was given change, the earlier guidance would no longer be effective; and[45]
- any informal steer does not bind the courts.[46]

That any change to a project nullifies existing informal guidance seems entirely fair in the specific context of many FinTech projects. Risks, technology and target clients may evolve over relatively short periods of time and any reliance on existing informal guidance could result in delays in product launching or breaches in regulation if the FCA decided that was a justifiable enforcement action to take. In essence, the FCA's disclaimer on providing an informal steer is that (a) they are not bound by it; (b) they reserve the right to change their mind; and (c) anyone relies on the statement at their own risk. However, it would be equally fair that the FCA case officer promptly communicates any revisions to a FinTech initiative from whom an earlier informal steer was provided. Yet that is not offered. The greater picture is that a FinTech venture needs independent professional advice.

---

[43] Note that the FCA authorisation application fees vary between £1,500 and £25,000. See www.fca.org .uk/firms/authorisation/fee. Given most FinTech initiatives are employing cutting-edge technologies, it cannot be presumed that the fee will always be at or closer to £1,500. For anything assessed as 'moderately complex' the fee is £5,000.

[44] FCA GEN 1.2.2AR. Available at www.handbook.fca.org.uk/handbook/GEN/1/?view=chapter.

[45] FCA SUP 9.4.2G.

[46] Sections 26–27 FSMA 2000.

The FCA has published additional Direct Support criteria for initiatives from established SME firms it especially wants to support, simultaneously acknowledging that any project must be (a) innovative, and (b) of benefit to consumers. Clearly some of the aims are focused on mitigating the economic consequences of the Covid-19 pandemic. The FCA is especially interested in projects aimed at helping or improving:

- access to credit or funding for consumers or small businesses;
- individuals or companies to access cash, charitable donations, government aid or other financial help;
- distributing funds or other forms of support during periods of isolation;
- the speed or efficiency in assessment and resolution of insurance claims;
- identifying vulnerable customers;
- identifying online frauds.[47]

7.3.2   FCA Advice Unit

The second alternative service offered is an FCA Advice Unit (the 'Advice Unit'). This comprises of two main services, namely (a) regulatory feedback, and (b) the publication of resources provided by the Advice Unit. To qualify for regulatory advice a firm must:

- have an automated proposition, meaning the core element(s) for the customer are automated, where viability may require assessment and fact finding in the target market;
- have a clear proposal, including a completed assessment on how regulations may apply to their business model;
- have a product that has the potential to deliver lower cost advice or lower cost guidance to unserved or under-served consumers;
- have a project that demands regulatory input, because the planned model raises difficult or new questions;[48]
- have a project focused on an FCA listed subsector, namely debt, general insurance, investments, mortgages, pensions (accumulation/

---

[47]   See www.fca.org.uk/firms/innovation/direct-support.

[48]   The Advice Unit is also willing to assist firms that want guidance rather than regulated advice, and is also willing to assist unauthorised firms not seeking authorisation. It is likely the widening of the scope enables unauthorised firms to be guided to seek authorisation.

decumulation) and protection; and[49]

- have a product with a genuine consumer benefit.

Assuming the Advice Unit's eligibility criteria are met the subsequent advice can include:

- an initial meeting with the Advice Unit, and if needed other FCA specialists;
- input from the Financial Ombudsman Service on the factors it may take into account when considering a potential complaint relating to advice given through an automated model;[50]
- if the firm is currently unauthorised, support on how to apply for authorisation;
- on-going engagement and a dedicated point of contact to provide periodic regulatory explanations; and
- specific feedback on the regulatory implications of the model, which among other things, could include guidance and informal steers.[51]

Turning to the publication of resources to assist firms, this refers to finalised FCA guidance (the 'Finalised Guidance') and policy documents. The most valuable of these is, in my view, a chapter in the Finalised Guidance based on case studies drawn from questions and answers of past communication with the Advice Unit.[52] In addition, the Finalised Guidance provides an important reminder that financial regulation applies neutral treatment to technology. In a section entitled 'Design of Client Interface' they advise 'the suitability requirements for [fully automated] streamlined advice are the same as for all other forms of investment advice; in other words, our rules are technology neutral and the mode of distribution or method of communicating with the client do not change the requirement that firms only recommend those services or financial products which are suitable'.[53]

Further, the Finalised Guidance also provides a helpful reminder for firms dedicated to investment advice or portfolio management ser-

---

[49] If a firm's planned automated product is not in a subsector listed by the Advice Unit, in that situation the firm applies to Direct Support as described earlier in this chapter.

[50] See www.financial-ombudsman.org.uk/.

[51] See www.fca.org.uk/firms/innovation/advice-unit.

[52] FCA FG17/8 (2017), Streamlined Advice and Related Consolidated Guidance, especially chapter 5, at 50–56.

[53] Ibid., at 10.

vices. Namely, existing regulations require automated or semi-automated systems to be assessed to the same standards of suitability when compared with making personal recommendations.[54]

7.3.3   Digital Sandbox Pilot

Launched by the FCA and the City of London Corporation in April 2020, the Digital Sandbox Pilot Scheme (the 'Digital Sandbox') is markedly different from the FCA Sandbox. The Digital Sandbox provides earlier stage innovators with digital resources, including cloud computing, synthetic data, a marketplace of over 300 APIs and a collaborative platform.[55] Within this digital ecosystem participants have an opportunity to establish proof of concept. By which is meant they may not yet have proven technical feasibility. In contrast, all FCA Sandbox participants have proof of concept.

The Digital Sandbox scheme allows participants also to promote the early stages of their projects to the FCA and other interested subsector actors. Applicants to the Digital Sandbox had to meet the following four criteria: (a) being genuinely innovative, so not found in the existing market; (b) beneficial to UK financial services consumers; (c) the solution requires a Digital Sandbox to develop or improve it; and (d) having clearly defined development objectives and a plan to bring the project to market.[56]

The first 28 participants can be viewed on the Digital Sandbox website. For ease of reference the diverse projects have been divided into three categories, namely (a) applications focused on anti-fraud or AML; (b) SME lending; and (c) applications that attempt to mitigate some element of consumer vulnerability, such as assessing credit risk or managing debt.[57] In the event that a participant's project is judged successful, this is likely to increase the FCA's confidence in admitting it to the UK Sandbox. Further, the relatively high profile nature of assessment by the FCA in partnership with the City of London Corporation can only increase the chances of raising capital or collaborating with established regulated firms.

---

[54]   Article 54(1) MiFID Org Regulation and COBS 9A.2.23.
[55]   See www.digitalsandboxpilot.co.uk/features.
[56]   See www.digitalsandboxpilot.co.uk/faqs.
[57]   See www.digitalsandboxpilot.co.uk/meet-the-teams.

Perhaps a memorable analogy for the Digital Sandbox is that of a crash dummy used in the automotive sector. No human is involved in evaluating the safety of the motor car being tested. But non-human financial services testing in this context of synthetic data for simulating investor and consumer behaviour allows participants to increase their chances of achieving a credible proof of concept.[58]

Digital Sandbox applications are jointly assessed by the FCA and the City of London Corporation, and an advisory panel comprising all or some of the following actors: the National Economic Crime Centre, UK Finance, City of London Police, Fair4, All Finance, StepChange, Citizens Advice, Innovate Finance, the Confederation of British Industry and ScaleUp Institute. The eclectic nature of the advisory panel reflects a strong societal theme throughout this initiative. Of special note is the involvement of Innovate Finance, a non-profit financial technology organisation that plays an important role by increasing access to capital for its FinTech membership. Current Innovate Finance members include Barclays, HSBC, IBM, Trade Ledger and Transferwise.[59]

Although Digital Sandbox is focused on proof of concept testing with synthetic data, it provides a deceptively agile way for firms to progress FinTech projects. Any firm admitted to the Digital Sandbox programme is simultaneously permitted to use the FCA's Direct Support or Advice Unit services. The programme has proven to be a success and is scheduled to become a permanent benefit to FinTech start-ups and new initiatives by incumbents. Each Digital Sandbox cohort has the valuable opportunity of establishing trust with UK financial services regulators. Further, given sustainability and climate change are likely to be running themes, participants can only attract more investors.[60]

---

[58] The FCA Sandbox is focused on participants that have already achieved proof of concept, so Digital Sandbox is providing an additional entrepreneurial support by allowing participants that are seeking to prove technical feasibility.

[59] See www.innovatefinance.com/about/.

[60] FCA and City of London Corporation (2021) Supporting Innovation in Financial Services: the Digital Sandbox Pilot. This is a detailed joint report covering feedback from participants, lessons learnt and recommendations. Available at www.fca.org.uk/publication/corporate/digital-sandbox-joint-report .pdf.

7.4   Multi-jurisdictional Sandbox options

Globally, the FCA Sandbox programme was a first mover initiative. Many other leading financial services market regulators, including Singapore and the US have followed suit with their own versions. Senior legal counsel and compliance officers should, in my view, be involved early on in commercial strategic discussions about FinTech expansion across borders. For instance, senior managers leading such projects need to factor in (a) evidence of general innovation across an economy, and (b) regulatory intelligence on the FinTech programme level of experience of each home regulator.

Table 7.1 captures the top 10 ranked leading innovative countries out of 131 economies measured by the annual metric-based exercise[61] carried out between Cornell University, INSEAD Business School and the United Nations World Intellectual Property Organization (WIPO). This ranking is called the Global Innovation Index ('GII').[62]

Nine out of the top 10 countries in Table 7.1 have established sandbox programmes. The inference is that FinTech businesses growing in these leading innovative jurisdictions where there are established FinTech pro- grammes are well supported by their relevant home regulators. Germany is the exception out of these top 10 by not offering a formal regulatory sandbox for financial services. However, it cannot be ignored that it remains an innovation powerhouse and has led on plenty of FinTech areas, for example implementing High Frequency Trading laws when the UK and other economies were slow to do so.[63]

---

[61] WIPO (2020) Global Innovation Index 2020.

[62] The GII metrics are complex. Five categories of input data are examined, namely institutions, human capital and research, infrastructure and market sophistication. Two output categories are also included, that of knowledge and technology, and creativity. See GII 2020, at 14.

[63] An important summary of German plans, including legal analysis has been published by the Federal Ministry for Economic Affairs and Energy (2019) entitled Making Space for Innovation – The Handbook for Regulatory Sandboxes. See www.bmwi.de/Redaktion/EN/Publikationen/Digitale -Welt/handbook-regulatory-sandboxes.pdf?__blob=publicationFile&v=2.

Table 7.1   The top 10 innovative countries

Country	Global Innovation Index ranking	Sandbox or equivalent?
Denmark	6th	Yes, est'd 2019
Finland	7th	Yes, est'd 2016
Germany	9th	No, but offer equivalent 'practice laboratories' (Reallabore)
Netherlands	5th	Yes, est'd 2017
Singapore	8th	Yes, est'd 2016
South Korea	10th	Yes, est'd 2019
Sweden	2nd	Yes, est'd 2018
Switzerland	1st	Yes, est'd 2016
UK	4th	Yes, a UK brainchild in 2014
USA	3rd	Yes, Arizona was the first state-level programme est'd in 2018[1]

Note: [1] Lim Byungkwon and Charles Low have provided a detailed summary of both federal and state-level US sandboxes. See Madir, J (ed.) (2021) *FinTech – Law and Regulation* (Edward Elgar), at 14.44–14.55.

7.5   FCA bilateral agreements

Given the cross-border efficiency of FinTech activity, the FCA has also already signed bilateral FinTech cooperation agreements with nine other jurisdictions.[64]

For instance, in February 2018 the FCA signed a FinTech cooperation agreement with the US Commodity Futures Trading Commission (CFTC).[65] The FCA's global plan is to test innovation simultaneously in more than one market in conjunction with the relevant regulators from

---

[64] Singapore signed a FinTech cooperation agreement with the UK in 2016. Available at www.mas .gov.sg/news-and-publications/media -releases/2016/First ever FinTech bridge established between Britain and Singapore.

[65] USCFTC and FCA (2018) Cooperation and the Exchange of Information on Financial Technology Innovation, 19 February 2018. Available at www.fca.org.uk/publication/mou/FCA-cftc-co-operation -agreement.pdf.

each jurisdiction. This will not be without regulatory challenges. For instance, US FinTech growth is held back by a number of conservative legislators at both federal and state levels.[66]

7.6 Global financial innovation network

In early 2018, the FCA first presented the concept of a global sandbox. By the end of that year, in collaboration with 11 other national regulators, the FCA proposed forming a Global Financial Innovation Network (GFIN).[67] The logic is to build on existing collaborative relationships. For example, if a UK firm wanted to set up a FinTech business targeting Middle East markets, its project could be trialled by the FCA in conjunction with the Dubai Financial Services Authority (DFSA) the UAE regulator and other relevant national regulators in that region.

In 2019 GFIN was formed and its terms of reference agreed. The primary functions of GFIN are to:

- facilitate regulators cooperating and sharing business, innovation and technology information from their markets, and to provide accessible regulatory contact information for firms;
- provide a forum for collaboration and information sharing on regulatory technology ('RegTech'), including the sharing of lessons learned; and
- provide firms with an environment to conduct cross-border trials.[68]

The notable benefit for GFIN member regulators is a multilateral approach to advancing FinTech flowing from the pooling of knowledge as well as widened communication channels between regulators and other stakeholders. For any FinTech firm the potentially pivotal advantage is testing innovative projects across borders. The majority of FinTech projects are international by design, whether for B2B or B2C markets, even if they are initially scaled to one jurisdiction. The GFIN presents 'the possibility of conducting trials in multiple jurisdictions simultaneously for those firms

---

[66] Madir, J (ed.) (2021) *FinTech – Law and Regulation* (Edward Elgar), at 14.44–14.55.
[67] GFIN (2018) Consultation Document.
[68] GFIN (2019) Terms of Reference for Membership and Governance of the Global Financial Innovation Network, at 2.

in a position to do so, or the detailed sharing of the outputs of local tests with the other regulators in the network'.[69]

Consistent with the second principle of its terms of reference, GFIN has invested efforts into lessons learned from collaboration. For example, in 2020 it published a paper entitled 'Cross-Border Testing: Lessons Learned – GFIN Reflects on the Cross-Border Testing Pilot'. In this paper it was raised that in 2019 there was no regulatory compendium that firms could examine to efficiently check how each member regulator governs FinTech firms and what support is offered.[70] Consequently, a regulatory compendium is now available on the GFIN website.[71]

The range of financial services regulators committed to the GFIN cross-border testing work is impressive, and includes regulators in Africa, Asia, Australia, other European countries, the Middle East, and North America. The 2019 GFIN pilot revealed that on average, applicants were filing four to six applications to different regulators. In many cases this resulted in duplication of work setting out their business model and planned FinTech innovation. However, GFIN currently provides an efficient single application form where applicants can select all the participating cross-border testing regulators to whom they wish to apply, negating the inefficiency of communicating the same application to each regulator. It has been confirmed by GFIN that there is no maximum number of participating regulators which an applicant can apply to, although detailed justification for each choice is required.

An on-going commercial challenge for regulated firms will be how to maximise the benefits of cross-border testing from a coordinated speed to all targeted markets viewpoint. By which is meant there might be a viable service to offer that is approved in one market but not in others. For example, it is memorable that when the original GFIN concept was agreed between 12 national regulators, the Australian Securities and Investment Commission (ASIC) attached an appendix to underline the very different way that FinTech firms are treated in the federal jurisdiction.[72] In short,

---

[69] Ibid., at 7.

[70] GFIN (2020) Cross-Border Testing: Lessons Learned – The Global Financial Innovation Network Reflects on the Cross-Border Testing Pilot.

[71] See www.thegfin.com/compendium.

[72] GFIN (2018) Consultation Document, at Appendix II.

ASIC introduced FinTech products and services regulation that allowed unauthorised (unlicensed) firms to provide advice and deal in a specified list of products for up to 12 months.

This original ASIC guidance was withdrawn in 2020 and replaced by an enhanced regulatory sandbox (ERS) that extends the unlicensed period to up to 24 months along with an expanded list of exempted products.[73] ASIC's ERS is the opposite of the UK approach. The FCA first tests FinTech initiatives with a limited number of consumers. In contrast, ASIC is allowing unauthorised firms to experiment across a market with an aggregate client exposure of AU$5,000,000.[74] For a firm that wants to develop products and services in both these forward looking jurisdictions, there are obvious challenges to cross-border testing. There are advantages and disadvantages to both jurisdictional approaches, but FinTech initiatives may be forced to compromise into conducting sequential tests. For example, in the scenario of a FinTech planning to operate in Australia and the UK, a decision could be rationally made to focus first on the ASIC ERS or the FCA's UK Sandbox, followed by the other programme.

The FCA's support of global innovation has made GFIN a rapid, evolving success. Currently, GFIN has over 60 members, and this number will only increase, because the 2020 Covid-19 pandemic acted as a catalyst for advancing regulatory sandbox initiatives. This conclusion is based on evidence from a sample of 75 regulators asked to provide answers as part of a statistical survey. The sandbox initiatives included providing both more 'real-time' support and fast-track policies. Impressively, planned FinTech initiatives were accelerated by 36 per cent.[75] Inevitably, there will always be some cultural and political barriers for some regulators to participate efficiently as part of GFIN, but when national self-interests are to maximise borderless digital FinTech offerings, that logically involves cross-border cooperation.

---

[73] See https://asic.gov.au/for-business/innovation-hub/enhanced-regulatory-sandbox/.

[74] See https://download.asic.gov.au/media/5763135/comparison-asic-sandbox-enhanced-regulatory-sandbox-published-25-augus.

[75] Cambridge Centre for Alternative Finance (2020). See www.jbs.cam.ac.uk/faculty-research/centres/alternative-finance/publications/2020-global-covid-19-fintech-regulatory-rapid-assessment-study/.

7.7   Final points

In less than five years the UK Government has pioneered and expanded the FCA Sandbox programme to be the busiest in the world. In the Kalifa Report of early 2021 there are many important proposals that will further enhance the UK's leading position. From a regulatory viewpoint, the most notable recommendations are:

- for the UK Sandbox to be available on a rolling basis;[76]
- offering support not only for original first mover initiatives, but also other innovative projects that may be similar to first mover innovations;
- creating a dedicated space in the regulatory sandbox for specific priority FinTech areas, with specialist support where necessary; and
- a regulatory scalebox initiative which aims to support FinTech firms at the growth phase, so that there is greater efficiency in the process of continuous growth after the start-up period.[77]

Within less than three months of the Kalifa Review's publication, the UK Government announced its commitment to implement the noted recommendations.[78] In my view, the Kalifa Review hits the target three out of four times on these points. A revised UK Sandbox programme on a rolling basis, supporting a wider range of innovative companies and scalebox are all sensible policy and regulatory changes. The third point on priority FinTech areas refers to areas identified by the UK Government as deserving special focus. The Kalifa Review concludes that two priority FinTech areas are digital identity and data standards. This conclusion is based on the premise that private companies are not well placed to develop public infrastructure standards. In my view, that is a moot point, given the pioneering application of private finance initiative (PFI) in the UK achieved not only many outstanding successes, but also numerous failings. Nevertheless, there is certainly value in a range of governmental actors, such as the Department for Business,

---

[76] As mentioned earlier in this chapter this recommendation was implemented from 2021, so applications can now be made on a rolling basis.

[77] City of London and Innovate Finance (2021) Kalifa Review of UK Fintech, at 36. https://assets .publishing.service.gov.uk/government/uploads/system/uploads/attachment_data/file/965032/Kalifa _Fintech_Review_Final_Report.pdf.

[78] *The FinTech Times* (2021) Rishi Sunak Announces New Plans to Boost Fintech at UK Fintech Week, 19 April 2021.

Energy and Industrial Strategy, HM Treasury, ICO and others, providing evidence-based reports on what areas of FinTech are contributing to digital public infrastructure.[79]

---

79 City of London and Innovate Finance, (2021) Kalifa Review of UK Fintech, at 24.

8. Trading platforms

This chapter focuses on current financial regulation that attempts to keep pace with technology-driven trading platforms across diverse asset classes. This includes commodities, relatively new-fangled cryptoassets, equities, fixed income and foreign exchange, as well as derivatives products referenced to all of these asset classes. The term trading platform is used interchangeably with 'electronic market', 'multilateral trading system'[1] and 'trading venue'.

The multi-faceted nature of trading platforms means that many of the subjects addressed in other chapters of this book contain valuable insights for legal and compliance functions. These include preparing financial regulation advice, drafting contract clauses, M&A due diligence, dispute resolution, and contributing to policies and standard operating procedures.[2]

8.1 Introduction

The journey of capital markets trading reminds us all how brilliant human ingenuity can be. Evolving from coffee house to open outcry to voice trading, and now platform-based forums. Since the beginning of this century the processes have become exponentially more complex and yet more efficient and flexible. There are now thousands of trading possibilities compounded by a frequency of trading with a meaningful volume of data to aid decision making. The dawn of this fourth Industrial Revolution can be traced to the start of this century.[3]

---

[1] Article 4(19) MiFID II, EU 2014/65, multilateral system 'means any system or facility in which multiple third-party buying and selling trading interests in financial instruments are able to interact in the system'. See www.legislation.gov.uk/eudr/2014/65/article/4.

[2] Note especially Chapter 10 Competition, Chapter 5 Cyber security and Chapter 6 Data protection.

[3] The term fourth industrial revolution has its inspiration from the German government's 'Industrie 4.0' originating in 2011.

When analysing financial services regulation in the context of trading platforms, there are numerous risks for regulated firms contracting with any platform. Further, the regulatory drivers and in turn the detailed legislation and rules illuminate that trading platforms are assessed as significant risks at the systemic level and to the integrity of the financial system. The consistent explicit and implied regulator motivations when addressing the evolving dynamism of trading platforms are fairness and systemic risk management. This is evident from both Bank of England and FCA cooperation with the London-based Systemic Risk Centre (SRC).[4]

Before addressing the regulatory detail, it is worthwhile making brief reference to what a stock exchange is in the 21st century given they are numerous and play an important role in country, regional and global economic stability. Many European cities and several US cities have operated a public stock exchange for between two and four centuries, Amsterdam acting as first mover in 1602. While these primary trading venues remain important symbols of nearly all nation states, their continuing contribution to technological progress cannot be overlooked. Each stock exchange is the source of reliable information on asset prices, especially equities and fixed income. In this sense, the data on stock exchanges is of increasing importance to their revenues, and to the functioning of many other secondary trading platforms.

The World Federation of Exchanges (WFE), the global industry group for exchanges and central counter-parties, issued a statement in early 2019 capturing the contemporary essence of a stock exchange as (a) a producer

---

[4] The London School of Economics and Political Science (LSE) formed the SRC in 2013 to examine the threat of 'systemic failure in the financial system spilling over into the real economy'. Founding partners of the SRC include the Bank of England, FCA and the European Central Bank. IHS Markit is also a partner. SRC publish many papers on specific financial subsector risks. For example, risk surrounding HFT. Several of their key personnel, for example Jean-Pierre Zigrand, have been very influential experts at the Bank of England and across UK government. See www.systemicrisk.ac.uk/about-centre -src.

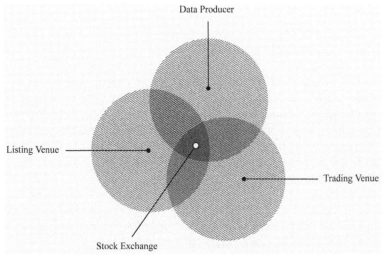

Source: © Iain Sheridan (2021).

Figure 8.1   *The 21st century stock exchange*

of data, (b) a listing venue and (c) a trading venue (see Figure 8.1).[5] In the WFE's analysis, stock exchanges are:

- creating information (data products) in the form of prices of traded shares, which but for their roles would not exist;
- creating data products as an integral part of the process of bringing together buyers and seller;
- ensuring the integrity of data products by carrying out a number of crucial functions, including market surveillance and robust information technology infrastructure;
- creating quality data products that have an economic value licensed for a fee; and
- providing free data products on delayed time basis, typically to con-

---

[5]   Arguably the key attributes of data in the context of a stock exchange is that it is reliable, trusted, and provides the constituents of indices that form many derivatives products. A listing venue's key attributes are to set down pre-condition criteria, consistent due diligence levels and on-going trading regulations. Trading venues must be technically reliable and trusted.

sumers who are willing to wait a short time for it.[6]

8.2   Financial regulation

Turning to the regulatory detail, there are three main types of trading platform relevant to a regulated firm.[7] If a regulated firm seeks to trade equities, fixed income or any other asset in the UK or the EEA,[8] the opportunities for doing so on an unregulated market are far narrower. The reason is that the EU regulatory stance, and by extension transposed in the UK, requires trading activity to take place on one of three regulated platform venues.[9]

First, a regulated market (RM) is a stock exchange as captured earlier in Figure 8.1, with primary market functions and secondary trading functions.[10] RM refers to a multilateral system that is:

- managed or operated by a market operator that facilitates the bringing together of multiple third-party buying and selling interests in financial instruments;

---

[6]   WFE (2019) WFE Statement Clarifying the Nature of Stock Market Data. See www.world-exchanges .org/our-work/articles/wfe-statement-clarifying-nature-stock-market-data. This statement was subsequently reproduced in WFE (2019) WFE Position Paper on Importance of Valuing Stock Market Data Correctly.

[7]   The regulation of trading platforms is also subject to competition regulation. Chapter 10 Competition includes reference the strong likelihood of trading platform mergers coming under the scrutiny of the regulators.

[8]   There are currently minimal differences in the treatment of regulated platforms in the UK compared with the EEA, because the UK implemented the EU regulations governing the three types of trading, namely RMs, MTFs and OTFs, all covered in this chapter.

[9]   The main exception to this regulatory perimeter based on venues is the functioning of considerable private OTC trading, and semi-private Systematic internaliser (SI). As a brief explanation, under the Article 4(20) MiFID 2014/65 definition an SI is an investment firm that substantially and systematically 'deals on own account when executing client orders outside a RM, an MTF or an OTF without operating a multilateral system'. Substantiality is calculated applying one of two OTC trading volume tests. An SI is semi-private for several reasons. For example, because of the transparency rule under Article 14(1) MiFIR 2014/600, which requires SIs to publish quotes on a range of instruments, including depository receipts, equities and ETFs 'for which there is a liquid market'. Further, under Article 18(1) MiFIR 2014/600, SIs are also required to publish their quotes for bonds, derivatives, emission allowances and structured products.

[10] Based on ESMA statistics for the trading year 2019, the European market contained 135 RMs. Source: ESMA (2020) EU Securities Markets ESMA Annual Statistical Report, at 5.

- based on a trading system operating by its own non-discretionary rules that effect a contract over the financial instruments admitted to trading under its rules and/or systems;
- authorised and functions regularly and in accordance with applicable regulation.[11]

The organisational requirements of RMs are well established, including the requirement from 2007 to have 'sound management of the technical operations of the system, including the establishment of effective contingency arrangements to cope with the risks of systems disruptions'.[12] However, the importance of technology in capital markets has subsequently dramatically increased and the organisational requirements currently also include:

- being adequately equipment to manage the risks exposures, to implement appropriate arrangements and systems to identify all significant risks to its operation;
- having effective measures to mitigate risk exposures; and
- having effective arrangements to facilitate the efficient and timely finalisation of the transactions executed under its systems.[13]

8.3 Systems resilience, circuit breakers and electronic trading

For RMs, the technology-based regulations represent, on first reading, a formidable legal burden to audit; check for implementation and ensure all relevant aspects are recorded in a written agreement. These include:

- to have in place a written agreement with all participating firms;
- to have in place effective arrangements, procedures and systems, including requiring members or participants to carry out appropriate testing of algorithms and providing environments to avoid disorderly trading conditions;
- to have in place effective systems, procedures and arrangements to reject orders that exceed pre-determined volume and price thresholds

---

[11] Article 4(21) MiFID II EU 2014/65. To clarify, 'functions regularly and in accordance with applicable regulation' refers to the requirements under Articles 44–56 EU 2014/65.

[12] Article 39(c) MiFID I EU 2004/39, repealed by MiFID II EU 2014/65 on 15 May 2014.

[13] Article 47(1) MIFID II EU 2014/65.

or are clearly erroneous;

- when ordered by a regulator to be able temporarily to halt or constrain trading if there is a significant price movement in a financial instrument;
- when ordered by a regulator to ensure that the parameters for halting trading are appropriately calibrated in a way which takes into account the liquidity of different asset classes and sub-classes;
- to have in place the necessary systems and procedures in place to ensure that it will notify competent authorities in order for them to coordinate a market-wide response;
- to have in place systems to limit the ratio of unexecuted orders to transactions that may be entered into the system by a member or participant;
- to be able to slow down the flow of orders if there is a risk of its system capacity being reached;
- to limit and enforce the minimum tick size that may be executed on the market;
- to have in place effective systems procedures and arrangements to ensure that members or participants are only permitted to provide direct electronic access services;
- to have set appropriate standards regarding risk controls and thresholds on trading via direct electronic access;
- to have arrangements in place to suspend or terminate the provision of direct electronic access by a member or participant to a client in the case of non-compliance; and
- to be able to identify, by means of flagging from members or participants, orders generated by algorithmic trading, the different algorithms used for the creation of orders and the relevant persons initiating those orders.[14]

All the above requirements are a challenge for legal and compliance functions supporting the trading venue to verify implementation and annually re-check. Yet they cover the minimum expectations. The second bullet point requiring venue members to carry out appropriate testing of algorithms and to ensure that algorithmic trading systems cannot create or contribute to disorderly trading conditions is executed with a short

---

[14]   Article 48 MiFID II EU 2014/65.

form for the prospective venue member to fill out, sign and return.[15] For legal counsel and compliance officers acting for venue members, the mandatory written agreement needs to reflect the above obligations.

Further, three commercial scenarios to these regulations provide the venue provider with discretion to charge higher fees, namely (a) for a placed order that is subsequently cancelled; (b) when there is a high ratio of cancelled orders to executed orders; and (c) for high frequency algorithmic trading technique.[16] Legal counsel for both sides need to confirm that any higher fee charges are agreed and recorded in the written agreement.

8.4   Multilateral trading facility

The second longest established type of trading platform,[17] the Multilateral Trading Facility (MTF),[18] refers to 'a multilateral system, operated by an investment firm or a market operator, which brings together multiple third-party buying and selling interests in financial instruments'.[19] Two key aspects are that MTFs, similar to RMs, are subject to non-discretionary rules and that the contract between the platform provider and the buyer or seller must comply with a broad range of rules that include organisational and algorithmic trading requirements.[20] An active market example is Turquoise MTF,[21] which trades, among other things, 4,500 equities with access to 19 markets.[22]

---

[15]   An example of an algorithm testing form can be downloaded to view at https://regulatory.tpicap.com/ icap/uk/tpicapukmtf, under the file name Algorithm Policy.

[16]   The logic of discretion to charge a higher fee for HFT is that this activity places a greater burden on system capacity.

[17]   Based on ESMA statistics for the trading year 2019, the European market contained 223 MTFs. Source: ESMA (2020) EU Securities Markets ESMA Annual Statistical Report, at 5.

[18]   The MTFs were introduced under MiFID I in 2007. The aim was to stimulate greater competition in trading so that trading choices were no longer revolving around primary RMs.

[19]   Article 4(22) MiFID II EU 2014/65.

[20]   Title II MiFID II EU 2014/65. These rules also apply to OTFs.

[21]   In fact as part of its strategic decision making Turquoise operates two MTFs, one regulated by the FCA and one regulated by Autoriteit Financiële Markten (AFM) and De Nederlandsche Bank (DNB). See www.lseg.com/markets-products-and-services/our-markets/turquoise/turquoise-trading-services.

[22]   See www.lseg.com/areas-expertise/our-markets/turquoise.

Investment firms and market operators operating an MTF must:

- in addition to meeting the requirements laid down in Articles 16 and 18 of MiFID II, establish and implement non-discretionary rules for the execution of orders in the system;[23]
- ensure that the rules referred to in Article 18(3) MiFID II, governing access to an MTF, comply with the conditions established in Article 53(3) MiFID II, governing competence, organisational arrangements, reputation and sufficient resources;[24]
- manage the risks to which it is exposed, to implement appropriate arrangements and systems to identify all significant risks to its operation, and to put in place effective measures to mitigate those risks;
- have effective arrangements to facilitate the efficient and timely finalisation of the transactions executed under its systems; and
- have available, at the time of authorisation and on an on-going basis, sufficient financial resources to facilitate its orderly functioning.[25]

8.5   Organised trading facility

The third venue, the Organised Trading Facility (OTF) was introduced in 2018, and refers to 'a multilateral system which is not a regulated market or an MTF and in which [there are] multiple third-party buying and selling [of] interests in bonds, structured finance products, emission allowances or derivatives'.[26] An active market example is TP ICAP OTF, which trades bond, credit, equity and foreign exchange (FX) derivatives.[27] In terms of the actual instruments traded, an authoritative report shows that across the EEA in 2019, so at that time the EEA included the UK, 148,000 bonds were available for trading on MTFs, and only 22,000 bonds were offered on OTFs.[28] Clearly, this just under 7:1 ratio may change over time.

---

[23] Article 19(1) MiFID II EU 2014/65.

[24] Article 53 MiFID II EU 2014/65.

[25] Article 19 MiFID II, EU 2014/65.

[26] Article 4(23) MiFID II 2014/65.

[27] See https://tpicap.com/tpicap/regulatory-hub/icap-securities-otf. For the benefit of US readers, an OTF is similar to a swap execution facility (SEF). Both an OTF and an SEF provide trading services for derivatives.

[28] ESMA (2020) EU Securities Markets ESMA Annual Statistical Report, at 11.

8.6 Comparing MTFs with OTFs

For readers new to MTFs or OTFs or both, their differentiation is not a logical thought process quickly understood by reference to the regulation alone. In my view, the differences are memorably clarified based on understanding (a) the policy reasoning behind the introduction of OTFs; (b) decision making on seeking to establish an OTF must be explained to the relevant regulator; and (c) understanding what an OTF can do compared with an MTF.

First, the EU policy objectives driving the introduction of OTFs in 2018 are fairness and transparency. These policy aims have their roots in the market activities before, during and after the Global Financial Crisis, when massive volumes of over-the-counter (OTC) trading went largely unreported. Non-equity trading played a role in the Global Financial Crisis, so there was a need also to address this previous omission. To maximise the amount of trading occurring on venues not already caught by MTFs, the OTF seeks to fill the regulatory gap in an era of greatly increased reliance on technology.

Of special concern to the EU was so-called broker crossing networks.[29] They concluded that 'any trading system in financial instruments, such as entities currently known as broker crossing networks, should in the future be properly regulated and be authorised under one of the types of multilateral trading venues or as a systematic internaliser'.[30] Table 8.1 indicates the concept of 'lit' trading venues, by which is meant venues that are 'lit' (light venues) require pre-trade transparency on orders and pricing. In contrast, dark venues do not. Consequently, with 72 OTFs established across the EU in 2019, the volume of broker crossing networks has already started to reduce.[31]

---

[29] Broker crossing network (BCN) can be defined as 'a subset of an investment bank operator's electronic platform where third-party orders can be matched anonymously using reference prices taken from selected lit markets'. In essence, an in-house broker matches buyers and sellers of stock directly in this pool without any external trading venue involvement. Access to the pool is determined by the broker who has discretion as to who can interact with the pool and who cannot. Source: FCA (2016) UK Equity Market Dark Pools – Role, Promotion and Oversight in Wholesale Markets, at 48–50.

[30] EU MiFIR 2014/600, at Recital 6.

[31] ESMA (2020) EU Securities Markets ESMA Annual Statistical Report, at 5.

Table 8.1 *Light and dark venues*

Market type	EU total	Lit	Discretionary trading	Matched principal trading[1]	Equity trading	Derivatives	Bonds
Regulated Market	135	Yes	No	No	Yes	Yes	Yes
MTF	223	Yes	No	No	Yes	Yes	Yes
OTF	72	Yes	Yes	Yes[2]	No	Yes	Yes
Systematic Internaliser (SI)	216	Yes	Yes	Yes	Yes	Yes	Yes
Broker crossing networks	Not known	No	Yes	Yes	Yes	Yes	Yes

Notes: [1] Under Article 4(1)(38) MiFID II 2014/65 'matched principal trading' means 'a transaction where the facilitator interposes itself between the buyer and the seller to the transaction in such a way that it is never exposed to market risk throughout the execution of the transaction, with both sides executed simultaneously, and where the transaction is concluded at a price where the facilitator makes no profit or loss, other than a previously disclosed commission, fee or charge for the transaction'. [2] Article 20(2) MiFID II 2014/65. The OTF is permitted to do matched principal trading subject to derivatives subject to mandatory clearing obligations. However, this permission does not extend to derivatives subject to mandatory clearing obligations.

Second, as captured in Table 8.1, there are distinct characteristics of an OTF compared with an MTF.[32] The power of an OTF to implement discretionary trading rules is significant given the same power does not exist for RMs and MTFs. The discretion means that an OTF provider can negotiate with its participants, decide whether to place or retract an order, and choose which orders to match in its system.

Other specific requirements for OTFs are that they are not permitted to trade equities, but are explicitly permitted to deal in OTFs focused on bonds and derivatives. Further, the same legal entity cannot operate both an OTF and an Systematic Internaliser (SI).[33]

The third element is to appreciate that an OTF is not an optional decision from the choices of RM and MTF, but occurs by default. There is a requirement that the applicant firm provides a detailed explanation setting out its reasoning why the planned trading platform cannot operate as an MTF or RM. This explanation is not only made when applying for authorisation from the FCA or PRA; but also if requested by the relevant regulator it has to be made at any point once authorised.[34] By way of example, if a trading venue wanted to deal on its own account for sovereign debt for which there is no liquid market, this is a specific activity that can only be carried out on an OTF.[35]

8.7   Detailed requirements for RMs, MTFs and OTFs

The immensely detailed requirements imposed on investment firms carrying out algorithmic trading is contained in the RTS 6, also called delegated regulation.[36] This vital RTS deals with five discrete topics, namely: (a) general organisational requirements focused mainly on the compliance function; (b) testing; (c) Direct Electronic Access; (d) regulated

---

[32]   Article 19 MiFID II EU 2014/65, deals with MTFs, and Article 20 MiFID II 2015/65 with OTFs.

[33]   Article 20(4) MiFID II EU 2014/65.

[34]   Article 20(7), (2) MiFID II EU 2014/65. In fact Article 20(7) also requires a detailed explanation on why the system cannot operate as an SI, where own account dealing takes place involving trading against proprietary capital.

[35]   Article 20(3) MiFID II EU 2014/65. Note that no other type of own account trading is permitted on an OTF.

[36]   Delegated Regulation EU 2017/589.

firms as general clearing members; and (e) High Frequency Algorithmic Trading (HFT).

Specific RM technology requirements are covered by this delegated legislation that also applies to MTFs and OTFs. The following summary of the relevant 28 Articles of RTS 6 has proven to be a useful aide memoire when setting out to review trading platform terms and conditions and rule books, whether RTS, MTF or OTF.

8.8   Contractual risks specific to MTFs and OTFs

When MiFID II came into force in 2018, my advice to investment banks included how to manage proposed penalty clauses in both the standard agreements and in the trading platform rules of several leading providers. From one angle, running any trading platform is a tremendous responsibility when each can form a significant market for equities, fixed income and structured products. Therefore, there is potential logic in the deterrent effect of some financial punitive measures. However, penalty clauses do need careful assessment, because under English law they are generally unenforceable.[37]

The established four tests to determine if something is likely to be assessed as a penalty clause are:

- weigh up if the stipulated sum is an unconscionable amount in comparison with the greatest likely loss to occur that can be proved to follow from the breach;
- presume the clause to be punitive if the breach of it only concerns the non-payment of money and the consequence of such a breach is the provision of a larger sum;
- presume the clause is punitive if it was payable in numerous scenarios of varying seriousness; and
- treat the clause as non-punitive if your reasoning is based solely on the

---

[37] For a recent interesting technology case that mentioned the issue of penalty clauses, see *Triple Point Technology, Inc v PTT Public Company Ltd* [2019] EWCA Civ 230 (5 March 2019). In this judgment the word 'penalty' within a software development contract focused on commodities trading applications was assessed not to amount to a penalty clause, but was a lawful provision for liquidated damages.

Table 8.2   *Algorithmic trading rules summary*

Article	Subject matter	Requirement(s)
1	General organisational	Establish and monitor trading systems and trading algorithms proportionate to complexity, nature and scale.
2	Role of compliance	Have at least a general understanding of how the algorithmic trading systems and its algorithms function.
		Continuous contact with persons within the firm who have detailed technical knowledge of the firm's algorithmic trading systems and algorithms.
		Continuous contact with the regulated firm's person(s) who have access to the 'kill functionality'.
3	Staffing	Sufficient staff with the necessary technical knowledge and skills to (a) manage relevant algorithms and trading systems; (b) test and monitor the algorithms and trading systems; (c) understand the trading strategies deployed via the algorithms and trading systems; and (d) manage the regulated firm's legal obligations.
		Ensure staff's skills remain up-to-date through continuous training and regularly evaluate their skills, especially about market abuse and submission systems.
		Ensure assigned compliance and risk staff has (a) sufficient knowledge of algorithmic trading and strategies; (b) sufficient skills to follow up on information provided by automatic alerts; (c) sufficient authority to challenge staff responsible for algorithmic trading where such trading creates disorderly trading conditions or suspicions of market abuse.
4	IT outsourcing and procurement	Regulated firms remain responsible for procured hardware and software.
		Regulated firms shall have sufficient knowledge and documentation to ensure effective compliance concerning procured hardware and software used in algorithmic trading.

Article	Subject matter	Requirement(s)
5	Testing and deployment of trading algorithms, strategies and systems	Before deployment or a substantial update of a trading algorithm or algorithmic trading strategy, the regulate firm must establish methodologies to develop and test (a) algorithms; (b) strategies; and (c) systems. The algorithmic strategy and systems methodologies shall ensure they: (a) behave as intended; (b) comply with the all the rules of this RTS; (c) comply with the rules of the trading venues accessed; (d) do not contribute to disorderly trading conditions; (e) continue to work in stressed market conditions; and (f) possess a kill switch.
6	Conformance testing	Need to perform conformance testing for both trading venue and direct market access. This includes the first time access is attempted and also when there are material changes to either the trading venue, direct market access or the regulated firm's algorithms, strategies or systems. Two basic elements to verify are (a) interaction with trading venues matching logic, and (b) quality of data flow processing from the trading venue.
7	Testing environments	The testing environment must be separated from the environment in which the regulated firm operates, comprising of all analysis systems, databases, data capture, hardware, market data, order routing to trading venues, post-trade processing systems, risk control systems and software.
8	Controlled deployment of algorithms	Before deploying a trading algorithm the regulated firm must set limits on (a) number of instruments traded, (b) price, value plus number of order, (c) strategy positions, and (d) number of trading venues to which orders are sent.

Article	Subject matter	Requirement(s)
9	Annual self-assessment and validation	Regulated firm must assess and confirm compliance with the fundamental rules on algorithmic trading.[1]
		The self-assessment as a minimum must cover an analysis of Annex I criteria to the regulations.[2]
		A validation report is to be completed by the risk function.[3]
		If the regulated firm's has an internal audit function, it must audit the validation report.[4]
		Senior management must approve the validation report.[5]
10	Stress testing	First test based on running the highest number of messages received and sent by the regulated firm in last six months multiplied by two.
		Second test based on running the highest volume of trading reached by the regulated firm in past six months multiplied by two.[6]
11	Management of material changes	Any planned material change to algorithmic trading must be reviewed by a designated senior manager.
		Procedures must include the communication of planned changes to compliance and risk functions.[7]
12	Kill functionality	In an emergency, to be able to immediately cancel unexecuted orders submitted to trading venues ('kill functionality');
		The ability to identify which trading algorithm and which trader, trading desk or, where applicable, which client is responsible for each order that has been sent to a trading venue.[8]

Article	Subject matter	Requirement(s)
13	Automated Surveillance System (ASS) to detect market manipulation	Regulated firm must monitor all trading activity that takes place through its trading systems, including that of its clients, for signs of potential market manipulation as defined in the relevant market abuse regulation.[9]
		The ASS shall be adaptable to changes to the regulatory obligations and the trading activity of the regulated firm.
		Review the automated surveillance system at least once a year.
		Using a sufficiently detailed level of time granularity, the ASS shall be able to read, replay and analyse order and transaction data on an *ex post* basis, and where relevant able have capacity to operate in an automated low-latency trading environment.
		Staff responsible for monitoring all the ASS aspects shall report to the compliance function any trading activity that may not be compliant with the regulated firm's policies and procedures or with its regulatory obligations.[10]
14	Business continuity arrangements	Appropriate to the complexity, nature and scale of the business.
		To be reviewed annually.[11]
15	Pre-trade controls on order	Price collars, which automatically block or cancel orders that do not meet set price parameters.
		Maximum order values, which prevent orders with an uncommonly large order value from entering the order book.
		Maximum order volumes, which prevent orders with an uncommonly large order size from entering the order book.
		Maximum messages limits, which prevent sending an excessive number of messages to order books pertaining to the submission, modification or cancellation of an order.[12]

Article	Subject matter	Requirement(s)
16	Real-time monitoring	To be undertaken by the trader in charge of the trading algorithm or algorithmic trading strategy, and by the risk management function or by an independent risk control function established for the purpose of this provision. That risk control function must be able to challenge the trader as appropriate and necessary within the organisational governance framework (see entry 1 in this table).[13]
		Real-time alerts shall be generated within five seconds after the relevant event.[14]
17	Post-trade controls	Regulated firm must continuously operate the post-trade controls.
		Where a post-trade control is triggered, appropriate action may include adjusting or shutting down the relevant trading algorithm or trading system or an orderly withdrawal from the market.
		Post-trade controls shall include the continuous assessment and monitoring of market and credit risk of the regulated firm in terms of effective exposure.
		For derivatives, the post-trade controls shall include controlling the maximum long and short and overall strategy positions, with trading limits to be set in units that are appropriate to the types of financial instruments involved.
		Post-trade monitoring shall be undertaken by the traders responsible for the algorithm and the risk control function.[15]

Article	Subject matter	Requirement(s)
18	Security and limits to access	Implement an IT strategy with defined objectives and measures which is in compliance with the regulated firm's risk strategy.
		The IT strategy must comply with an effective IT security management, including authenticity, confidentiality and integrity.
		Promptly inform the competent authority of any material breaches of its physical and electronic security measures.
		Provide an incident report to the competent authority.
		Annually undertake penetration tests and vulnerability scans to simulate cyber attacks.[16]
19–23	Direct Electronic Access (DEA)	DEA provider[17] shall establish policies and procedures to ensure that trading by its clients via DEA complies with the trading venue's rules so as to ensure the DEA provider meets its own regulatory requirements.[18]
		Effective controls, monitoring and systems in place to ensure client suitability, limits and credit thresholds are set, and activity is monitored.
		Responsible for ensuring clients comply with regulation and the rules of the trading venue.
		Binding written contract covering DEA rights and obligations in place between the trading venue member and each client.[19]
		Notify the regulator to confirm fact are providing DEA and specify the trading venue(s).[20]
		DEA provider is responsible for the effectiveness of pre-trade and post-trade controls, whether these are set by or offered by the trading venue.
		Real-time on-going monitoring required of all client trade controls.[21]
		DEA provider must have control to automatically block or cancel orders from individuals[22] who operate trading systems that submit orders related to algorithmic trading and which lack authorisation to send orders via DEA.[23]

Article	Subject matter	Requirement(s)
		Automatically block or cancel orders from a DEA client which that client is unauthorised to trade.
		Automatically block or cancel orders from a DEA client that breach the risk management thresholds of the DEA provider.
		Stop order flows transmitted by its DEA clients.
		Suspend or withdraw DEA if not satisfied that continued access would be consistent with its rules and procedures for fair and orderly trading and market integrity.
		Whenever necessary, review the internal risk control systems of DEA clients.[24]
		If permitting a DEA client to provide its DEA access to its own clients ('sub-delegation'), then must be able to differentiate DEA client orders from the sub-delegatee.[25]
		DEA provider shall conduct a due diligence assessment of its prospective DEA clients.[26]
		DEA to annually review its due diligence assessment.[27]
24–27	Regulated firms acting as general clearing members	System must be subject to appropriate due diligence assessments, controls and monitoring.[28]
		Need initial due diligence assessment of a prospective clearing client, taking into account the complexity, nature, and scale of its business.[29]
		Annually conduct due diligence review on clearing client.[30]
		Set out and communicate to its clearing clients appropriate trading and position limits.[31]
		Clearing service terms must not only be published, but also made with reasonably commercial terms.[32]
28	HFT record content and format	Immediately after submitting a HFT order, the regulated firm records the details of the order in a set format.[33]
		Records must be kept for five years.[34]

Notes: All Articles in the table refer to EU 2017/589 unless otherwise stated. [1] Article 17 EU MiFID 2014/65 are the core algorithmic trading requirements. [2] Annex I set out criteria based on complexity (9), nature (12) and scale (14) of the regulated firm's algorithms, strategies, and systems.

[3] Article 9(1). See Article 9(3). Further, Article 9(2) requires the annual assessment to be carried out within the framework of a risk management function as set out in Article 23(1) EU Delegated Regulation 2017/565. Article 23(1) requires a regulated firm to establish an independent risk function. However, under Article 23(2), if the complexity, nature and scale of the business mean it is unrealistic to establish a risk function, the firm still needs to implement risks policies and procedures in compliance with Article 23(1), and which are upon request, verifiable by the regulator. [4] Article 9(3). [5] Article 9(3). [6] Article 10. The stress testing must be based on ensuring resilience as set out in Articles 12–18. [7] Article 11. [8] Articles 12(1)–(2). [9] The market abuse regulation that applies is Article 12 EU 2014/596, which is an extremely long definition of market manipulation to apply for full compliance with Article 13 (EU 2017/589). Later in this chapter the section entitled Market Abuse provides a summary. It is essential to read the full text, but for ease of general reference my summary is as follows. Market manipulation covers scenarios affecting a broad range of financial products based on five scenarios, namely (a) false or misleading signals; (b) securing a price at an abnormal level; (c) activity or behaviour based on a fictitious device or other form of deception; (d) disseminating information that gives or is likely to give a false or misleading impression; and (e) transmitting false or misleading information in the context that manipulates benchmark calculation. [10] Article 13(1)–(8). [11] Article 14 (1)–(4). [12] Article 15. [13] Article 16(2).

[14] Article 16(5). [15] Article 17. [16] Article 18. [17] In essence, a trading venue member permits its client to use its trading code to directly transmit trade orders to the trading venue. This arrangement is called Direct Market Access (DMA). [18] Articles 19–23. [19] Contracts between DEA providers and its clients may not make reference to DEA, but only used the commercial term DMA. [20] Article 19 requires compliance with Article 17(5) EU 2014/65. These first five points summarise Article 17(5). [21] Article 20. [22] Note this appears to be a cyber security measure given the regulation specifies 'individuals' not just clients. See Chapter 5 Cyber security. [23] Article 21(1)(b). [24] Articles 21(1)(c)–(g). [25] Article 21(4). [26] Article 22. [27] Article 23. [28] Article 24. [29] Article 25(1). [30] Article 25(2). [31] Article 26. [32] Article 27. [33] The prescribed format for recording HFT orders is set out in tables 2 and 3 of Annex II of MiFID II Delegated Regulation 2017/589. To speedily make sense of Annex II, when you first glance at it note that Annex II Table 1 is simply the legend for Tables 2 and 3, so that all three tables can be kept in portrait format. [34] Article 28.

impossibility of precisely pre-estimating the true loss.[38]

The primary question to ask is whether the stipulated sum is an unconscionable amount or not. Further, the four-fold test works best with ordinary commercial contracts, but raises the question can this apply equally to complex 21st century trading platforms? Bargaining power matters here, but as an English High Court judge has recently observed 'in a negotiated contract between properly advised parties of comparable bargaining power, the strong initial presumption must be that the parties themselves are the best judges of what is legitimate in a provision dealing with the consequences of breach'.[39]

In sum, negotiating on behalf of established asset managers and investment banks is especially important, because their bargaining power will exceed or match that of any existing trading platform provider. Conversely, other regulated firms, for example FinTech SMEs, may be better placed to expect empathy in High Court litigation concerning penalty clauses in standard terms.

8.9   Algorithmic trading requirements

Turning to specific trading venue risk issues relevant to trading venue providers and its members, these include (a) algorithmic trading; (b) HFT; (c) market abuse; (d) circuit breakers; and (e) speedbumps. Firstly, for conducting algorithmic trading the fundamental requirements for investments firms include implementing, preventing or setting:

- effective systems and risk controls relevant to its business service to ensure that its trading systems are resilient;
- effective systems and risk controls suitable to the business it operates to ensure that its trading systems have sufficient capacity;
- appropriate trading thresholds and limits;
- the transmission of erroneous orders or the systems otherwise functioning in a way that may create or contribute to a disorderly market;

---

[38] *Dunlop Pneumatic Tyre Co Ltd v New Garage & Motor Co Ltd* [1914] UKHL 1, [1915] AC 79 (1 July 1914) per Lord Dunedin, at paragraph 4.

[39] *Cavendish Square Holding BV v Talal El Makdessi* (Rev 3) [2015] UKSC 67 per Lord Neuberger, at 35 (4 November 2015).

- effective systems and risk controls to ensure the trading systems cannot be used for any purpose that is contrary to market abuse regulation;[40]
- effective systems and risk controls to ensure the trading systems cannot be used for any purpose that is contrary or to the rules of a trading venue to which it is connected;[41]
- effective business continuity arrangements to deal with any failure of its trading systems; and
- testing and properly monitoring systems to ensure that they meet all the already outlined requirements.[42]

8.10 HFT

HFT is arguably the greatest priority to regulators given it is an actual or perceived cause of market volatility, which could potentially amount to systemic risk. HFT is a subset of algorithmic trading. An accurate caricature of HFT is that of proprietary trading with high daily volumes of orders utilising spread and arbitrage strategies.

Based on a definition relied on by the US Securities and Exchange Commission (SEC) for more than 10 years, HFT typically has the following five characteristics, accepting that not all five need be present for activity to qualify:

- exceptionally high-speed computers used for generating, routing and executing orders;
- use of co-location services and individual data feeds to minimise network and other types of latencies;
- very short time-frames for establishing and liquidating positions;
- high volumes of orders that are cancelled shortly after submission; and
- daily flat position, with the aim of minimising overnight un-hedged positions.[43]

---

[40] Regulation (EU) No. 596/2014.

[41] Trading platform rules are a discrete topic dealt with later in this chapter.

[42] Article 17(1) EU 2014/65.

[43] SEC (2020) Staff Report on Algorithmic Trading in US Capital Markets, at 38. See www.sec.gov/files/Algo_Trading_Report_2020.pdf.

HFT activities vary tremendously. Nevertheless, from a memorable formulaic viewpoint, Equation 8.1 illustrates that HFT is typically achieved by the interaction of several variables, most significantly with low latency, and without human involvement:

$$HFT = \frac{(A \times V) - H}{L} \qquad (8.1)^{44}$$

Where A is automated orders; V is the high volume of orders; H is the absence of human involvement; and L is the common denominator of latency.[45]

From a regulatory viewpoint, a regulated firm would be judged to carrying out HFT activities based on the following characteristics:

- computer infrastructure intended to minimise network and other types of latencies, achieved by co-location or proximity hosting or high-speed Direct Electronic Access (DEA);
- system-determination of order initiation, generation, routing or execution without human intervention; and
- high message intra-day rates which constitute orders, quotes or cancellations.[46]

The consequence of HFT is that such a business activity must be authorised by the FCA and is subject to more onerous reporting requirements.[47] The incremental costs involved in regular reporting to the FCA or PRA are unclear. However, an authoritative UK Government Office for Science report on HFT concluded that the extra compliance requirements were a substantial financial burden.[48]

---

[44] © Iain Sheridan (2021).

[45] In electronic engineering, Moore's law states that the capacity of semiconductors, so chip power, perennially doubles every 18 months to two years. Consequently, latency halves, albeit this appears to occur every 36 months. See Linton, O, and Mahmoodzadeh, S (2018) 'Implications of High-Frequency Trading in Security Markets', *Annual Review of Economics*, Volume 10, at 242.

[46] Article 4(40) MiFID II EU 2014/65.

[47] Article 17(2) MiFID II EU 2014/65 deals with the additional compliance requirements.

[48] UK Government Office for Science (2012) The Future of Computer Trading in Financial Markets – An International Perspective, at 99. A discipline maintained throughout all chapters of this book is to rely on the most up-to-date sources, given technology in the financial services sector moves so quickly. However, the depth and quality of this 2012 UK government research led by the UK Government's Chief Scientific Adviser is a rational exception. Based on 50 working papers assembled by over 150

Further, given financial market use of technology continuously expands and improves, the definition of HFT will change. For example, the current criteria for high message intra-day rates on trading venues is at least (a) two messages per second with respect to single products, and (b) four messages per second with respect to all financial instruments.[49] The relevance of these criteria has already been questioned, because ever-increasing speed of execution is available to an expanding population of market participants.[50] Further, trading activity that applies HFT techniques must comply with not only the general rules relevant to algorithmic trading, but also specific rules for HFT.[51] However, the EU supplementary regulation on algorithmic trading continues to apply.[52]

8.10.1 Market abuse

EU market abuse regulation transferred into UK law was established as a 'common regulatory framework on insider dealing, the unlawful disclosure of inside information and market manipulation (market abuse) as well as measures to prevent market abuse to ensure the integrity of financial markets in the Union and to enhance investor protection and confidence in those markets'.[53] The market abuse definition has five elements:

- entering into a transaction, placing an order to trade or any other behaviour which gives, or is likely to give, false or misleading signals as to the supply or demand for, or price of a financial product(s);
- securing, or is likely to secure, the price of a financial product(s) at an abnormal or artificial level;
- entering into a transaction, placing an order to trade or any other activity or behaviour which affects or is likely to affect the price of a financial product(s) based on a fictitious device or any other form of deception or contrivance;

---

independent academics from over 20 countries, its main focus is the effect of HFT. Further, its timeframe was from 2012 to 2020. See www.gov.uk/government/uploads/system/uploads/attachment _data/file/289431/12-1086-future-of-computer-trading-in-financial-markets-report.pdf.

[49] Article 19(1) MiFID Org Regulation EU 2017/565.

[50] ESMA (2020) MiFID/MiFIR Review Report on Algorithmic Trading, at 24. See www.esma.europa.eu/ sites/default/files/library/esma-70-156-2368_mifid_ii_consultation_paper_on_algorithmic_trading .pdf.

[51] See FCA CP 15/43, at 8.27, December 2016.

[52] EU 2017/589 as summarised earlier in this chapter.

[53] Article 1 EU 2014/596.

- disseminating information, including rumours, via digital media or by any other means, which gives, or is likely to give, false or misleading signals as to the supply of, demand for, or price of a financial product(s); and
- transmitting false or misleading information or providing false or misleading inputs concerning a benchmark, or any other behaviour which manipulates benchmark calculation.[54]

Relevant to trading venues, the threat of HFT market abuse, whether actual or perceived, has been examined at a level of unprecedented depth.[55] An authoritative conclusion reached under the leadership of the UK's Chief Scientific Officer is that:

> This qualitative evidence consistently indicates high levels of concern. Claims of market manipulation using HFT techniques are reported by institutional investors such as pension funds and mutual funds in different countries … Even if not backed by statistical evidence, these perceptions need to be taken seriously by policy makers because, given that the true extent of abuse is not precisely known, it is perception that is likely to determine the behaviour of liquidity suppliers. High perceived levels of abuse may harm market liquidity and efficiency for all classes of traders.[56]

While it is conceded that the qualitative evidence mentioned above is not easy to interpret unambiguously, it is consistent with three different 'scenarios' that counsel will benefit from understanding how its regulated firm mitigates the legal risks.

First, Scenario A, high frequency traders take advantage of slower agents through a speed advantage. This is a consistent claim of buy-side regulated firms. With the exception of at least one strategy,[57] low latency is inessential, but speed of computer function may increase profitability. Referring back to the earlier summary of market abuse, such strategies are based on 'false or misleading signals'. Example strategies include 'layering' and 'spoofing'.

---

[54] Article 12 EU 2014/596.
[55] UK Government Office for Science, The Future of Computer Trading in Financial Markets – An International Perspective.
[56] Ibid., at 12.
[57] The exception pinpointed is 'quote stuffing', when exceptionally high quantities of order messages flood competing trading venues with noise.

Second, in Scenario B HFT transforms the trading environment, especially order flow, in ways that facilitate market abuse or increase the perceived extent of abuse. This behaviour, especially if conducted through liquidity supply by temporarily modifying quotes following detection of sustained attempts to buy or sell the asset,[58] may amount to market abuse, because attempted profit derives from artificially pushing prices away from the levels warranted by their natural demand and supply. For example, in the time span of one second the commitment to buy a stock can be processed, but within that period of time a very high percentage of the liquidity can disappear and move the price.

Third, Scenario C concerns other market developments that have accompanied the growth in HFT which may also contribute to an increase in the perceived or actual presence of market abuse. The complexity evolves disentangling these other factors from HFT. An example of a connected market development is the fragmentation of liquidity across trading venues.[59] Another example is the buying of shares in a listed equity share when large short positions exist. If the buying of shares was based on a coordinated attempt to inflate the share price fuelled by extensive promotion on social media, that may amount to market abuse. This specific fact pattern was found in the 2021 inflation of the share price in GameStop by 1,745 per cent.[60]

8.10.2 Circuit breakers

Trading venue providers employ various mechanisms in an attempt to manage extreme volatility. Circuit breakers are commonly implemented to limit order books in a way that allows (a) a cooling-off period, and (b) an auction to pool liquidity and calm volatility. For example, the LSE's FTSE 100 circuit breaker thresholds are triggered based on two criteria. These are (a) the dynamic threshold for FTSE 100 shares is breached when a potential order book trade price is more than 3 per cent from the last executed order book trade price, and (b) the static threshold for FTSE 100 shares is breached when a potential order book trade price is

---

[58] This strategy is also termed 'liquidity detection'.

[59] UK Government Office for Science, The Future of Computer Trading in Financial Markets – An International Perspective, at 91.

[60] ESMA (2021) Statement on Episodes of Very High Volatility in Trading of Certain Stocks. Introductory Statement on GameStop.

more than 8 per cent away from the opening price established in the last auction.[61]

The FCA has provided an incisive analysis on the functioning of circuit breakers. This analysis was based on a sample of 51 incidents of circuit breakers triggered on the LSE in FTSE 350 securities over an 18 month period. This analysis was based on proprietary FCA data made up of consolidated order book and trade data from the major UK equity trading venues – the LSE, Turquoise[62] and BATS Europe,[63] and linked dark pools. Further, data was consolidated from the lit order books of all three of these MTFs. As charted in Figure 8.2, in the FCA sample the number of transactions increases significantly just before the circuit breaker is triggered. FCA analysis concludes that 'during the LSE call auction period, trading on MTF venues tends to dry up and is mostly limited to HFTs trading in low volume on Chi-X. HFTs participate in the auctions in relatively low volumes and when continuous trading resumes, their trading patterns normalise.'[64]

Others capital markets experts have commented on circuit breakers as creating imperfect gravitational or magnetic effects on trading where the act of halting trading accelerates the price changes or moves the price more than it would have in the absence of such an automated non-human intervention. The same experts also take the view that 'during the Sterling Flash Crash the implementation of trading halts in the CME [Chicago Metal Exchange] futures market contributed to the collapse of the spot market'.[65] Although it is important to highlight that the Sterling Flash Crash revolves around a far narrower time window of analysis and based on one event.[66] Whatever the role of circuit breakers they need scrutiny by compliance officers to understand what risks they present, especially how evolving technology will act as a catalyst to require threshold changes.

---

[61] Available at https://docs.londonstockexchange.com/sites/default/files/documents/n1114.pdf.

[62] Majority owned by the LSE. See www.lseg.com/markets-products-and-services/our-markets/turquoise/turquoise-trading-services.

[63] See www.cboe.com/europe/equities/overview/.

[64] FCA (2017) Catching a Falling Knife – An Analysis of Circuit Breakers in UK Equity Markets.

[65] Linton, O, and Mahmoodzadeh, S (2018) 'Implications of High-Frequency Trading in Security Markets', *Annual Review of Economics*, Volume 10, at 253.

[66] For an extensive text and graph explanation of the Sterling Flash Crash see BIS (2017) The Sterling 'Flash Event' of 7 October 2016, available at www.bis.org/publ/mktc09.pdf.

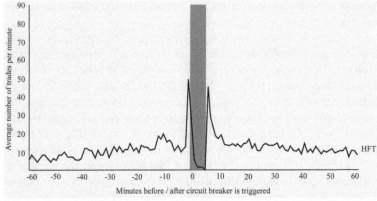

Source: FCA (2017) Catching a Falling Knife: An Analysis of Circuit Breakers in UK Equity Markets. See www.fca.org.uk/publications/research/analysis-circuit-breakers-uk-equity-markets.

Figure 8.2   *MTF trades*

8.10.3 Speedbumps

Under MiFID II and the EU Markets in Financial Instruments Regulation (MiFIR) the EC must, after consulting ESMA, present reports to the European Parliament and the Council on rules concerning the impact of algorithmic trading including HFT. A recent ESMA consultation paper on algorithmic trading provided an important section on the regulatory treatment of trading speedbumps together with questions communicated to market participants.[67]

A speedbump is a mechanism that allows trading platforms that implement them to delay orders before they enter the matching engine for execution. The rationale for implementing speedbumps is to reduce the technological advantages of HFT trading strategies. Speedbumps can be either (a) symmetric, meaning they apply equally across all orders, or (b) asymmetric whereby they target specific types of orders, for example only aggressive ones.[68]

---

[67] ESMA (2020) Consultation Paper MiFID II/MiFIR Review Report on Algorithmic Trading, at 318–321.

[68] Ibid., at 318–319.

Currently, neither the UK nor EU financial regulations specifically address how speedbumps should be regulated, although MiFID II has general organisational provisions that certainly cover the management of conflicts of interest. It is likely that regulatory changes may occur in the near future so both the UK and EU approaches require monitoring. Interestingly the Association for Financial Markets in Europe (AFME), a leading capital markets industry body, takes the view that trading platforms should be left to innovate.[69]

---

[69] AFME (2021) Response to ESMA (2020) Consultation Paper MiFID II/MiFIR Review Report on Algorithmic Trading, at 33.

9. Innovation protection

From global asset managers and investment banks, to platforms and start-up FinTech firms, regulated firms increasingly rely on adding business value from technical innovation. These revenues are principally created on the basis of computer science, or more precisely digital engineering. In this context, the prime mind-set of any legal counsel is to think in terms of (a) confidentiality; (b) IP; and (c) trade secrets – three key ways either to licence or protect products.[1]

9.1   Introduction

A former president of the UK Supreme Court gave a speech at the Royal Society, entitled 'Science and Law: Contrasts and Cooperation'. He observed:

> both scientific thinking and legal thinking rely in general on logical reasoning and on the evaluation of evidence. Scientists and lawyers each search for and assess hard facts from which they can establish the truth, whether of a particular theory or in a particular case, and they each use principles and reasoning to enable them to reach what they hope is the right conclusion.[2]

In essence, both law and science apply accepted principles and logical reasoning to facts supported by evidence, then reach conclusions. Remembering that there are things in common between law and science is important for legal counsel acting for regulated firms.

---

[1]   Of course most intellectual property performs both functions at the same time. Licensed to others and protected by law against unlicensed use. An authoritative and in-depth work on all types of intellectual property with extensive case law referencing is Cornish, W, Llewelyn, D, and Aplin, T (2019) *Intellectual Property: Patents, Copyright, Trade Marks and Allied Rights*, 9th edn. (Sweet & Maxwell).

[2]   David Neuberger QC, Hon FRS (2015) Science and Law: Contrasts and Cooperation. See www.supremecourt.uk/docs/speech-151124.pdf.

Acknowledging these similarities, it is also valuable to remember an essential difference between law and computer engineering. Specifically, the key mind-set of all engineers, including software engineers, is to think in terms of systems.[3] To solve anything well in engineering requires factoring in that the problem to be solved is linked to other systems. To be precise this mind-set is called modular systems thinking.[4] Issues concerning protecting innovation in this chapter depend to some degree on the input of computer engineers, typically software engineers.[5] There are common habits of thinking between lawyers and engineers, but in my experience systems thinking has to be equally factored in as an important element. Therefore, the common threads weaving through this chapter are professional cooperation, IP protection and systems thinking. In combination, the rule-based, protective mind-set of the legal counsel, coupled with the modular systems thinking of software engineers, maximise the value of innovation in any regulated firm.

9.2   Core IP

The types of IP which can be protected by registration or not can be mesmerising for financial regulation counsel. Figure 9.1 captures the three recurring elements. In an era of increasing reliance on machine learning, this trio are the vital ingredients of many financial services initiatives.

---

[3]   As an illustration of system thinking, if you add a piece of software to a system, there may be some immediate advantage to the end user, but how that software interacts with other software and how much hard disk storage and processing power is required potentially affects the performance of existing software. Everything is a module, a part of a system. To the competent engineer there is always more to changing a system than can be immediately seen. Modular systems thinking is how good engineers create better solutions. In contrast, the law, perhaps with the exception of litigation, has no moving parts that need to be constructed, deconstructed and tested to verify how the solutions function in practice.

[4]   Madhaven, G (2017) *Think Like An Engineer – Inside the Minds That Are Changing Our Lives* (OneWorld), at 21.

[5]   There is also the important role of data scientists, especially with the increasing use of machine learning in investment and trading activity.

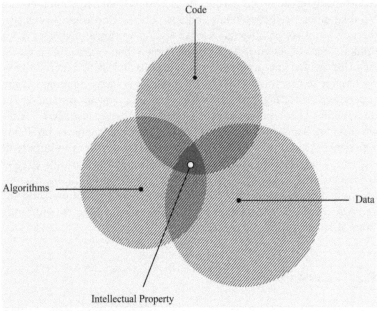

Source: © Iain Sheridan (2021).

Figure 9.1   Vital IP ingredients

9.3   Confidentiality

An essential way of maximising protection is to manage how employees and third-parties are held accountable for maintaining confidentiality. English law on confidentiality is multi-faceted.[6] The requirements to prove breach of confidentiality are threefold:[7]

- the information must be of a confidential nature;
- the information must have been communicated in circumstances indicating an obligation of confidence; and[8]
- there must be an unauthorised use of the information to the detriment

---

[6]   For an authoritative exploration of all aspects, see Phipps, C, and Harman, W (2019) *Toulson & Phipps on Confidentiality*, 4th edn. (Sweet & Maxwell).

[7]   *Coco v A N Clark (Engineers) Ltd* ChD 1968.

[8]   There is no generally established precise test provided by the High Courts to decide if circumstances indicate an obligation of confidence. However, in *Argyll v Argyll*, cited by Megarry J in *Coco v Clark*,

of the person communicating it.[9]

9.4   Case study on Goldman Sachs

The theft of valuable source code from a software developer in the Goldman Sachs New York office in 2009 was something that could occur in any regulated firm.[10] The facts highlight the challenges of trade secret protection.[11] To summarise, in May 2007 Sergey Aleynikov started employment at Goldman Sachs as a computer programmer. He was hired to develop Goldman Sachs's HFT software.[12] The computer code for Goldman Sachs's HFT system was pivotal to successful trading, and therefore constantly updated. However, employees were not permitted to remove a copy of any source code from Goldman Sachs's network and all signed agreements acknowledging this rule.

To carry out his software development work, Aleynikov had complete access to the HFT source code stored in Goldman Sachs's software repository. In the spring of 2009, Aleynikov accepted an offer of employment at Teza Technologies (Teza), a Chicago-based start-up firm. Teza had no connectivity, equipment or software for HFT at the time. Its founder planned to develop HFT trading software. On 5 June 2009, his last day of work at Goldman Sachs, Aleynikov uploaded a large quantity of Goldman Sachs's HFT source code, via a website, to a subversion repository.[13] Aleynikov compressed the data from Goldman Sachs's source code repository into files, and uploaded the source code to a German server.

---

an objective test was proposed based on when a reasonable person would realise information was given in confidence: *Argyll v Argyll* [1967] Ch 302.

[9] The Trade Secrets (Enforcement, etc.) Regulations 2018, SI 2018/597, came into force in 2018, so operate in parallel with the common law. Case law indicates that common law principles are unaffected: *Shenzhen Senior v Celgard* [2020] EWCA Civ 1293.

[10] *People v Aleynikov*, 2018 NY Slip Op 03174 [31 NY3d 383] 3 May 2018 Fahey, J, Court of Appeals. See http://courts.state.ny.us/Reporter/3dseries/2018/2018_03174.htm.

[11] The facts of this Goldman case also highlight that cutting-edge technologies, in this example HFT, are often evolving for many years before they become mainstream challenges for regulators. The original system was acquired by Goldman when it acquired a pioneering algorithmic trading company, Hull Group Inc, for $531 million in 1999.

[12] HFT is a subset of algorithmic trading. An accurate caricature of HFT is that of proprietary trading with high daily volumes of orders utilising spread and arbitrage strategies. Chapter 8 Trading platforms includes a detailed explanation of HFT.

[13] A subversion repository is a remote server to which a user can transfer code.

Subsequently, Aleynikov downloaded the source code to his home computers. On 9 June 2009, Teza created an account on a website that allowed companies to share source code within a select group of users. Aleynikov then placed HFT software in a source code repository on that website.

In late June 2009, Goldman Sachs's information security personnel discovered that unauthorised transfers of data from Goldman Sachs's repository had occurred in the early evening of 5 June 2009 totalling 17.5 megabytes of data. Goldman Sachs identified the device from which the transfers had been made as Aleynikov's work computer.

After FBI investigations, a 2010 federal trial resulted in Aleynikov's conviction for theft of the source code. In 2012 Aleynikov was acquitted of that decision by an appellate court. A subsequent 2015 New York state jury found Aleynikov guilty of stealing Goldman Sachs's HFT source code. In sum, it was difficult and time consuming for Goldman Sachs to seek redress for the source code theft. Yet all regulated firms have to ruthlessly follow through on IP theft as an on-going deterrent.

9.5   Mitigating information leakage

While both English civil and criminal law provide some deterrence to technology-based trade secrets, human nature means that some individuals are still going to risk misappropriating trade secrets and passing on confidential information. Respecting information is a habit that can be cultivated. In financial services the resource advantages of an employer may not be enough to stop all leakage, but in my experience there are effective ways to mitigate information leakage. To provide just one example, it is sensible to ask the Chief Executive Officer to meet all new employees, welcome them to the firm and politely remind them that confidentiality is treated seriously. It may not seem intuitive to ask a busy Chief Executive Officer to support the legal function in this practical way, but when you remind the Chief Executive Officer about the cost savings from less information leakage on strategic innovation they will thank you. Ultimately, breaches of confidentiality are down to conduct, and leadership is a powerful influence.

9.6   Trade secrets

A report commissioned by the international law firm CMS Cameron McKenna Nabarro Olswang LLP and written by The Economist Intelligence Unit covers the degree to which firms identify intangible assets as trade secrets. The report was based on a survey of 314 senior corporate executives located in China, France, Germany, Singapore, the UK and the US, and across six sectors.[14] While this extensive survey did not include the financial services sector the results indicate that cyber security is the main concern for the way trade secrets are revealed.[15]

Trade secrets are a broad category of IP. The WIPO has observed that any confidential business information that provides an entity with a competitive edge may be classed as a trade secret. When a trade secret is used by another entity other than the owner or without the owner's permission, this amounts to a violation of that secret. Article 39.2 of the Agreement on Trade-related Aspects of Intellectual Property, produced by the World Trade Organization, provides the following three general standards for any legal counsel to follow in the process of deciding whether something is a trade secret:

- the information must be valuable;
- the information must be secret, in the sense that its precise dimensions or form are only accessible or known in the circles of people that normally deal with the kind of information in question; and
- the owner must have taken reasonable steps to keep it secret.

9.7   English law and trade secrets

The laws that deal with each violation will vary with the specific facts of each case. Trade secrets are governed by laws on breach of confidence, breach of contract and industrial espionage. Listed below are some aspects of a regulated firm's business that may contain trade secrets:

- source code;
- algorithms that form part of machine learning and other AI

---

[14]   CMS (2021) Open Secrets? Guarding Value in the Intangible Economy, at 9.
[15]   Chapter 5 Cyber security provides important related material on how to protect against cyber attacks.

applications;

- designs and drawings of inventions some of which, whether in draft or final version, form part of an innovation;
- business strategies, for example the decision to use a specific over-looked business process known in the market and unprotected by IP, in combination with another licensed protected business process;[16]
- charts or flow diagrams setting out the operations management of how a regulated firm controls data and develops products based on data;
- company procedure manuals, for instance policies on developing, monitoring and registering IP based on the contributions of several in-house functions; and
- commercial IP valuation based on internal and external legal function audits.

The decision flowchart, Figure 9.2, provides legal counsel with a checking process to assist in the decision making on whether to attempt to manage a trade secret, or alternatively file a patent. The legal function also has to assess if the granting of a patent is a realistic prospect based on statute and case law, so the outcome can often be no patent filing and trade secrets that remain vulnerable. Often it may be better, for commercial, efficiency and time reasons, to maintain a new concept under trade secret clauses in contracts with employees and other entities commissioned to work on behalf of the regulated firm. The details of the development and imple-mentation of a trade secret policy for the regulated firm is beyond the scope of this chapter. However, a rigorous trade secret policy will include all of the following measures:

- developing a corporate culture that thinks about protecting informa-tion forming part of a trade secret;
- installing information systems with technical measures, such as encryption and security entry procedures, commensurate with the different functions and types of information that flow around the reg-ulated firm and between the regulated firm and its external advisers and business partners;
- maintaining individual trade secrets among only the necessary minimum number of employees and including brief notices to remind

---

[16] An example might be the use of a licensed SAP system in combination with other innovative software overlooked by competitors.

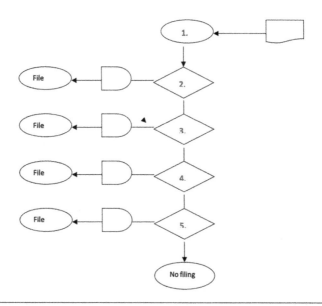

1. *Development team starts the process by providing information to the legal function on a new commercially valuable concept.*

2. *Is the trade secret vulnerable to being intentionally or unintentionally revealed to a 3rd party? If yes, then file.*

3. *Can the product be reversed engineered? If yes, then file.*

4. *Is it likely that a competitor will independently invent the new concept? If yes, then file.*

5. *Is maintaining the trade secret impractical or too costly? If yes, then file.*

Source: © Iain Sheridan (2021).

Figure 9.2   *Trade secret or patent decision tree*

them not to communicate the content of communication concerning the trade secret to others inside and outside the regulated firm;
• prioritising business secrets based on the estimated value of each one;
• putting in place confidentiality agreements with employees with

knowledge of trade secrets;[17]
- training employees on the protection of trade secrets; and
- signing non-disclosure agreements with all business partners.

9.8 Accessing and protecting data

It is helpful to first define data. An authoritative industry definition is that it concerns 'reinterpretable representation of information in a formalised manner suitable for communication, interpretation, or processing'. Importantly, the processing can be processed by humans or automatically.[18] For all regulated firms 'using rich information streams to make decisions is superior to relying on money alone'.[19] Further, the significance of data is also changing with rapidity. It has been incisively said that the 'informational centre of gravity in markets is moving away from money', because it is the new fundamental market force.[20] Data is often also described as the new oil. Yet both these comparisons miss the multi-dimensional nature of data, which can include financial services data sets that can potentially be monetised in the short, medium and long term. For example, consider the dimensions of the FTSE 100 Index, and its constituent data and combined level indicator over time.

The value of data is to measure it as a unique asset class often with third-party rights. These characteristics need to be factored into any commercial assessment. Under statute, in the context of IP rights, a database is a collection of independent works, data or other materials that are (a) arranged in a systematic or methodical way, and (b) individually accessible by electronic or other means.[21] From a technical viewpoint 'systematic and methodical' can be encapsulated in the term data structure. By which is meant the data is organised and not randomly placed in a file. There is a consistency, method, and a system how data can be processed at great

---

[17] Specific reference to a number or code that is the reference of the trade secret reduces the chance of the employee building a case of accidental disclosure.

[18] ISO/IEC 2383-1:1993. Information Technology: Vocabulary: Part 1: Fundamental Terms. See www .iso.org/obp/ui/#iso:std:iso-iec:2382:ed-1:v1:en or see www.iso.org/standard/63598.html.

[19] Mayer-Schönberger, V, and Ramge, T (2018) *Reinventing Capitalism* (John Murray), at 139.

[20] Ibid.

[21] Article 6, The Copyright and Rights in Databases Regulations 1997, SI 1997/3032. See www.legislation .gov.uk/uksi/1997/3032/regulation/6/made.

Table 9.1   *FinTech competitors*

Regulated firm	Services	Est'd	Regulated by	Location	Disruptive Impact
Atom	FinTech	2014	FCA, PRA	Durham	4
Marcus[1]	FinTech	2018	FCA, PRA	Milton Keynes	2
Monzo	FinTech	2015	FCA, PRA	London	3
Revolut	FinTech	2015	FCA	London	3
Starling	FinTech	2014	FCA, PRA	London	4
Wise	FinTech	2011	FCA	London	5

Note: [1] Marcus is a subsidiary of Goldman Sachs.

speed by a computer without error. To illustrate, Table 9.1 is an example of a data structure.[22] This is a simplified example given any working financial services database would be based on multiple interlinked data structures.

9.9   Copyright protection

Under the Berne Convention for the Protection of Literary and Artistic Works ('the Berne Convention'), 176 UN member states apply the same standards of national treatment to copyright authors.[23] Copyright protects the structure of data.[24] So again looking at in the example of Table 9.1, the format of that database presented is potentially protected but not the data itself. However, to gain copyright protection any database needs to be original and based on 'the author's own intellectual creation'.[25] So if the far right-hand column, Disruptive Impact rating, is based on an original formula for determining the disruptive level of a regulated firm, it would be copyright protected.[26]

---

[22]   A software developer would describe a data structure as a 'table'.

[23]   Berne Convention for the Protection of Literary and Artistic Works (1979). See https://wipolex.wipo .int/en/treaties/textdetails/12214. Note this came into effect in 1984.

[24]   An authoritative two volume practitioner reference book on all aspects of copyright is Harbottle, G et al. (2021) *Copinger and Skone James on Copyright* (Sweet & Maxwell).

[25]   Section 3A(2) Copyrights, Designs and Patents Act 1988.

[26]   The protection period is long, based on 70 years from the date the author dies.

9.10 Database rights

Under UK regulations,[27] there is an automatic database right given to the producer of the database that lasts for 15 years.[28] Further, a substantial change to the database based on a significant investment would be classed as creating a new database that would qualify for its own 15 years of protection.[29] To qualify, 'there has to be substantial investment in obtaining, verifying or presenting the contents of the database'.[30] The assessment of substantial investment is both a qualitative and a quantitative standard.[31] For example, look again at the far right column of Table 9.1 recording a Disruptive Impact rating. That column records the degree of disruption by each venture to incumbent competitors. The level of disruption is based on 1 being the lowest level and 5 being the highest. Imagine if the final rating required paying 30 investment bank analysts to text their monthly view on the disruptive value of each of these regulated firms based on their own calculations and individual analysis. This effort in obtaining the Disruptive Impact rating metric and including it in Table 9.1 would potentially qualify as a substantial investment on qualitative terms.[32]

In the financial services sector the use of database rights are often pivotal to the revenue streams of both licensor and licensee. In the context of equity indexes that form part of derivative products, a Dutch court has already concluded that efforts made by Euronext in checking the accuracy of index components forming the AEX index and linked options database amounted to a substantial investment, and therefore a database right.[33]

---

[27] Copyright and Rights in Databases Regulations (CRDR), SI 1997/3032. These Regulations became law in the UK in 1998, implementing the EU Database Directive 96/9/EC. From 1 January 2021, a UK database owner no longer benefits from protection throughout the EEA. However, for databases created before 2021 the EEA-wide protection remains.

[28] Section 17 CRDR, SI 1997/3032.

[29] Section 17(3) CRDR, SI 1997/3032.

[30] Section 17 CRDR, SI 1997/3032.

[31] *British Horse Racing Board (BHB) v William Hill* [2004] ECR I-10415 ECJ. The ECJ held that the financial investment made in the collection of the contents was the relevant focus.

[32] *Football Dataco v Stan James* [2013] EWCA Civ 27.

[33] *Euronext v TOM & BinckBank* [2015] Case/Registration No. C/09/442420/HA ZQ 13-152 (Dutch language judgment).

9.10.1 What constitutes a breach of a database right?

The database right protects the owner from qualitative and quantitative 'extraction' or 're-utilisation' of all or a substantial part of the database.[34] Substantial copying can be based on several criteria, including the financial and human resource investment put into obtaining data even though the data might form a small percentage of the total data. In a memorable court decision, just 6,000 records from a database with 43,000 records, 13.9 per cent, was considered substantial because to obtain it required thousands of staff and thousands of phone calls.[35]

Further, repeated and systematic extraction of insubstantial parts of a database may also amount to breach.[36] This in my view is clumsy drafting, and it would have made more sense to refer to 'any part of a database'. Nevertheless, this rule provides for a database right owner to expect a user of data that has repeatedly and systematically taken from its database to ask permission to do so, and also allows it to charge a licence fee for that access. Referring back to the Table 9.1 example, if the Disruptive Impact rating was based on a significant investment, the extraction of that metric could potentially qualify.[37]

9.10.2 The evolving legal treatment of databases

The technology affecting database rights and their legal treatment constantly evolves. For example, intuitively from a technological viewpoint a PDF document is not a database. The PDF file format was developed by Adobe Systems in 1993, and then released as an open standard in 2008.[38] The PDF file format has evolved to allow data to be easily converted from PDF text to another format. Although unintuitive, case law has classed a PDF document as a form of database. The legal reasoning is based on the

---

[34] Section 16(1) CRDR, SI 1997/3032.

[35] *Beechwood v Guardian* [2010] EWPCC 12.

[36] Section 16(2) CRDR, SI 1997/3032.

[37] Under Section 12(1) CRDR, SI 1997/3032 'Extraction' means 'the permanent or temporary transfer of all or a substantial part of the contents of a database to another medium by any means or in any form'. In an English case concerning geospatial addresses, the High Court confirmed that the fact the extracted data was viewed then discarded did not prevent it from being treated as an infringing extraction. The data was transferred to the operating memory of a computer – another medium: *77m Ltd v Ordnance Survey Ltd* [2019] EWHC 3007 (Ch).

[38] ISO 32000-1:2008. See iso.org/standard/51502.html, https://wipolex.wipo.int/en/treaties/textdetails/12214.

view that 'informative values' do not change with the medium of delivery, whether digital or paper. Any recorded data structure can potentially be a database. In 2017, an English High Court judge concluded that a PDF of a spreadsheet could be a database because 'the contents of the PDF can be accessed, either through electronic conversion, through digital character recognition, or old-fashioned reading or re-typing'.[39] It is also notable that the EU is in the process of reviewing the EU Database Directive, which in part reflects the evolution of what qualifies as a database and the commercial value of data.[40]

9.11 Text and data mining

When the investment and marketing of AI in regulated firms has increased so significantly, it is understandable to realise there is too much emphasis on data mining. A hugely respected Turing Award[41] winning AI expert, Judea Pearl, underlined the realities when he reminded that 'causal questions can never be answered from data alone. They require us to formulate a model of the process that generates the data, or at least some aspects of that process.' Big Data is the first step not the last.[42] Given producing negligent machine learning models has potentially serious legal consequences, legal counsel needs to be part of both the data mining and model formation decision making at every stage.

Regulated firms seeking to lever machine learning and other AI applications generally need to rely on some data sets from outside their own four walls. New legislation attempts to manage the use of data by businesses without thwarting the advancement of public institutes involved in data mining that has wider societal benefits. In the EU digital content copyright is protected, while EU copyright regulations allow for limited use by all entities of protected works without the author's permission. However,

---

[39] *Technomed Ltd & Anor v Bluecrest Health Screening Ltd & Anor* [2017] EWHC 2142 (Ch) per HHJ Stone at 69.

[40] EC COM (2020) 690, Commission Work Programme 2021, A Union of Vitality in a World of Fragility, at Annex I, Section 6.

[41] The AM Turing Award in an annual prize awarded by the Association of Computing Machinery. In computer science circles it is considered to the 'Nobel Prize of Computing'.

[42] Pearl, J (2019) *The Book of Why – The New Science of Cause and Effect* (Penguin), at 351.

beyond the limited use level only non-commercial institutes are exempt.[43] Therefore, regulated firms accessing public data will need to negotiate public-private agreements to avoiding infringing IP.

9.12   Patents

The management of patents in the context of a regulated firm requires teamwork between the financial regulation legal counsel and the instructed patent attorney. There is a distinct career path of patent attorney because the management of patent applications requires a blend of at least engineering or science tertiary education, and nuanced processes on specific, tactical drafting. So while this section provides an accurate high-level summary, it is important to underline the necessity to obtain specialist patent attorney advice before lodging any application.[44]

The monopoly granted to a patent extends to 20 years,[45] but the commercial motivations driving regulated firms to make patent applications is more realistically anchored in much shorter time-frames. While there are exceptions, if granted, a patent would provide some 24–36 months' protection from competitors to the patent owner before competitors are able to work around the patent or advance the state of the art and have their own patent granted.

For FinTech businesses seeking more funding there is certainly a pattern of venture capital firms assessing a patent portfolio as a reliable metric on which, among other evidence, to make investment decisions. To be clear, that portfolio might initially be one patent given it is often one very clever idea that needs protection. In such a scenario, the first step is to produce an invention disclosure report. This report is a confidential document written by the in-house inventor for exclusive reading by the in-house legal counsel and external patent attorney. This confidential document is

---

[43]   Article 3 EU Directive 2019/790 provides an exception for institutes involved in scientific research.

[44]   The probability of obtaining a commercially useful patent is significantly increased by the use a registered patent attorney. This is because the drafting of a patent specification requires a mix of legal and technical skills. For an objective summary on this topic produced by the UK Intellectual Property Office see www.gov.uk/guidance/why-you-should-use-an-ip-attorney.

[45]   Section 25 Patents Act 1977.

used to decide if a patent application should be lodged or if an alternative type of protection should be deployed.

In terms of legal principles, the UK has its own established case law and statutory framework.[46] It also makes reference to many EU court decisions. However, when business leaders discuss with legal counsel how best to strategically and tactically protect innovation, most realise that there is not always a good chance that computer driven innovations, especially computer programs, can be patented.[47] The same barrier to patentability applies to business methods. Under English statute,[48] a patent may be granted only for an invention[49] when (a) the invention is new;[50] (b) it involves an inventive step;[51] (c) it is capable of industrial application;[52] and (d) it does not fall within an exception.[53]

The exceptions of most relevance to regulated firms are business methods and computer programs. Given any business method will at least in part rely on some computer programming the policy-based objection is that

---

[46] Ibid., at Section 1(2). The grant of a patent for it is not excluded because it is a '(a) a discovery, scientific theory or mathematical method; (s) a literary, dramatic, musical or artistic work or any other aesthetic creation whatsoever; (c) a scheme, rule or method for performing a mental act, playing a game or doing business, or a program for a computer; (d) the presentation of information'.

[47] The EPO provides a succinct summary of the key challenges of hardware and software patentability. See www.epo.org/news-events/in-focus/ict/hardware-and-software.html.

[48] Section 1(1) (a)–(d) Patents Act 1977.

[49] The concept of an invention is not a defined term forming part of any initial judicial analysis. See *Biogen Inc v Medeva plc* [1996] UKHL 18, (1997) 38 BMLR 149, [1997] RPC 1 per Lord Hoffman, at 46, who advised all judges to 'put on one side their intuitive sense of what constitutes an invention until they have considered the questions of novelty, inventiveness and so forth'.

[50] Section (2)(1) Patents Act 1977 states that 'an invention shall be taken to be new if it does not form part of the state of the art'. Section 2(2) elaborates that the state of the art includes any invention made public in any way, so including oral and written communication, before the priority date. So for any readers new to English patent law it is crucial to note that novelty is lost if the invention is divulged before filing. Many inventors have made this mistake.

[51] *Pozzoli v BDMO* [2007] EWCA Civ 588, at 23.

[52] This is broadly construed and certainly covers any practical or useful innovation that forms all or part of a financial service.

[53] Section 1(2) Patents Act 1977 the exceptions are: anything which consists of '(a) a discovery, scientific theory or mathematical method; (b) a literary, dramatic, musical or artistic work or any other aesthetic creation whatsoever; (c) a scheme, rule or method for performing a mental act, playing a game or doing business, or a program for a computer; (d) the presentation of information; but the foregoing provision shall prevent anything from being treated as an invention for the purposes of this Act only to the extent that a patent or application for a patent relates to that thing as such'. The words 'as such' are especially important and are elaborated on later in this chapter.

most programming is a set of instructions which theoretically can be carried out by a human.[54] Patentability of excluded subject matter is not allowed. However, where a computer program is making a clear technical contribution, for example increasing the speed at which it functions, that is patentable.[55]

For FinTech firms the cost-benefit analyses of attempting to obtain one or more patents, typically for machine learning and other AI applications, are an important part of funding strategy and medium term success. Many FinTech firms can expect to pay up to £20,000 to file a patent based on the combined fees for the essential financial regulation lawyer advice plus the patent attorney fees. Patenting is not a low cost form of protection, but given the power and signalling of the monopoly it provides that makes sense, albeit it is not without risk. If the patent application fails there would be sunk legal patent attorney costs and a considerable loss of time.

From the stance of a regulated firm researching the recurring challenges of patenting its inventions, a valuable document to read is the lost appeal by Merrill Lynch in its attempt to obtain a patent for an automated securities trading system. This example shows immense innovative foresight, but unfortunately in the view of the Court of Appeal the invention was merely a program on a conventional computer, and lacked the technical contribution required to grant a patent.[56] In a similar case that involved the rejection of a patent application by Bloomberg the judge put it this way: 'a claim to a programmed computer as a matter of substance is just a claim to the program on a kind of carrier. A computer on a kind of carrier, which, if run, performs a business method, adds nothing to the art that does not lie in excluded subject matter'.[57]

---

[54]   The increased use of machine learning does not fit that generalisation. However, machine learning, and other AI applications are based around algorithms and models which are also needed to prove there is a technical effect to be granted a patent.

[55]   *Aerotel/Macrossan* [2006] EWCA Civ 1371.

[56]   *Merrill Lynch's Application* [1989] RPC 561. The Court of Appeal held that the invention lacked patentability, because it failed to contribute a technical effect. For readers less familiar with the name Merrill Lynch, before the Global Financial Crisis it was a globally respected and innovative investment bank. In 2008 it was acquired by Bank of America.

[57]   *Bloomberg LLP v Cappellini's Applications* [2007] EWHC 476, per Pumfrey J, at 9.

Based on a UK Court of Appeal level judgment of two different patent applications relevant to both business methods and computer programs, the following four-step approach applies:

- properly construe the claim;
- identify the actual contribution;
- ask whether the contribution falls solely within excluded subject matter; and
- check whether the actual or alleged contribution is technical in nature.[58]

In a Court of Appeal case where the focus of analysis was solely a computer program, the judges reached the conclusion that is was acceptable to combine the third and fourth steps.[59] Therefore, an assessment of a patent's technical effect forms part of deciding if it falls within one of the excluded subject matters. So it would be an error for a patent examining officer or court to dismiss an application on the basis of the view that it concerned excluded subject matter with no consideration on whether a technical contribution had been made or not. The conclusion reached by the Court of Appeal was that the computer program made a technical contribution and was patentable. An important observation included that:

> a computer with this program operates better than a similar prior art computer. To say 'oh but that is only because it is a better program – the computer itself is unchanged' gives no credit to the practical reality of what is achieved by the program. As a matter of such reality ... there is a faster and more reliable computer.[60]

It is worth also mentioning that while the patent examiners are bound by legal precedent and have to follow the decisions of the higher courts, each examination is expected to be judged on its own merits. By which is meant, different cases decided on different facts and inventions may

---

[58] *Aerotel Ltd v Telco Holdings Ltd & Ors Rev* 1 [2006] EWCA Civ 1371. When looking for other analyses of this case, note that two separate cases were heard as one appeal. So it is referred to as *Aerotel/Macrossan*. See www.bailii.org/ew/cases/EWCA/Civ/2006/1371.html.

[59] *Symbian Ltd v Comptroller General of Patents* [2008] EWCA Civ 1066. See www.bailii.org/cgi-bin/format.cgi?doc=/ew/cases/EWCA/Civ/2008/1066.html&query=(symbian).

[60] *Symbian Ltd v Comptroller General of Patents* [2008] EWCA Civ 1066 per Lord Neuberger, at 56.

not assist, and whether a patent application is granted is an inherently uncertain process.[61]

Given the nature of both innovation and technology, court decisions on patentability constantly evolve, although the four-step approach outlined above is still applied. Of special note in the context of the financial services sector is a decision in a case concerning a stock market index. The company Research Affiliates created an index based on the accounts and other data found in a company annual report to select individual stocks. Subsequently, each stock was weighted and added to an index. Its competitive advantage was based on lower volatility compared with traditional indices relying on price or market capitalisation such as the FTSE or NASDAQ indices. The hearing officer held that the invention failed the earlier mentioned 'excluded subject matter' third step.[62] Consequently, it was unpatentable.[63]

This Research Affiliates case is especially important because, more recently, indices have exploited machine learning technologies which are complex, technical in nature but still need to be assessed for patentability based on existing English law. For example, Equbot has collaborated with HSBC to market AiPEX, an AI-powered equity index comprising of 250 US publicly listed companies.[64] This works by an AI algorithm selecting constituents of the AiPEX on a monthly basis. The AiPEX is the first financial services index to use IBM Watson as part of its data analysis process. In short, AI and especially machine learning are increasingly parts of patent applications, but they are not in any sense automatically assumed to be patentable.

9.13 The US position on business methods and software patents

Given the importance of the US market and the significant activity of US asset managers, global investment banks, platforms plus FinTech SMEs in the UK and vice versa, there is logical interest in clients wanting to know

---

[61] *Research In Motion UK Ltd v Inpro Licensing SARL* [2006] EWHC 70 per Pumfrey J, at 186.

[62] *Aerotel/Macrossan* [2006] EWCA Civ 1371.

[63] *Research Affiliates LLC v Commissioner of Patents* [2014] FCAFC 150.

[64] See http://aipex.gbm.hsbc.com.

how the US compares with the UK approach. Briefly, the US statute does not exclude business methods or computer programs from patentability. Consequently, there are a high number of US granted patents covering one or both. However, US courts are reluctant to grant patents for purely abstract ideas, although some degree of abstractness would not preclude an application from being granted.

In an important US Supreme Court decision, the patent claims centred on 'managing the consumption risk costs of a commodity sold by a commodity provider at a fixed price'. In substance, the patent application was based on hedging risk for consumers in the commodity markets by instructing the use of well-known random analysis techniques to help establish some of the inputs into the hedging equation.[65] The US Supreme Court rejected an established 'useful, concrete and tangible result' test from an earlier decision concerning State Street Bank.[66] In its place the bench unanimously emphasised a well-established 'machine-or-transformation' test. Further, it was held that a business method judged to be an abstract idea is not patentable.[67]

9.14 Patent application options and lifespan

Compared with other leading FinTech jurisdictions, such as Singapore and the US, the strategic process of making patent applications to protect innovation in the UK is markedly different. This is because the UK is a member of the European Patent Convention (EPC).[68] The EPC allows any signatory country to file a patent application with the European Patent Office (EPO) in Munich with the aim of having a patent granted

---

[65] *Bilski v Kappos*, 561 U.S. 593 (2010). See www.supremecourt.gov/opinions/09pdf/08-964.pdf.

[66] *State Street Bank & Trust Co v Signature Financial Group, Inc* 927 F. Supp. 502, 38 USPQ2d 1530 (D. Mass. 1996).

[67] The weight of this decision is underlined by the fact all the judges of the Supreme Court addressed the issues, referred to as an *en banc* decision.

[68] The 17th edition of the European Patent Convention is available at www.epo.org/law-practice/legal-texts/epc.html.

for one or more EPC member states.[69] If granted, the patent covers all the signatory jurisdictions designated by the applicant.[70]

9.15 Employer and employee entitlement

The role of employees as inventors is not a straightforward issue.[71] The employee needs to be incentivised, but simultaneously the regulated firm has invested salary and other benefits, which mean a balance needs to be struck between fair treatment of employees versus revenue. Common law provides many useful cases on the issue of employee inventions. However, for many decades statute has also governed.[72] In the case study below surrounding a trading system at the LIFFE the reading of the relevant sections of statute were covered. In that court case it was also made clear that while employee duties are primarily captured in contracts of employment, the reality is that over time roles evolve, making it unsafe to rely on only contractual terms.[73]

9.15.1 Case study on the LIFFE

The appellant Dr Pavel Pinkava was employed by the LIFFE, the operator of the London Futures Exchange, as a manager in its Interest Rate Product (IRP) Management Team in July 2001. In July 2004 he invented a novel electronic trading system for various financial instruments. He was promoted to senior manager in the same team on 13 September 2004.

---

[69] Current EPC member states include all the EEA, Albania, North Macedonia, Monaco, San Marino, Switzerland, Turkey and the UK. To check for future additional member states see www.epo.org/about-us/foundation/member-states.html.

[70] For an authoritative article-by-article analysis of the EPC, see Visser, D et al. (2019) *Visser's Annotated European Patent Convention* (Kluwer Law International).

[71] A recent Supreme Court decision dealt with the issue of the Section 40 Patents Act 1977 requirement to compensate employee patents that have contributed an outstanding benefit to the employer. See *Shanks v Unilever Plc & Ors* [2019] UKSC 45.

[72] The Patents Act 1977 was made law on 1 June 1978. For an in-depth analysis of the Patents Act 1977 in this context, see Johnson, P (2021) 'From Banks to Shanks; the History of Employee Awards for Patented Inventions under the Patents Act 1977', *Queen Mary Journal of Intellectual Property*, Volume 11, Issue 2.

[73] *LIFFE Administration and Management v Pavel Pinkava* [2007] EWCA Civ 217.

In January 2005 Pinkava was advised by the LIFFE that he was entitled to be the owner of the invented IRP trading system. On 23 April 2005 Dr Pinkava filed four applications for US patents covering the trading system.[74] Thereafter, the LIFFE terminated Pinkava's employment on 13 July 2005. One week later, LIFFE also started proceedings claiming to be entitled to the confidential information relating to the system devised by Pinkava and the patent applications based on it. Subsequently, at a first instance hearing instigated by Pinkava claiming ownership of the four US patents, the judge concluded that:

- the inventions were not made in the course of the normal duties of Pinkava as an employee of the LIFFE;[75]
- the inventions were made as part of duties specifically assigned to him;[76] and
- the circumstances were such that an invention might reasonably be expected to result from the carrying out of the specific duties.[77]

At first instance, the LIFFE was held to be the owner of the inventions claimed in the US patent applications. The appeal by Pinkava was dismissed. However, a different conclusion was reached, specifically that the US patents belonged to the LIFFE because each invention was made in the course of Pinkava's normal duties.

The issues in the LIFFE case are recurring ones in the financial services sector, and increasingly so in FinTech environments where software developers may have a portfolio of work with more than one employer. In sum, if the employee activity is part of their general duties or specially assigned duties, for example a software developer dedicated to trading system advances, any patent linked to either focus is the property of the employer. As the statute makes clear, 'any other invention made by an employee shall, as between him and his employer, be taken for those purposes to belong to the employee'.[78]

---

[74] As discussed earlier in this chapter, Section 1(2)(c) Patents Act 1977 excludes such patents under English law. But they are available under US law. For example, in 1999 Amazon was granted a patent for its one-click buying invention (US Patent US5960411A). This patent expired in 2017. However, for financial services business with an interest in the US market, the granting of US patents for business methods and computer programs is increasingly harder.

[75] Section 39(1)(a) Patents Act 1977.

[76] Section 39(1)(a) Patents Act 1977.

[77] Section 39(1)(a) Patents Act 1977.

[78] Section 39(2) Patents Act 1977.

9.16   Case study on *Thaler v Comptroller*

The issue of how AI machine learning should be treated in the context of patent ownership was raised by a Dr Stephen Thaler before the Patents Court.[79] To summarise the facts, Thaler developed a machine learning-based computer program which he called 'DABUS'. In his patent application, Thaler described DABUS as a creativity machine. In essence, DABUS used artificial neural networks to generate ideas. Then a second artificial network identified ideas it measured to be novel compared with the second artificial network's pre-existing knowledge.[80] Thaler submitted the patent application naming DABUS as the inventor primarily based on the view that DABUS independently conceived of the inventions it generated.

Under statute, there are three persons that may be granted a patent, namely (a) the inventor or joint inventors; (b) any person(s) based on domestic law, foreign law, convention, treaty or under an agreement;[81] and (c) any successors of (a) or (b).[82] Principally based on this section, the judge concluded:

> DABUS is not a person, whether natural or legal. DABUS is not a legal person because (unlike corporations) it has not had conferred upon it legal personality by operation of law. It is not a natural person because it lacks those attributes that an entity must have in order to be recognised as a person in the absence of specific (statutory) legal intervention.[83]

This decision confirms that under English law a patent inventor must be either a natural or legal person, and that a machine has no legal personality.[84]

Of special interest to regulated firms investing in machine learning development, Thaler's appeal did not include arguments on whether the

---

[79]   *Thaler v Comptroller of Patents, Designs and Trade Marks* [2020] EWHC 2412 (Pat).

[80]   Chapter 12 Machine learning considers the central legal and regulatory issues on machine learning.

[81]   In the vast majority of situations this person will be an employer.

[82]   Section 7(2) Patents Act 1977.

[83]   *Thaler v Comptroller of Patents, Designs and Trade Marks* [2020] EWHC 2412 (Pat) per Smith J, at 34.

[84]   Section 7(1) Patents Act 1977 only states that the patent applicant must be a 'person'. There was no argument in this appeal that DABUS was a person or had 'legal personality' in the corporate law sense of that word.

human controlling a machine that creates an invention can be the inventor for the purposes of patent ownership. Thaler's patent application made explicit that he was not the inventor – the inventor was DABUS. Further, he was not arguing that the machine's patent was being transferred to him to make him the owner of the machine's invention.[85] These two points may seem surprising, even metaphysical ones, but commercial fortunes may be lost or won from an inaccurate understanding of how English law develops its classification of legal personality and machine learning technology. Legal counsel will need to monitor how that issue is dealt with by UK patent assessors and in any future appeals.[86]

9.17 Auditing

The starting point for protecting the IP of any regulated firm is to understand and record precisely what a company owns, what trade secrets it needs to protect, what patents it has filed and what other IP it has registered. Therefore the legal function in cooperation with research, product development and other front office business functions need to conduct regular audits of its IP. The way to conduct an IP audit is: (a) first to answer a number of internal audit questions, and then (b) to go on to answer a number of external audit questions that focus on licensing and third-party IP. The questions that need to be answered for the internal audit are set out in Table 9.2.

Regularly answering the above questions can act as the most effective form of IP protection by preventing expenditure on negotiating or litigating disputes. Amongst the questions in Table 9.2 there is no hierarchy of importance. For example, checking that all contracts with subcontractors adequately cover ownership can be valued as the most key question for financial services businesses developing products and systems with proprietary information. However, many of the most valuable corporate IP

---

[85] Section 30(1) Patents Act 1977 allows for the transfer of patent ownership: 'Any patent or application for a patent is personal property ... and any patent or any such application and rights in or under it may be transferred'.

[86] No doubt any future machine learning appeal will include reference to *Yeda Research and Development Company Ltd v Rhone-Poulenc Rorer International Holdings* [2007] UKHL 43. At 20 Lord Hoffman concluded 'The inventor is defined in section 7(3) as "the actual deviser of the invention". The word "actual" denotes a contrast with a deemed or pretended deviser of the invention.'

Table 9.2   Internal audit questions

Internal audit questions	Document, policy or person confirming answer
Who owns the IP?	
Has the regulated firm any obsolete IP?	
If others use the regulated firm's IP what are the terms?	
Do contracts with employees or subcontractors adequately cover ownership?	
Has the regulated firm proper procedure when disclosing confidential information?	
Has the regulated firm sufficient protection where it matters most, especially core IP?	

assets are protected by trade secrets, so rigorous procedures for keeping commercially sensitive information within a regulated firm and setting out clearly what can and cannot be externally disclosed can be more important.

There needs to be constant monitoring of IP law, including litigation rules, in the countries in which the regulated firm markets products and services. That may reduce the risk of disputes and on the occasions when litigation cannot be avoided, the cost of litigation. For instance, currently the registration of European patents are granted by the EPO in Munich, Germany providing patent protection across the 31 contracting countries that apply this continental system. However, infringements are litigated on a country-by-country basis, often resulting in unpredictable outcomes because each jurisdiction may reach a different outcome.

Turning to external auditing, the legal function needs to answer a number of external audit questions that focus on third party IP and licensing. The questions that need to be answered for the external audit phase are listed in Table 9.3.

Potentially the most valuable external audit questions are the last two questions in Table 9.3 because considerable IP expense can be saved by researching into and then using lower cost IP, rather than entering into

Table 9.3   *External audit questions form*

External audit questions	Document, policy or person confirming answer
Does your Company use or intend to use third-party IP?	
Is the IP properly protected?	
Are proper licensing agreements in place?	
What precisely has been licensed?	
Is all non-core IP being fully exploited?	
Is it possible and safe to lower the cost of IP?	
Are regular searches conducted of IP databases relevant to the regulated firm's existing and planned products?	

or extending IP licensing agreements made with more expensive third parties. Costs are secondary to effective legal advice, contract formation and risk management by the legal function, but such measures are important incremental contributions to sustaining competitiveness.

9.17.1 Practical implementation

A sample confidential in-house checklist for signing-off by both the legal counsel conducting the audits and the Head of Legal function is set out in Table 9.4. The Head of Legal will look to ensure the process of internal audit is regularly completed and remains confidential.

The legal counsel or team of lawyers conducting the audit should state the objective of the audit. For example, that the task is the '8th Formal Annual Audit'. They should also sign off the report attaching a one page executive summary explaining what has been audited, the IP issues the audit has raised, and also recommend ways of improving both the exploitation and protection of the regulated firm's IP, as well as stating the timescale for the implementation of suitable improvements.

The completion, signing and circulation of a succinct executive summary to senior management will also play a useful role in highlighting this valuable preventative role played by the legal function. To whom this exec-

Table 9.4   *IP audit*

This confidential document and the attached summary are for the view of the
following staff only: [insert name]; [insert name]; [insert name].

IP audit task	Type of evidence	Date reviewed
Patents held and filed.		
Patent renewals.		
Review of patent licensing arrangements.		
Search for patents dealing with the same activity.		
Check trademark names are registered, including all Internet-based domain names.		
Check all relevant trademark names are renewed.		
Discuss future product plans and launches with business units.		
Review trademark and design right licensing arrangements.		
Check legitimate trademark and design right usage.		
Search registers for similar marks or design rights registered by competitors.		
Check copyright notices comply with the Company standard.		
Identify copyrights of commercial value.		
Confirm ownership of copyrights.		
Review copyright licensing arrangements.		
Review confidentiality agreements with employees, subcontractors and joint venture partners.		

I confirm that all the above checks have been carried out. Any necessary
action has been taken or the date of any future action has been recorded
before the next scheduled review.

......................., Legal Counsel

Signed...........................

I have discussed the process and completion of this audit with the above Legal Counsel. I am satisfied that checks have been carried out and that any appropriate action has been taken.

…………………….., Head of Legal

Signed……......................................

WARNING: This checklist and attached summary are the confidential property of [insert full regulated firm name]. Its contents must not be sent or communicated to any person or entity that is not listed at the top of this page. If you have any query concerning this document please contact the Legal Department at email address [ ] or on telephone number [ ].

Source: © Iain Sheridan (2021).

utive summary is circulated needs to be stated precisely, indicating that the summary is highly confidential and not to be forwarded electronically or on paper to any employee, director or external adviser or consultant without the prior permission of the Head of Legal.

9.18   Final points

The FCA introduced the concept of a compliance culture. When first introduced, this was the equivalent of wearing in a new shoe – strange and uncomfortable. However, over time, whether in an asset manager, bank or platform, the substance of legal risk management is accepted as being at least half about how humans think and act to implement regulation. Equally, in my experience, there is significant value in cultivating the addition of an innovation protection culture.

As regulated firms rely more and more on technological advantages, such as data analytics and machine learning, cultivating an innovation protection culture becomes critical to revenues.[87] That requires financial regulation legal counsel to have more understanding of these main areas of IP. In a larger regulated firm there may continue to be dedicated IP/IT counsel. For most regulated firms, including the global leaders, it will

---

[87]   As Steven Woolley, a mercurial former Head of Compliance of ICAP once remarked to me, 'there is probably nothing more overlooked and problematic than the protection and valuing of ideas'. In 2016 ICAP was acquired by Tullett Prebon to become TP ICAP, globally one of the leading trading platforms.

always be extremely valuable to have financial regulation lawyers able to spot IP risks and opportunities as early as possible.

10. Competition

Exceptionally high value mergers and acquisitions in the financial services sector have tended to revolve around stock exchanges. However, the power of digital technology is changing that, especially with the exponential increase of client and consumer business occurring over the Internet. The regulated firms under the most competition scrutiny from regulators are leading incumbents, including the largest asset managers, investment banks, price comparison platforms and trading platforms.

10.1   Introduction

Legal counsel and compliance officers can find themselves working to support an acquisition or a merger. In either scenario, they need to have some understanding of current and likely future competition law that may affect expansion plans with different time scales, risk management choices and strategy up to board level.[1] In the UK financial services sector competition is concurrently managed by the Competition and Markets Authority (CMA) and the FCA.[2] The detailed legislative interplay between UK regulators on competition is helpfully explained in a summary by the FCA.[3] Further, an updated Memorandum of Understanding between the CMA and the FCA provides practical detail on their concurrent powers.[4] Table 10.1 captures the remit of the CMA, FCA and the Payment Systems Regulator (PSR).[5]

---

[1]   An authoritative and in-depth work on all aspects of competition is Scott, A et al. (2021) *Encyclopaedia of Competition Law* (Sweet & Maxwell).

[2]   Section 54(1)(j) Competition Act 1998; and Sections 234I to 234O FSMA 2000.

[3]   FCA FG15/8. (2018) FCA's Powers and Procedures under the Competition Act 1998.

[4]   CMA and FCA (2019) Memorandum of Understanding between the Competition and Markets Authority and the Financial Conduct Authority – Concurrent Competition Powers.

[5]   PSR (2021) CP21/7, Consultation Paper – Our Proposed PSR Strategy, at 1.13, sets out the PSR's proposed five year strategic plan. One of its four strategic priorities is to promote competition in the payment systems subsector.

Table 10.1   *Regulator functions*

Regulator	Areas of responsibility and focus
CMA	Competition powers across all sectors of the economy. Promoting competition for the benefit of consumers by investigations into businesses, investigating all market sectors, actions against businesses and producing policy papers. Focus of CMA advice to FCA concerns acts or omissions that 'may cause or contribute to the prevention, restriction or distortion of competition'.[1]
FCA	Concurrent powers with CMA.[2] Competition powers across the financial services sector. Promoting competition for the benefit of consumers by investigations into businesses, financial services sector investigations, actions against firms and producing policy papers.
PSR	Concurrent powers with CMA.[3] Competition powers focused on payment systems.[4] Promoting competition for the benefit of consumers by investigations into businesses, investigating all payment systems issues, and producing policy papers.[5]

Notes: [1] Section 140B(5) FSMA 2000. See www.legislation.gov.uk/ukpga/2000/8/section/140B. To clarify, the CMA will in the majority of situations be advising the FCA, but under the FSMA, s. 140A1(b), it also has the remit to advise the PRA. Further, under regulation 4 of the Competition Act 1998 (Concurrency) Regulations 2014, the CMA must inform in writing any UK regulator of cases over which there is concurrent jurisdiction. [2] Section 234J FSMA 2000. [3] Section 66 Financial Services (Banking Reform) Act 2013. [4] See Chapter 11 Payment services. [5] Section 50 Financial Services (Banking Reform) Act 2013 is a detailed list of competition objectives that includes the promotion of effective competition in the market for payment systems, ease of market entry for new participants, and the extent to which competition is encouraging innovation.

10.2 FCA and CMA approaches to competition

The FCA's focus on competition law[6] is not just a prosecutorial deterrent. In fact it has considerable scope to alter potential anti-competitive behaviour by issuing advisory or on notice letters. Neither type of letter

---

[6]   Details on how the FCA can use its concurrent powers are summarised in FCA FG15/8, FCA's Powers and Procedures under the Competition Act 1998.

is a formal decision.[7] With either letter the FCA can influence changes in all regulated firms levering technology as part of their revenue generating strategies.

The CMA 'has powers to initiate market investigations, gather and appraise evidence and also impose structural and behavioural remedies'.[8] Arguably it is not just a matter of good law and guidelines, given the CMA needs access to independent information on pricing along with insights to make balanced decisions on when anti-competitive practices exist. Absent such roles, there is a real risk 'that sector regulators, even the most dedicated ones, may fail to understand and predict market dynamics'.[9] However, evidence from the CMA's responses to a House of Lords investigation into online platforms reveals an organisation aware that over-zealous regulation may stifle innovation.[10] This online platform report recorded that the CMA focused on the potentially anti-competitive effects of 'disproportionate regulatory mechanisms', which could have 'the counterproductive effect of "locking-in" a particular market structure', and thereby 'insulate incumbent on-line firms from dynamic competition that would otherwise benefit consumers'.[11]

There has already been CMA scrutiny of trading platforms, namely the acquisition by Tullett Prebon plc of ICAP plc's broking and information businesses. As part of that merger process, instead of applying its own anti-competitive remedies to a merger scenario,[12] the CMA accepted appropriate 'undertakings in lieu' aimed at mitigating or preventing the substantial lessening of competition expected to occur from the impact of the merger.[13] Those published undertakings may assist counsel working

---

[7]   An advisory letter has an educational aim. In contrast, a notice letter requires the firm to reply with an explanation on its acts, omissions and remedial plans. See FCA FG15/8, at 3.12.

[8]   Guidelines for Market Investigations: Their Role, Procedures, Assessment and Remedies, CC3 (Revised) (April 2013). See www.gov.uk/government/organisations/competition-and-markets -authority.

[9]   Ezrachi, A, and Stucke, M (2016) *Virtual Competition – The Promise and Perils of the Algorithm-Driven Economy* (Harvard University Press), at 216.

[10] House of Lords, Online Platforms and the EU Digital Single Market, 10th Report of Session 2015–16, 20 April 2016 – HL Paper 129.

[11] HL Paper 129, Competition and Markets Authority – Written evidence (OPL0055), at paragraph 45.

[12] Sections 22 and 33 Enterprise Act 2002. See www.legislation.gov.uk/ukpga/2002/40/section/22; and www.legislation.gov.uk/ukpga/2002/40/section/33.

[13] Section 73 Enterprise Act 2002. See www.legislation.gov.uk/ukpga/2002/40/section/73.

with platforms in the planning phase of a merger.[14] More generally, they can assist any regulated firm in gaining insights into the 'undertakings in lieu' process.

10.3   Regulations compared

In the context of cross-border financial services it is useful to see how UK law compares with the EU, US and China. It is beneficial to have a broader understanding of the reasons for one of these actors taking enforcement action or blocking a planned acquisition or merger. In sum, Table 10.2 illustrates that it is not necessarily always politics that drives decisions, but the legal principles and jurisprudence can be equally influential. In turn, knowing this may assist in anticipating if proposals made by clients are likely to be accepted by regulators and commercially progress.[15]

10.4   UK competition law

From a UK perspective, the concept of dominance has its roots in EU case law. Dominant market position has been consistently defined as 'a position of economic strength enjoyed by an undertaking which enables it to prevent effective competition being maintained on the relevant market by affording it the power to behave to an appreciable extent independently of its competitors, customers and ultimately of its consumers'.[16] Further, it is also important to emphasise that based on CMA guidance, dominance is inextricably linked to substantial market power.[17]

In the context of financial services there is the initial logic of thinking about market economic strength and substantial market power as rele-

---

[14]   CMA (2016) Undertakings Given by *Tullett Prebon plc* and *ICAP plc* to the Competition and Markets Authority Pursuant to Section 73 of the Enterprise Act 2002. See https://assets.publishing.service.gov .uk/media/57da7601ed915d6c2f000056/tullett-icap-final-undertakings.pdf.

[15]   The comparison table of UK, China, EU and US regulations does not include reference to state aid principles.

[16]   Case 27/76 *United Brands v Commission* [1978] ECR 207, [1978] 1 CMLR 429.

[17]   At the risk of being accused of pedantry, the CMA guidance was in fact that of the Office of Fair Trading (OFT), the predecessor to the CMA. See OFT (2004) Abuse of a Dominant Position – Understanding Competition Law, at 13.

Table 10.2　　*Key aspects of competition law in China, the EU, the UK and the US*

Jurisdiction	Aspects relevant to the financial services sector
UK	Prohibition on the abuse of a dominant position within the UK. The abuse may include, among other things, unfair pricing or other unfair trading conditions, applying dissimilar conditions to equivalent transactions, and making contracts subject to acceptance by the counter-party of supplementary obligations which commercially or practically have no connection with the contract subject matter.[1] Prohibition on agreements or practices in the UK that potentially affect or actually distort, prevent or restrict competition.[2] A completed merger may result in a substantial lessening of competition within any UK market.[3] An imminent merger may result in a substantial lessening of competition within any UK market.[4] A turnover test – based on greater than £70 million turnover of the entity being taken over.[5] If a proposed acquisition or merger is considered to pose an unacceptable risk to national security, the National Security and Investment Act 2021 (NSIA 2021) provides the power to block the transaction.[6] The relevant percentage share ownership or voting rights tests are from 25% or less to more than 25%, from 50% or less to more than 50%, or from less than 75% to 75% or more.[7] In addition, there are another two acquisition situations that require mandatory notification. First, where the acquisition of voting rights enable a person to 'secure or prevent' the passing of any class of resolution under the entity's constitution.[8] A turnover test – based on greater than £1 million to £70 million turnover for specifically listed technology activities, including AI, cryptographic authentication and QC.[9] In the alternative, a share of supply test – based on a completed or anticipated merger that creates a new entity supplying greater than or equal to 25% of the total UK market or greater than or equal to 25% of a substantial part of a UK market.[10]
China	Prohibition on the abuse of a dominant position based principally on control of price, quantity or terms of trade, or to influence the ability of another entity to enter a market.[11] Special turnover threshold tests apply to the financial services sector.

Jurisdiction	Aspects relevant to the financial services sector
EU	Prohibition on the abuse of a dominant position within the EU internal market.[12] Note there is no attempted monopolisation law. Prohibition on agreements or practices within the EU that potentially affect or actually distort, prevent or restrict competition.[13]
US	Prohibition on every contract, combined arrangement or conspiracy in restraint of trade.[14] Prohibition on monopolising or attempting to monopolise or conspiring to monopolise.[15] Mergers and acquisitions that substantially lessen competition.[16]

Notes: [1] Section 18 Competition Act 1998. [2] Section 2 Competition Act 1998. [3] Section 22 Enterprise Act 2002. [4] Section 33 Enterprise Act 2002. [5] Section 23(b)(i) Enterprise Act 2002. [6] Importantly, The City Code on Takeovers and Mergers (the 'Code'), deriving its statutory basis under Chapter 1 of Part 28 (sections 942 to 965) of the Companies Act 2006, will not have specific amendments covering how the NSIA 2021 interacts with the Code. However, the Code Committee has produced valuable guidance of what it expects professional advisers, including legal counsel, to advise clients to do. This guidance is summarised in Takeover Panel RS 2020/1 (2021) Conditions to Offers and the Offer Timetable, at 1.18. [7] Section 8(2)-(5) NSIA 2021, covered in detail later in this chapter. [8] Section 8(6) NSIA 2021. [9] Sections 23(b)(ii) Enterprise Act 2002 and Section 23(1)(b) Enterprise Act 2002 listing the qualifying technologies and contexts of their research or use. [10] Section 23(4A) Enterprise Act 2002. In *Sabre Corporation v Competition and Markets Authority* [2021] CAT 11, the Competition Appeal Tribunal judgment confirmed there is no de minimis threshold to this ≥25 per cent share of supply test. The CMA investigated the proposed acquisition of a target company that represented less than 1% of the pre-merger market supply. Although it is important to note that Sabre Corporation had a pre-merger supply that was already above 25%. The CMA's investigation resulted in the deal not proceeding. [11] Article 17 of the PRC Anti-Monopoly Law 2007, applying throughout the PRC with the exceptions of Hong Kong (SAR) and Macau. An authoritative book on this subject is Kikkoris, I, Maniatis, S, and Wang, X (2019) *Competition Law and Intellectual Property in China* (Oxford University Press). In Chapter 10 entitled 'Abuse of Dominance and Intellectual Property in China', at 196, the authors point out that 'China is still a comparatively new player in the antitrust world but it has grown quickly and it is currently one of the most important emerging jurisdictions for antitrust enforcement ... Intensifying enforcement action in China over recent years suggests that IP-centred, or related, business models and practices will face growing antitrust scrutiny over the next few years.' Readers may logically assess IP-centred businesses as patent-driven telecommunications companies and software providers. However, financial services business models relying on algorithms and databases will equally need to take legal advice in both their home jurisdiction and China before implementing long term strategies. [12] Article 102 Treaty on the Functioning of the European Union (TFEU). [13] Article 101 TFEU. [14] Section 1 Sherman Antitrust Act 1890. [15] Section 2 Sherman Antitrust Act 1890. [16] Section 7 Clayton Antitrust Act 1914 as amended.

vant to a handful of market leaders, whether asset managers, investment banks or platforms. However, as technology becomes a central part of competitive advantage, it is likely that some smaller regulated firms will come under the scrutiny of the CMA and FCA; for example, if any asset manager or established FinTech firm enters a joint venture with Ali Baba, Amazon, Apple, Facebook, Google or Microsoft to provide advisory services based on machine learning applications not available to any other asset manager.

10.4.1 Consequences of anti-competitive behaviour

The CMA has wide powers of enforcement. Regulated firms can potentially overlook that the CMA's power to just investigate can cause significant cost and loss of time. That decision alone will tie up considerable senior management time and legal resources.[18] Added to these immediate pressures is a power to publish notice of an investigation.[19] During investigations the CMA can impose interim measures stopping potential anti-competitive behaviour until a final decision is made.[20] It can also accept appropriate commitments from an entity under investigation to take specific action or refrain from taking such action as appropriate.[21]

In terms of financial penalties, the CMA has power to impose a penalty of up to 10 per cent of annual worldwide group turnover.[22] In the example of ComparetheMarket, its imposition of a 'most favoured nation' (MFN) clause in its contract with insurance providers resulted in a £17.9 million fine.[23] For the benefit of readers outside the UK, ComparetheMarket is a well-established price comparison platform.[24] In brief, the facts were that ComparetheMarket breached competition law by imposing wide MFN clauses on providers of home insurance published on its platform. These MFN clauses prohibited the insurance providers from offering lower prices on alternative price comparison platforms. Further, ComparetheMarket's price position created by the MFN clause meant that the growth of competitors was slowed in a subsector where

---

[18] Section 25 Competition Act 1998.
[19] Ibid., at Section 25A.
[20] Ibid., at Section 35.
[21] Ibid., at Section 31A.
[22] Ibid., at Section 36.
[23] CMA (2020) CMA Fines *ComparetheMarket* £17.9m for Competition Law Breach.
[24] ComparetheMarket is regulated by the FCA. See www.comparethemarket.com.

ComparetheMarket was already strongly positioned. From a consumer perspective, the CMA concluded that the MFN resulted in higher insurance premiums.

Memorably, as a precursor of how UK regulators view technology, the CMA's enforcement statement in the ComparetheMarket case concluded that 'digital markets can yield great benefits for competition, and therefore for consumers. We are determined to secure those benefits, and to ensure that competition is not illegitimately restricted. Today's action should come as a warning – when we find evidence that the law has been broken, we will not hesitate to step in and protect consumers.'[25]

10.4.2 FCA enforcement

In December 2019, in its first competition law decision, the FCA found that three asset managers, Hargreave Hale Ltd ('Hargreave'), Newton Investment Management Limited ('Newton') and River and Mercantile Asset Management LLP ('RAMAM'), breached FCA rules. In brief, the anti-competitive acts consisted of the sharing of strategic information, between competing asset managers during (a) an initial public offering (IPO), and (b) one placing, just before the share prices were set. The firms disclosed or accepted what should have been confidential bids, namely the price they were willing to pay and to a lesser extent their preferred volume. Consequently, each firm got to know another's plans during the IPO or placing process when they should have been competing for shares.[26]

The commercial harm of these actions was asset managers undermining a process by which prices should have been left to natural market dynamics. At any IPO or placing each issuer is attempting to raise the maximum amount of capital. The divulging of confidential buying intentions is more likely than not to reduce the share price achieved. Each investment manager increased its profit and potentially increased the cost of finance for the capital raising company.[27]

---

[25] CMA (2020) CMA Fines *ComparetheMarket* £17.9m for Competition Law Breach.

[26] FCA (2019) FCA Issues its First Decision under Competition Law. See www.fca.org.uk/news/press-releases/fca-issues-its-first-decision-under-competition-law.

[27] Ibid., 47.

The FCA fined Hargreave £306,300 and RAMAM £108,600. The FCA did not impose a fine on Newton because it was given immunity under the competition leniency programme. By which is meant when a business that has been involved in alleged cartel activity assists the FCA with its investigation, in return that regulated firm may be granted immunity from penalties or a significant reduction in penalty.[28]

Significantly, the most senior FCA strategy director highlighted that:

> this is our first case using our competition law powers and demonstrates our commitment to taking enforcement action to protect competition. Asset managers must take care to avoid undermining how prices are properly set for shares in both IPOs and placings. Failure to do so risks them acting illegally. The FCA will act when markets that play a vital role in helping companies raise capital in the UK's financial markets are put at risk. We can also take regulatory action against an individual and did so here with respect to some of the same facts.[29]

The reference to individuals affected by the decision concerned a £32,200 fine imposed on a former fund manager at Newton concerning his conduct in relation to an IPO and a placing. On two occasions, the former Newton fund manager submitted orders as part of a book build for shares that were to be quoted on public exchanges. Before the order books for the new shares closed, the fund manager contacted other fund managers at competitor firms and attempted to influence them to cap their orders at the same price limit as his own orders. In so doing, the FCA viewed his actions as an attempt to use collective power, behaviour that potentially undermined the integrity of the market and the book build process.[30]

In the FCA's judgement, the fund manager failed to observe proper standards of market conduct. He was also found to have acted without due skill, care and diligence by failing to give proper consideration to the risks of engaging in these communications.[31] On this decision, the FCA head of enforcement commented that 'this matter underscores the importance

---

[28] FCA (2018) FG15/8: The FCA's Concurrent Competition Enforcement Powers for the Provision of Financial Services – A Guide to the FCA's Powers and Procedures under the Competition Act 1998.

[29] FCA (2019) FCA Issues its First Decision under Competition Law, by Christopher Woolard, at that time acting as the FCA's Executive Director of Strategy and Competition.

[30] Ibid.

[31] FCA (2019) FCA Fines Former Fund Manager Paul Stephany. See www.fca.org.uk/news/press-releases/fca-fines-former-fund-manager-paul-stephany.

of fund managers taking care to avoid undermining the proper price formation process in both IPOs and placings'.[32] The increasing role of technology in both IPOs and book building processes requires additional caution by fund managers.

10.4.3 Merger activity involving specific technologies

Before July 2020, the merger test threshold for merged businesses being referred to the CMA for investigation was a turnover exceeding £70 million.[33] However, since 20 July 2020 the turnover test has been amended to a turnover exceeding £1 million for the following activities:[34]

- AI research;
- cryptographic authentication research;
- ownership, development or supply of IP concerning the functional capability of computer processing units, instruction set architecture units and any code that provides low level control for such units;
- QC research;
- any services employing QC communication or simulation; or quantum resistant cryptography;
- any services employing AI; and
- any services employing cryptographic authentication.

Additionally, regulated firms and start-ups seeking to expand in the financial services sectors with a turnover figure below the £1 million threshold may still be investigated at the discretion of the Secretary of State on the grounds of public interest. In this context, original AI projects and quantum cryptography may experience special attention regardless of their turnover level.[35]

There is also a merger test based on 'share of supply'. Specifically, the threshold is based on services supplied in the UK amounting to at least 25 per cent of the UK market or a 'substantial part of the UK'.[36] This second share of supply test may seem an unlikely consideration in financial

---

[32] Ibid., comment by Mark Steward, Executive Director of Enforcement and Market Oversight at the FCA.

[33] Section 23(1)(b) Enterprise Act 2002.

[34] The Enterprise Act 2002 (Turnover Test) (Amendment) Order 2020.

[35] Section 42 Enterprise Act 2002.

[36] Section 23(4A) Enterprise Act 2002.

services markets. However, with stock exchanges and other trading platforms this would be relevant. For example, the TP ICAP platform group amounts to one-quarter or more of MTFs in London.[37]

10.4.4 The National Security and Investment Act 2021

The flawed £1 million threshold test added into the Enterprise Act 2002 has been superseded in the context of cutting-edge technologies by the introduction of the National Security and Investment Act 2021 (NSIA 2021).[38] The NSIA 2021 creates a new regime for vetting both foreign and national investment in the UK. While the main political driver behind the NSIA 2021 is national defence and security, it will certainly play a role in the make-up of actors supplying technology not only to established regulated firms but also new FinTech ventures.

Covering 17 sectors including AI, computing hardware, cryptographic authentication, data infrastructure and quantum technologies, the NSIA 2021 introduces a mandatory notification regime. Therefore, sectors that are potential long-term levers of competitive advantage in the financial services sector will all be scrutinised by the Secretary of State. If a proposed acquisition or merger is considered to pose an unacceptable risk to national security, the NSIA 2021 provides the power to block the transaction.

10.5 Competition and algorithms

The vision that algorithms driven by computers should be essential components of financial services markets has been the focus of brilliant minds for several decades,[39] although the pace of technology and its costs meant that human decision making based on analysis and experience

---

[37] Available at https://assets.publishing.service.gov.uk/media/57da7601ed915d6c2f000056/tullett-icap -final-undertakings.pdf. See also Chapter 8 Trading platforms.

[38] The NSIA 2021 was enacted on 29 April 2021, and was made effective on 4 January 2022.

[39] For instance, in his 1975 Nobel Prize Lecture entitled 'Mathematics in Economics: Achievements, Difficulties, Perspectives', the Russian economist Leonid Kantorovich shared his understanding and ambition for algorithms optimising the market challenges of prediction and allocation. See www .nobelprize.org/nobel_prizes/economic-sciences/laureates/1975/kantorovich-lecture.html.

continued to determine investment advice and trading up until the turn of this century.

10.5.1 Case study on Athena Capital Research

The use of algorithms in capital markets in the context of competition law demonstrated that early legal counsel advice and decision making really matter. For instance, a SEC case against Athena Capital Research ('Athena') is illustrative of how human-controlled algorithms levered on technology can have anti-competitive effects.[40]

The Athena case concerned HFT on the NASDAQ.[41] The facts were that Athena, a quantitative investment manager, implemented a manipulative HFT scheme on almost every trading day for a six-month period, namely June to December 2009.[42] The Athena algorithm made large purchases or sales of stocks in the last two seconds of NASDAQ trading. The Athena strategy was to make a profit by driving the closing price either higher or lower in the last two seconds of trading.

To understand how Athena made a profit it is necessary to briefly explain how NASDAQ functions. Trading always ceases at 16:00 hours. Ten minutes before, at 15:50 hours, NASDAQ informs market participants of the predicted closing imbalances for each stock. Then at 16:00 hours the closing price of each stock is determined by NASDAQ's proprietary auction algorithm. The reasoning logic behind this auction algorithm is to minimise market volatility by matching as many buyers and sellers at the close of trading as possible.[43]

An example of Athena's strategy is set out in Table 10.3. The 15:50 hours published closing imbalance for eBay Inc (EBAY) was 224,638 Buy Imbalance. By which is meant NASDAQ predicted there would be 224,638 buy orders without matching sellers. At that same point in time Athena placed a Sell Imbalance order for 224,638 shares, simultaneously

---

[40] SEC (2014), In the Matter of *Athena Capital Research LLC*, Release No. 73369, 16 October 2014. See www.sec.gov/litigation/admin/2014/34-73369.pdf.

[41] Chapter 8 Trading platforms includes a summary of HFT and applicable financial regulation.

[42] www.athenacr.com.

[43] SEC (2014), In the Matter of *Athena Capital Research LLC*, Release No. 73369, 16 October 2014, at 6–7.

Table 10.3   *Athena HFT in the last two seconds*

Time	Order price	Quantity	Exchange
15:59:58.355	$23.81	11,200	BATS[1]
15:59:58.503	$23.81	22,400	BATS
15:59:59.403	$23.81	33,600	BATS
15:59:59.705	$23.81	5,600	NASDAQ
15:59:59.870	$23.81	28,000	BATS
15:59:59.950	$23.81	11,200	Nasdaq

Note: [1] BATS was acquired by CBOE in 2017.

placing an order for 85,300 shares at $23.56.[44] Just before 15:59:58, the National Best Offer[45] for EBAY was $23.58. Table 10.3 illustrates how in the last two seconds of trading Athena's HFT algorithm was able to move the price of the EBAY stock.[46] Within this final two second window Athena's trading amounted to 71 per cent of the entire trading activity in EBAY stocks.[47]

At 15:59:59.963 the National Best Offer was $23.60. Thereafter, Nasdaq's closing auction algorithm matched as many buyers and sellers at a price nearest to the last trading price. Athena's Sell Imbalance orders were filled at $23.61. In sum, Athena's profit in the last two seconds of trading was $.03, because its HFT algorithm had driven the price from $23.58 to $23.60 – thereafter NASDAQ provided an auction price of $23.61.[48] Based on the evidence of internal emails, Athena referred to its HFT strategy as 'dominating the auction' and 'owning the game'.[49] The consequence of Athena's HFT activity was 'Cease and Desist Order' and censure by the SEC. While Athena did not admit guilt, it paid a US$1 million fine.[50]

---

[44] Ibid.

[45] The National Best Offer is the best available ask price made available to customers or brokers as required by US SEC rules.

[46] The two second time duration is not a typographical error.

[47] SEC (2014), In the Matter of *Athena Capital Research LLC*, Release No. 73369, 16 October 2014, at 6–7.

[48] Ibid.

[49] Ibid., at 7.

[50] Ibid., at 11.

Two points arise from the Athena case with potentially important consequences. First, given the subsequent advances in computer processing speeds, machine learning and cutting-edge communications such as 5G, the sophistication of algorithmic anti-competitive strategies may achieve considerable profits before regulators are able to spot the breach. Second, machine learning may present the risk of breaches because an algorithm develops in response to competitor algorithms that in combination amount to anti-competitive behaviour. This may occur because of tacit collusion, a market dynamic that is currently not unlawful.[51] To elaborate, the concept of tacit collusion refers to an outcome similar to express collusion or even a cartel which develops despite no express collusion between participants. By which is meant there is a complete absence of communication between competitors over pricing or market allocation, but the result is the same as unlawful express collusion.[52] Over time there is evidence of anti-competitive intent.

Tacit collusion can only take place in markets with price transparency. By which is meant, where competitors have real-time access to competitor prices. In financial markets all forms of trading venues are required to be transparent in detailed, specific ways.[53] Trading venues include RMs, MTFs, OTFs and SIs. The regulator's overarching aim is for 'a high degree of transparency ... This high degree of transparency should also establish a level playing field between trading venues so that the price discovery process in respect of particular financial instruments is not impaired by the fragmentation of liquidity, and investors are not thereby penalised.'[54]

In the context of machine learning, tacit collusion is likely to occur on trading venues. Each leading venue participant will have the resources

---

[51] Ezrachi, A, and Stucke, M (2016) *Virtual Competition – The Promise and Perils of the Algorithm-Driven Economy* (Harvard University Press), at 56–57.

[52] In *Brooke Group Ltd v Brown & Williamson Tobacco Corp*, 509 US 209 (1993) the US Supreme Court gave the following explanation: 'Tacit collusion, sometimes called oligopolistic price coordination or conscious parallelism, describes the process, not in itself unlawful, by which firms in a concentrated market might in effect share monopoly power, setting their prices at a profit-maximizing, supra-competitive level by recognizing their share economic interests and their interdependence with respect to price and output decisions and subsequently unilaterally set their prices above the competitive level.'

[53] For example, multilateral trading facilities (MTFs) and organised trading facilities (OTFs) both have extensive rules on transparency obligations and requirements. See Commission Delegated Regulation 2017/587 covering MTFs; and Commission Delegated Regulation 2017/583 applicable to OTFs.

[54] Recital 1, Commission Delegated Regulation 2017/583.

to programme their algorithms to maximise profits. Over time, the algorithm-based programs of each leading venue will have an acute understanding of competitor venue pricing of trading fees based on historic data, real-time data and sophisticated prediction of imminent pricing. Each algorithm will learn that rapidly matching the discounted pricing of competitors does not work, because the consequence is narrower profit margins. Equally, the algorithms will learn that if one venue increases its trading fees they can, with limits, follow suit. In sum, the risk of algorithm-driven markets in the context of high transparency is the likelihood of higher prices created by tacit collusion.[55]

After examining the threat of different types of tacit collusion, the CMA's conclusion was:

> the risks of collusion in real-world markets is unclear due to a relative paucity of empirical evidence ... there have been few enforcement cases by competition authorities against firms that used pricing algorithms to enforce explicit collusive agreements. It is as yet unclear that competition authorities can object ... to autonomous tacit collusion situations where, for example, there may not have been direct contact between two undertakings or a meeting of minds between them to restrict competition.[56]

The threat of tacit collusion while lacking empirical evidence still needs commercial consideration and regulator investment. A UK Treasury report on competition in digital markets takes the stance that 'should further evidence emerge of pricing algorithms tacitly co-ordinating of their own accord, a change in the legal approach may become necessary but the Panel [the body instructed to look into competition in digital markets] does not believe the evidence is sufficient to justify such a change at the current time'.[57]

---

[55] Ezrachi, A, and Stucke, M (2016) *Virtual Competition – The Promise and Perils of the Algorithm-Driven Economy* (Harvard University Press), at 61–62.

[56] CMA (2021) Algorithms: How They Can Reduce Competition and Harm Consumers, at 2.87.

[57] HM Treasury (2019) Unlocking Digital Competition, Report of the Digital Competition Expert Panel, at 110-111.

10.6   Tacit collusion incubators

In my view, when considering how effective traditional system-based computing is at facilitating HFT strategies, the sophistication and complexity of machine learning systems deserves pre-emptive risk investment by regulators. If we think back to the Athena HFT strategy case study, that was only one trading team. Based on SEC evidence from the investigation, one day's trading yielded a profit of $5,300.[58] The harm to market integrity caused by manipulations from, for example, a group of leading trading venues, could be of a different order of magnitude.

One viable way to manage the risk of tacit collusion is, in my view, for the FCA to invest in collusive simulations in the same spirit that it facilitates FinTech initiatives in the UK Sandbox programme. Many of the UK Sandbox participants, and also firms that applied to join and instead received FCA advice, rely on algorithms based on machine learning models. Additionally, it is notable that the CMA is already aware that pricing algorithms competing in simulations have revealed the ability to learn collusive strategies with punishment for deviation.[59] The insight value of regulatory incubators to understand tacit collusion has also been acknowledged by the Organization for Economic Cooperation and Development (OECD).[60]

10.7   Real-world simulations

A joint paper by the French and German national competition regulators provides, in my view, a practical approach that negates the potential UK Sandbox programme weaknesses of relying on an artificial setting with unrealistic inputs. Instead, one of the Franco-German proposals is to rely on predefined inputs that are assessed against the algorithm provided by the company using a relevant algorithm.[61] Further, the company might

---

58   SEC (2014), In the Matter of *Athena Capital Research LLC*, Release No. 73369, 16 October 2014, at 7.

59   CMA (2021) Algorithms: How They Can Reduce Competition and Harm Consumers, at 2.85.

60   OECD (2017) Roundtable on Algorithms and Collusion Algorithmic Collusion: Problems and Counter-Measures – Note by A Ezrachi and M Stucke, at 106. See www.oecd.org/officialdocuments/publicdisplaydocumentpdf/?cote=DAF/COMP/WD(2017)25&docLanguage=En.

61   Autorité de la Concurrence and Bundeskartellamt, Algorithms and Competition, at 71–72. Available at www.autoritedelaconcurrence.fr/sites/default/files/2019-11/2019-11-04_algorithms_and_competition.pdf.

provide an interface, such as an API for querying the algorithm or parts of it as it works on the firm's own system. This could be an existing commercial API or a newly established one for the specific benefit of the regulator. The Franco-German joint paper incisively points out that this API option might be particularly efficient for queries involving large sets of input parameters and potentially reduce the workload for the company providing the data as well.[62]

10.8 Legal tasks

From a short-term legal perspective, the risk of algorithmic tacit collusion amongst trading venues requires two tasks. First, there is a need to understand how the algorithms coded into trade pricing learn from competitor data. Second, contract drafting, whether from the perspective of a trading venue or imminent trading venue member, needs to include reference to liabilities and obligations on tacit collusion on pricing algorithms. In-house documentation to assist legal counsel in their due diligence and subsequent drafting includes, among other things:

- actual data sources;
- detail about the front office team that is dependent on the algorithm for revenue; .
- frequency of learning, recalibration or manual adjustments;
- front office specification provided to software engineers;
- functional specifications;
- log files documenting inputs and/or outputs;
- pseudo-code used during the development phase;
- usage patterns of the algorithm; and
- user guides or related technical documents.

From medium- and long-term viewpoints, tacit collusion requires really careful legal analysis on the liability of (a) colluding algorithms, and (b) the senior managers that approve the design of collusive models to provide and sell financial services. Some regulated firms have already raised that the legal definitions of 'agreement' and 'intention' will require

---

[62] Ibid.

special attention.[63] Readers of Chapter 4 Cryptoassets will be aware of the important role of the UKJT in producing a coherent and influential legal statement on the treatment of cryptoassets. In my view, there is a strong case for the UKJT to also enter the debate on tacit collusion.

10.9 Big Data and competitive realities

The term Big Data essentially refers to the collation and analysis of vast quantities of data primarily with the aid of algorithms. The anatomy of how Big Data is transforming capital markets is complex, because Big Data does not necessarily mean huge leaps in data quality. For instance, an eminent Harvard University statistics professor has pointed out that many current statistical measures covering errors and uncertainties are only meaningful when the sample data is perfect. He has observed that 'once we take into account the data quality, the effective sample size of a Big Data set can be vanishingly small'.[64]

As Big Data has risen in importance, so has the interest from established regulated firms to lever it, including by way of acquiring data and data science expertise. An existing example and pioneer is the LSE in its acquisition of Refinitiv.[65] The headline of this £22 billion acquisition, the joining of a world leading stock exchange with a world class data risk and analytics, belie the potential market influence. As captured in Figure 10.1, the synergies include the three main types of trading venues, RMs, MTFs and OTFs with world class data risk and analytics.

Despite this warranted scepticism, outside of the financial services sector there is a small cluster of immensely powerful platform providers, such as Amazon, Ant Group and Facebook that own vast data sets much of which is also qualitatively accurate. New UK and EU legislation is very likely to 'catch up' with this reality and provide structured ways for these uniquely large data sets to be shared with SMEs. Consequently, competition law is very likely to adjust to manage the dynamic of neither too little restric-

---

[63] CMA (2021) Algorithms: How They Can Reduce Competition and Harm Consumers – Summary of Responses to the Consultation, CMA 141con, at 3.39–3.30.

[64] Li Xiao Meng is the leading Statistics Professor at Harvard University. See 'Statistical Paradises and Paradoxes in Big Data', https://doi.org/10.1214/18-AOAS1161SF.

[65] See www.lseg.com/refinitiv-acquisition.

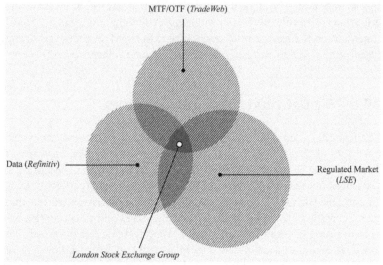

Source: © Iain Sheridan (2021).

Figure 10.1   *London Stock Exchange Group and Refinitiv*

tion on data sharing thereby stifling innovation, nor too much access, allowing SMEs and other regulated firms to free ride off the data owned by the largest platforms.[66] A leading competition law professor at Oxford University incisively put it this way: 'what we need to achieve from when we think of data sharing is this balanced approach when you try to leave sufficient incentives for the platforms and try not to harm their key activity, and at the same time create sufficient competitive pressure that reduces barriers to expansion and barriers to entry'.[67]

---

[66] The impact of the GDPR is also an easy to overlook added cost for SMEs. The cost of compliance with GDPR impacts younger SMEs which are often FinTech already burdened by compliance with myriad FSMA and FCA rules. For established asset managers, investment banks and platforms the costs are more easily absorbed so that can create a competition advantage.

[67] Slaughter and May (2021) Ariel Ezrachi, Professor of Competition Law, Oxford University, Regulating Digital – Competition and Privacy – the Best of Frenemies?, Podcast transcript, at 4.

10.10 Future competition and large FinTech firms

In 2020, a Digital Markets Taskforce (DMT) was formed and led by the CMA to examine how best to regulate the UK's dynamic digital ecosystem, made up of leading global companies, such as Alphabet, Amazon, Ant Group, Apple and Meta (previously Facebook Inc), and a myriad of SMEs and start-ups.[68] The key conclusions of the DMT included a proposal to form a Digital Markets Unit (DMU) within the CMA to, first, promote competition across digital markets. Consequently the DMU started functioning in non-statutory form in April 2021. Second, the DMU would oversee new regulation that includes the concept of a Strategic Market Status (SMS) designation for regulated firms that have substantial market power in at least one digital activity.[69] The SMS concept is not a regulation to date, but if followed through it would be relevant to the largest asset managers and banks that become dominant through the leverage of technology.

In the context of financial services it has been acknowledged that if a regulated firm was designated to have SMS, in the specific examples of payment services, cryptocurrencies, insurance or banking, the expert regulator is the FCA. The DMT put it this way: 'We expect the SMS regime to apply to only a limited number of the most powerful digital firms … It would be important for these activities to be regulated in a coherent way alongside wider sectoral regulation. Enabling the respective sectoral regulator to lead in relation to regulation of these activities would better enable coherent regulation.'[70]

Interestingly, in an independent report on regulating competition in digital markets by John Penrose MP, one of his key recommendations was that to prevent regulatory creep by the DMU it should be called the Network & Data Monopolies Unit (NDMU). Further that its powers should only apply to individual firms that own and run new network and data monopolies, rather than to the rest of the technology sector. This

---

[68] CMA (2020) A New Pro-competition Regime for Digital Markets.
[69] Ibid., at 7, paragraph 12.
[70] CMA (2020) Advice of the Digital Markets Taskforce. A New Pro-competition Regime for Digital Markets, at 77–78.

advice has not been followed, so the potential for regulatory creep by the DMU remains a possibility.[71]

Further, the EU has proposed the introduction of the Digital Markets Act designed to manage anti-competitive behaviour by the largest technology platforms.[72] The EU approach has some similarities when compared with the UK planned legislation. The EU focuses on strategic gatekeepers, defined as 'digital platforms with a systemic role in the internal market that function as bottlenecks between businesses and consumers for important digital services'.[73] The assessment criteria for gatekeepers includes, among other things, operating a platform with greater than 45 million monthly users in the EU or greater than 10,000 business users established in the EU in the last financial year.[74]

Of special note is the EU's plan for the Digital Markets Act to prevent anti-competitive behaviour by gatekeepers by way of *ex ante* regulation. This is planned to include the requirement that on being classified as a gatekeeper a regulated firm must comply, within six months, with a list of 'dos and don'ts'. For instance, one of the 'do' obligations for gatekeepers is to provide their business users with access to the data generated by their activities on the gatekeeper's platform.[75] Given the often considerable time lag between regulator investigations and final decision making, coupled with the fast-moving nature of digital technology, this is a potentially powerful legislative innovation. The potential consequences of non-compliance with the Digital Markets Act include fines and structural remedies, such as obliging a gatekeeper to sell a business, or parts of it.[76]

---

71 Penrose Report (2021) Power to the People. See https://assets.publishing.service.gov.uk/government/uploads/system/uploads/attachment_data/file/961665/penrose-report-final.pdf.

72 EC (2020) Digital Markets Act: Ensuring Fair and Open Digital Markets. See https://ec.europa.eu/info/strategy/priorities-2019-2024/europe-fit-digital-age/digital-markets-act-ensuring-fair-and-open-digital-markets_en.

73 EC (2020) The Digital Services Act package. See https://digital-strategy.ec.europa.eu/en/policies/digital-services-act-package.

74 Article 3(b) EU COM(2020) 842, final version of the proposed Digital Markets Act.

75 Ibid.

76 Ibid.

10.11 AI and competition law

The on-going challenge for regulators is to balance fairness with three equally important actors. First, there are consumers who have the least bargaining power and are least able to weather the consequences that a lack of competition and manipulation can have on their lives. Second, there are the regulated firms competing in each financial services sub-sector. Third, there are the leading incumbents that initially worked abnormally long hours and took high risks to develop their cutting-edge offerings. In sum, the point of balance is a complex triangular see-saw.

Turning to the regulatory risk viewpoint of machine learning, a key issue is how this competitive advantage opportunity may simultaneously increase the severity of regulator fines and other enforcement measures. Competition law does not yet specifically address the role of algorithms, but financial regulation does in capital markets.[77] However, under statute the FCA can take disciplinary action against any senior manager that 'did not take such steps as [he or she] ... could reasonably be expected to avoid the contravention occurring (or continuing)'.[78] The FCA Enforcement Division has provided some indirect guidance on FCA expectations concerning 'reasonable steps'.[79]

There is no reason to think that SMFs can ignore the introduction of investing or trading strategies reliant on machine learning without preparatory and on-going assessments of the impact. The complexity of this task is not something to understate, and the responsibility rests with senior authorised persons deciding to deploy machine learning strategies. The challenge has been analysed this way: 'Unlike humans, the computer does not fear detection and possible financial penalties or incarceration ... The computer can quantify the pay-offs that are likely achievable through

---

[77] Chapter 8 Trading platforms considers the regulation of algorithms in capital markets.

[78] Section 66A(5) FSMA 2000.

[79] From a transcript of an FCA Enforcement Director's speech the expectations include 'a person not exhibiting negligent behaviour, and evidence of asking questions and so informed and informing ... delegating when safe to do so to those who are well-placed, and only acting beyond expertise and experience with competent expert advice'. Available at www.fca.org.uk/news/speeches/tackling-hard -questions.

cooperation in future games, and opt for forbearance rather than punishing small deviations. It can also be more efficient in analysing pay-offs.'[80]

10.12 Big tech

The largest technology company operating platforms provide substantial benefits to consumers. That is, in part, based on the large pool of talented employees and contractors working on projects, and also massive annual R&D spending. However, there are also substantial anti-competitive risks. It has been memorably analysed that the largest platforms are:

> gate keepers ... and what happens is that within their own ecosystems they act as quasi-regulators. They set their own rules, they create the rules that govern the autonomy and as they do so, they also set the rules on what happens to data that they harvest or receive within their ecosystem ... often consent is either given as default, or might even be argued as forced consent, and it enabled them to leverage market power from one market to another within their own ecosystem.[81]

In sum, based on their growing dominance, the largest technology platforms are gaining increasing scrutiny from regulators which will in turn result in more regulation that specifically addresses competition issues unique to their gatekeeper bargaining power. Financial services is not immune to these regulatory changes given all large incumbent platforms seek to lever their existing vast customer bases, high quality data sets and trusted brands to offer credit, loans and payment systems.

---

[80]   Ezrachi, A, and Stucke, M (2016) *Virtual Competition – The Promise and Perils of the Algorithm-Driven Economy* (Harvard University Press), at 77.

[81]   Slaughter and May (2021) Ariel Ezrachi, Professor of Competition Law, Oxford University, Regulating Digital – Competition and Privacy – The Best of Frenemies?, Podcast transcript, at 6.

11. Payment services

For centuries it mattered where a bank or its branches were located. It was at these physical locations that a teller would 'over the counter' collect or pay you with cash, and where cheques would be simultaneously lodged. Even in the relatively recent past it mattered where a bank was located because their network of ATMs would provide cash at any time of the day.

11.1 Introduction

Currently, in diverse cultures, for example China and Sweden, the use of physical cash is swiftly diminishing. The UK is following suit. In 2009, 58 per cent of UK transactions used cash. In 2019, that reduced to 23 per cent.[1] The Covid-19 pandemic will have reduced that percentage down significantly. Replacing cash, consumers seek convenience and trust in new digital payment services to make local and cross-border purchases. In the UK, as captured in Figure 11.1, around 2017 the total number of debit card payments exceeded cash payments.[2]

This chapter addresses how financial regulation and UK regulators attempt to manage and plan to manage these rapidly burgeoning digital payment services providers. At the outset it is valuable to address how this is occurring so as to understand the interplay of regulation affecting FinTech payment services as a relatively new addition to financial services. Put in practical technological terms, virtually none of the current payment services platforms have much advantage without the evolution of smart phones as low-cost portable devices combined with the ability to process and store large volumes of data.[3]

---

[1] UK Finance (2020) UK Payment Markets Report 2020 Summary, at 4. See www.ukfinance.org.uk/system/files/UK-Payment-Markets-Report-2020-SUMMARY.pdf.

[2] Ibid., at 1.

[3] Note that this chapter is entitled payment services, not payment networks. An important HM Treasury documents incisively put it this way, 'a payment network describes the entirety of partici-

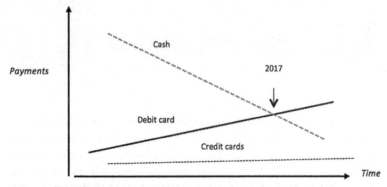

Note: This Figure is adapted from one that shows the number of payments for all types of payment methods, such as cheque and direct debit.
Source: Adaptation of UK Finance (2020) UK Payment Markets Report 2020 Summary, at 4. See www.ukfinance.org.uk/system/files/UK-Payment-Markets-Report-2020-Summary.pdf.

Figure 11.1   UK payment methods 2009–2019

11.2   Leading payment services providers

While there are many payment service providers, Table 11.1 provides an overview of some of the leading providers of special importance for the protection of consumers and the support of innovation across the UK.

It is worth emphasising that all the leading payment services firms shown in Table 11.1 are mature businesses in the UK with generally more than a decade of market activity. The exceptions are the two Chinese firms, Ali Pay and We Chat Pay,[4] which are extremely important in China and point to the potential trajectory of some of the Western equivalent regulated firms albeit in the context of hundreds of millions of customers across several jurisdictions. The technology-based success of both these Chinese behemoths influences UK regulators and the strategies of new UK FinTech regulated firms.

---

pants, processes and systems, and the links between them, which constitute the process for transmitting money from a payer to the payee using any particular payment instrument. It describes the entire chain from payer to payee.' HM Treasury (2020) Payments Landscape Review: Call for Evidence, Section 2.1, at 13.

4   WeChat Pay has more than 800 million users in mainland China.

Table 11.1   Leading payment services providers

Provider	Core service	Est'd
PayPal	Online money transfers	1998
Klarna	Online post purchase payments	2005
Amazon Payments	Online payment processing	2007
Google Wallet	Digital wallet and online payments	2015
WeChat Pay (Tencent)	Mobile payment App	2011
Square	Point of sale and online payments	2010
Ali Pay	Digital wallet and online payments	2004
Wise[1]	Online international money transfers	2011

Note: [1] Formerly called *TransferWise*. See www.wise.com.

Some of these new payment services are just one link in a payment chain made up of other activities which may be regulated by the FCA, supervised by the PSR or are unregulated. As a Bank of England report observed 'a typical "payment chain" … may now start with new non-bank entities using new technologies'.[5]

In the Chapter 1 reference was made to an established method applied by Japanese engineers called Ishikawa fishbone analysis.[6] A key critical thinking question for regulated firms to pose is where did things fall below perfection? Further, even though the users appear satisfied with the final outcome, what could have been done better? Figure 11.2 has adapted the Ishikawa fishbone to provide critical analysis techniques to payment services. It provides an opportunity to think across the vista of issues, some of which have interrelated risks and synergies.

The Ishikawa fishbone analysis starts with topics on the left-hand side tail. The order is not relevant, but from a logical structure it is easier to start with the treatment of 'Data', because the payer enters data in the form of his or her card details or other instructions and under agreed contractual

---

[5]   Bank of England (2019) Financial Policy Committee – Financial Stability Report, December 2019, at 83.

[6]   Ishikawa. K (1991) *Introduction to Quality Control* (Productivity Press).

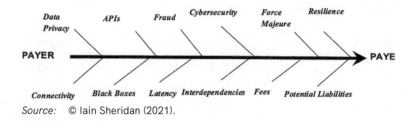

Source: © Iain Sheridan (2021).

Figure 11.2   Payments systems risks

terms over the Internet via a laptop, smartphone or tablet. A question to pose on Data is: has data privacy been maintained?

11.3   Summary of regulation

The three key pieces of regulation covering payment services are the Payment Services Directive (PSD 2),[7] PSD2-linked RTSs and the Electronic Commerce Directive. The main aims of PSD 2 include:

- contributing to a more integrated and efficient European payments market;
- encouraging lower prices for payments;
- improving the level playing field for payment service providers;
- making payments safer and more secure;
- promoting the development and use of innovative online and mobile payments; and
- protecting consumers.[8]

Table 11.2 sets out the main categories of payment service providers that are referenced in PSD 2, the PSD 2 supplementary regulations, such as the RTS, as well as related FCA rules and guidance.

---

[7]   EU Directive 2015/2366.

[8]   FCA (2021) Revised Payment Services Directive (PSD 2).

Table 11.2   *Payment Service Providers*

Service providers	Explanation
Account Information Service Providers (AISPs)	Payment service providers that provide account information services. These include a diverse range of financial institutions, including the authorised payment institutions, the Bank of England, credit institutions, the Post Office and small payment institutions.[1] An account information service is an online service to provide consolidated information on one or more payment accounts held by the payment service user with another payment service provider or with more than one payment service provider.[2]
Account Servicing Payment Service Providers (ASPSPs)	Payment service providers that provide and maintain a payment account for a payer.[3] Examples include banks and building societies. ASPSPs are required to allow customers to grant access to AISPs and PISPs (see below). In doing so the AISPs and PISPs can access the consenting customer's data and process payments on their behalf.[4]
Banking Service Providers (CMA 9)	The UK's nine largest banks and building societies, measured by the number of business current accounts and personal accounts ('CMA 9').[5] Under an order made by the CMA in 2017, the CMA 9 were required to develop and use open APIs through which they share data. The aim is for data to be shared (a) between these leading nine regulated firms; (b) with other payment providers; and (c) with third-party service providers, including price comparison websites, AISPs (see explanation above) and PISPs (see below).[6]

Service providers	Explanation
Card-based Payment Instrument Issuer (CBPIIs)	A payment instrument refers to a personalised device(s) and/or set of procedures agreed between the payment service user and the payment service provider that is used to pay for goods and services.[7]
Payment Initiation Service Providers (PISPs)	PISPs refers to a payment provider that provides payment initiation services. Payment initiation services refers to 'an online service to initiate a payment order at the request of the payment service user with respect to a payment account held at another payment service provider'.[8]

Notes: [1] Regulation 2(1) of the Payment Services Regulations 2017 (SI 2017/752). [2] FCA Handbook Glossary. [3] Article 4(17) EU Directive 2015/2366. [4] UK Finance (2020) PSD 2 Guidance – Open Access Guidance for Account Servicing Payment Service Providers, at 4. [5] Article 3.1.1, Retail Banking Market Investigation Order 2017. These are AIB Group (UK) plc, Bank of Ireland (UK) plc, Barclays Bank plc, HSBC Group, Lloyds Banking Group plc, Nationwide Building Society, Northern Bank Limited, The Royal Bank of Scotland Group plc and Santander UK plc. [6] CMA (2016) Retail Banking Market Investigation – Final Report, Section 13.5 Open Banking – Open API Standards and Data Sharing, Summary of Remedy, section 13.5 and Figure 13.1, at 441–442. [7] Article 4(14) EU Directive 2015/2366. [8] Regulation 2(1) of the Payment Services Regulations 2017 (SI 2017/752).

11.4 Scope of payment services

In both the UK and EU, the range of payments includes:

- account information services;
- execution of payment transactions, plus transfers of funds on a payment account with the user's payment service provider or with another payment service provider, including (a) credit transfers; (b) direct debits; and (c) payment cards;
- execution of payment transactions where the funds are covered by a credit line, including (a) credit transfers; (b) direct debits; and (c) payment card, or similar device;
- money remittance;
- payment initiation services;
- services enabling cash to be placed on a payment account, and the operational requirements for a payment account; and
- services enabling cash withdrawals from a payment account, and

operational requirements for a payment account.[9]

Beyond democratic governmental processes, actors influencing legislation include businesses and their lobbyists, consumer groups, E-money institutions and FinTech payments firms, financial institutions, especially banks and building societies, and payment institutions. Consultations by the key regulators, the FCA and the PSR, rely heavily on this mix of expertise and interests.[10] Regulation affecting payment service providers constantly evolves reflecting the millions of consumers and thousands of businesses that can benefit from digital technologies, but are also vulnerable to fraud.[11]

11.5 Strong customer authentication

Strong customer authentication (SCA) refers to two-factor authentication where 'two out of three' independent elements are chosen from (a) inherence; (b) knowledge; and (c) possession. The logic is that in the event of a breach of one element, security is not compromised. The three categories are:

- inherence, meaning something inherent to the payment service user, for example fingerprint, facial, iris or voice recognition;
- knowledge, that is something known only by the payment service user, for example a password or PIN number; and
- possession, so something held only by the payment service user, for example a smartphone or security token.[12]

The transposed EU Regulatory Technical Standards for Strong Customer Authentication and Common and Secure Open Standards of Communication is the main secondary EU legislation supplementing PSD 2 (the 'Strong Authentication RTS').[13] The Strong Authentication

---

9   EU Directive (EU) 2015/2366, Payment Services in the Internal Market, Amending Directive.
10   The PSR has concurrent powers with the FCA, and also with the CMA for competition issues. Chapter 10 Competition considers these issues and powers.
11   For the FCA, an accessible and safe payment subsector is an on-going top priority for 2020–2023. See FCA (2020) Business Plan 2020/21, at 16.
12   Regulation 2(1) of the Payment Services Regulations 2017, SI 2017/752.
13   The Strong Authentication RTS has been transposed into UK law by way of the Technical Standards on Strong Customer Authentication and Common and Secure Methods of Communication Instrument 2020 made by the FCA.

RTS details secure communication requirements between on the one hand

Account Servicing Payment Service Providers (ASPSPs) (typically established banks) and Account Information Service Providers (AISPs), Payment Initiation Service Providers (PISPs), and Card-based Payment Instrument Issuer (CBPIIs). These three payment service providers are collectively referred to as Third-party Providers (TPPs). Principally, the Strong Authentication RTS covers general authentication risk management, requiring all payment service providers to factor in the following:

- compromised or stolen authentication element lists;
- each payment transaction amount;
- known fraud scenarios relevant to payment services;
- malware infection signals in parts of the authentication procedure; and
- when an access device or software is provided by the payment service provider, a log of the use of the access device or the software provided to the payment service user, including any abnormal use.[14]

11.5.1 Changes to the Strong Authentication RTS

In early 2021, the FCA proposed important changes to the Strong Authentication RTS, which, if implemented, would make it different from the original EU RTS in some key aspects. Second, the FCA proposed changes to its established guidance covering payment services and electronic money ('FCA Approach Document').[15] For several years the FCA Approach Document has provided important detail on many complex payment regulations.[16] In an attempt to reflect the pace of technology, and encourage growth in open banking, the FCA has proposed changes to the Strong Authentication RTS, including:

- removal of the every 90 day re-authentication requirement when a customer is accessing payment account information through a TPP;

---

[14] Article 2(2) Strong Customer Authentication RTS, Commission Delegated Regulation (EU) 2018/389 with regard to regulatory technical standards for strong customer authentication and common and secure open standards of communication.

[15] FCA (2019) version 4, Payment Services and Electronic Money – Our Approach, The FCA's role under the Payment Services Regulations 2017 and the Electronic Money Regulations 2011.

[16] Ibid.

- certain ASPSPs must build dedicated interfaces, which are typically APIs;
- technical specifications and testing facilities; and
- static card data.[17]

11.5.2 The 90-day re-authentication rule

Turning first to the current 90-day re-authentication requirement, it is easier to first explain that the current rule allows a customer to access (a) account balance details, and (b) payment transactions covering the last 90 days.[18] For brevity and clarity, it is helpful to collectively term these two types of data as 'payment account information'. SCA is required when accessing payment account information not only for the first time, but also then every 90 days.[19]

This every 90 days re-authentication requirement has been impractical for many TPP regulated firms acting on behalf of a customer, because if the customer has not re-authenticated with its ASPSP, the TPP firm cannot access relevant data on that customer. Based on FCA assessments of reports from both AISPs and PISPs, the intended 'opening up' of the banking sector is not working as planned. The FCA concluded 'the potential loss of access to customer data as a result of a customer's failure to re-authenticate every 90 days has caused firms to delay or stop the launch of new products and services in the UK. As a result, the full benefits of open banking to UK consumers and competition are not being realised.'[20] Subsequently, the FCA has confirmed an exemption to the 90-day re-authentication requirement where a customer is using a TPP to indirectly access their accounts. The practical effect of this change means the payment provider is only applying strong authentication on the first occasion that the customer uses a TPP.[21]

---

[17] FCA CP 21/3 (2021) Changes to the SCA-RTS and to the Guidance in 'Payment Services and Electronic Money – Our Approach' and the Perimeter Guidance Manual, Chapter 3.

[18] Article 10(1) Strong Customer Authentication RTS, Commission Delegated Regulation (EU) 2018/389.

[19] Ibid., at Article 10(2).

[20] FCA CP 21/3 (2021) Changes to the SCA-RTS and to the Guidance in 'Payment Services and Electronic Money – Our Approach', at 3.9.10.

[21] Article 10A Technical Standards on Strong Customer Authentication and Common and Secure Methods of Communication (Amendment) Instrument 2021. Article 10A comes into force on 26 March 2022.

11.6   Dedicated API requirement

The Strong Authentication RTS also provides that an account-holding firm may provide such access via a dedicated interface, which is typically an API or via its customer-facing interface such as an online banking portal.[22] The FCA proposes that account-holding firms managing current accounts and credit card accounts for consumers and SMEs must build a dedicated interface which is typically an API.

The FCA points out that in combination with the changes to the 90-day re-authentication 'TPPs will also benefit from the mandated use of dedicated interfaces as barriers will be lowered … This will enable them to innovate, benefiting consumers and, in turn, the overall open banking ecosystem in the UK.'[23] The nine largest UK banks and building societies were already required to implement an API interface, so this is not significant to them. However, other regulated firms will be expected to make this change with perhaps an 18 month implementation timetable.[24] Beyond the nine largest banks and building societies, the FCA estimates that 252 small- and medium-sized ASPSPs are affected by this change.[25]

11.7   Testing facilities and technical specifications and requirements

Under the existing rules, ASPSPs that have implemented a dedicated interface must provide TPPs six months before the launch date with (a) a facility that enables them to test the technical solutions, and (b) the technical specifications of the chosen solutions.[26] Further, in the event that an

---

[22] Article 31 Strong Customer Authentication RTS, Commission Delegated Regulation (EU) 2018/389.

[23] FCA CP 21/3 (2021) Changes to the SCA-RTS and to the Guidance in 'Payment Services and Electronic Money – Our Approach', at 12.

[24] Notably, 'small payment institutions', 'small electronic money institutions', and EEA firms within the Temporary Permission Regime will not be subject to Article 31 of the Strong Customer RTS. See FCA CP 21/3 (2021) Changes to the SCA-RTS and to the guidance in 'Payment Services and Electronic Money – Our Approach' and the Perimeter Guidance Manual.

[25] FCA CP 21/3 (2021) Changes to the SCA-RTS and to the Guidance in 'Payment Services and Electronic Money – Our Approach', at 37. Notably, the FCA estimates that the 20 largest ASPSPs have already developed an API.

[26] Paragraph 21 Strong Customer Authentication RTS, Commission Delegated Regulation (EU) 2018/389. Note that in the FCA CP 21/3 publication, at Section 3.25, at 12, it states that the relevant article of the SCA-RTS is Article 31. That is a typographical error.

ASPSP's dedicated interface becomes unavailable, the ASPSP is required to adapt their own consumer interface for use by TPPs. This interface adaptation requirement has been termed the 'fall-back interface'.[27] The FCA has reflected on these testing and specification rules and reached the conclusion that they are a fetter on innovation, acting as a barrier to entry for new service providers. Further, that TPPs are unlikely to exploit testing facilities or technical specifications to perform testing before a product or service is launched. Consequently, the FCA proposes that both are made available to TPPs at the time of product or service launch. The FCA has projected that the number of regulated firms affected by these rule changes is 272 ASPSPs.[28]

11.8 Deemed authorised ASPSPs

Under the Temporary Permissions Regime ASPSPs located in the EEA with deemed authorisation are exempt from the rule requiring a fall-back interface. This exemption is conditional upon the ASPSP having proof of exemption from its home state competent authority. After 31 December 2020, so the end of the UK's exit transition period from the EU, the EEA ASPSPs have been required to set up a fall-back interface unless exempted by the FCA. The proposal by the FCA is to treat an EEA home state exemption as if it had been granted by the FCA.[29]

11.9 Contactless payments thresholds

Since 2020, a contactless payment card could be used for a single payment of up to £45 without SCA. The cumulative threshold limit was £130 or when up to five contactless payments have been consecutively made.[30]

---

[27] FCA CP 21/3 (2021) Changes to the SCA-RTS and to the Guidance in 'Payment Services and Electronic Money – Our Approach', at 12. Note there is an exemption application procedure from the fall-back interface under Article 33(6) of the SCA-RTS.

[28] FCA CP 21/3 (2021) Changes to the SCA-RTS and to the Guidance in 'Payment Services and Electronic Money – Our Approach, at 37.

[29] FCA CP 21/3 (2021) Changes to the SCA-RTS and to the Guidance in 'Payment Services and Electronic Money – Our Approach, at 14.

[30] Article 11 Strong Customer Authentication RTS, Commission Delegated Regulation (EU) 2018/389. See www.legislation.gov.uk/eur/2018/389/introduction.

However, from October 2021, HM Treasury and the FCA confirmed increases in the single and cumulative transaction thresholds for contactless payments, with single payments changing from £45 to £100, and cumulative ones from £130 to £300.[31] The projected number of regulated firms affected by this new exemption is 272 ASPSPs.[32] In my view, while the increase of thresholds provides convenience, it is more likely that both more consumer and SME card holders will become victims of stolen cards. Further, these changes may act as a catalyst for both more card theft and robbery. Put this way, if someone has in effect £100 on their person that is considerably more than £45. One solution, indeed innovative offering, would be to provide customers with the ability to set their own limit. From a financial regulation viewpoint this can be easily accommodated based on each customer choosing a limit confirmed with strong two-factor customer authentication.

11.10 Contractual terms

The treatment of single transactions is quite distinct, and logically requires a lower level of information.[33] For general contract condition requirements, the detail on communication requirements is increasingly important as desktop, laptop, smartphone or tablet-based interactions are the norm. It is well established under UK statute[34] and English case law that core contractual terms, including exclusion and restriction of liability clauses, must be prominent and transparent.[35] Further, there cannot be a significant imbalance in favour of the supplier of services.[36]

Recently the English High Court has added to established precedents with a case that focused on the treatment of 'clickwrap' terms and conditions for consumers.[37] This decision confirmed that courts assess the appear-

---

[31] FCA (2021) FCA Confirms the Increase in Thresholds for Contactless Payments. See www.fca.org.uk/news/press-releases/fca-confirms-increase-thresholds-contactless-payments.

[32] FCA CP 21/3 (2021) Changes to the SCA-RTS and to the Guidance in 'Payment Services and Electronic Money – Our Approach'at 37.

[33] Articles 44–49 EU Directive 2015/2366.

[34] Sections 62–64 Consumer Rights Act 2015.

[35] *Office of Fair Trading v Abbey National Plc* [2009] UKSC 6, and *Interfoto Picture Library Ltd v Stiletto Visual Programmes Ltd* [1987] EWCA Civ 6.

[36] *Director General of Fair Trading v First National Bank* [2001] UKHL 52.

[37] *Green v Petfre (Gibraltar) Ltd (t/a Betfred)* [2021] EWHC 842 (QB).

ance of a contract not just the substance of the terms and conditions. This means that the form of a contract will be scrutinised, including font sizes and formatting. Given the general small size of smartphone screens, the clarity of smartphone-accessed payment service contracts is an obvious area for especially careful checking. Further, from a regulatory stance, where applicable, the following information and conditions concerning communication must be made:

- the technical requirements for the payment service user's equipment and software, agreed between the parties for the transmission of information or notifications under PSD 2;
- the frequency and manner of communication provided or made available as required under PSD 2;
- the language or languages in which the contract will be concluded and communication will made throughout the duration of the contract; and
- the payment service user's right to receive, at any point during the contract, the contractual terms and information and conditions.[38]

11.11 Outsourcing arrangements

The increasing reliance on outsourcing as part of the operational fabric of many regulated firms makes this an important area for scrutiny by senior managers, and by extension legal counsel and compliance officers advising on compliance, contract or policy implementation.[39] All regulated firms undertaking outsourcing arrangements remain fully liable for the acts or omissions of agents.[40] Under PSD rules, outsourcing of important operational functions, such as technology, cannot be done if it affects 'materially the quality' of the regulated firm's internal control and dilutes the regulator's ability to monitor compliance with PSD rules.[41]

---

[38] Article 52(4) EU Directive 2015/2366. My summary omits something of importance if the PSD 2 text is referred to for exact detailed reproduction. In fact Article 52(4)(d) makes reference to Article 53, which in turn states: 'At any time during the contractual relationship the payment service user shall have a right to receive, on request, the contractual terms of the framework contract as well as the information and conditions specified in Article 52 on paper or on another durable medium.'

[39] Chapter 3 Cloud computing considers in detail the legal risk issues surrounding outsource arrangements.

[40] Article 20(2) EU Directive 2015/2366.

[41] Ibid., at Article 19(6).

When outsourcing important operational functions, the regulated firm must ensure:

- the arrangement cannot result in the delegation of responsibility by senior management;
- the relationship and obligations of the regulated firm towards its payment service users under PSD 2 is not changed;
- the conditions with which the regulated firm is to comply in order to be authorised and remain so in accordance with relevant sections of the PSD shall not be undermined; and[42]
- none of the other conditions under which the regulated firm was authorised to act as a payment services provider are modified or removed.[43]

11.12 Data protection

Readers will be conscious that the GDPR is centrally about individual human data treatment.[44] The treatment of data protection under PSD 2 is congruent with the GDPR requirement of explicit customer consent. Specifically, with explicit customer consent, the PSD 2 permits access, processing and storage of customer data for the provision of payment services.[45]

11.13 The EMR

The Electronic Money Regulations (2011/99) (EMR) have been an effective part of UK law for more than a decade.[46] The EMR is a transposition of the second directive covering the supervision of electronic money institutions,[47] namely e-money institutions or small e-money institutions (collectively 'EMIs'). In effect the EMR are the conduct of business rules for EMIs, as a third category of payment service provider. By which is meant

---

[42] Ibid., at Articles 5 to 37.
[43] Ibid., at Article 19(6).
[44] Chapter 6 Data protection considers these issues.
[45] Articles 94 and 20(2) EU Directive 2015/2366.
[46] Electronic Money Regulations 2011/99.
[47] Practitioners often refer to the second Electronic Money Directive as '2EMD'.

these are neither banks nor building societies. Under the EMR, electronic money, subject to exceptions, means electronically stored monetary value, including magnetically stored value, which is a claim on an EMI if (a) issued on receipt of funds with the aim of making payment transactions, or (b) accepted by a person other than the electronic money issuer.[48]

The EMR exceptions, concerning (a) intermediary transfer, and (b) as payment accepted by a third-party, have particular resonance in the context of technology. In summary, monetary value that is used to 'make payment transactions executed by means of any telecommunication, digital or IT device, where the goods or services purchased are used through a telecommunication, digital or IT device, provided that the telecommunication, digital or IT operator does not act only as an intermediary between the payment service user and the supplier of the goods and services'.[49]

This electronic communications exception takes on increasing significance with smartphone use and financial services.[50] For instance, a mobile telecommunications network provider can provide network coverage, and in addition digital downloads in the form of podcasts and video broadcasts. Further, it could use customer credit for mobile participation in video conference calls. With 5G, this mixture of services becomes a potent offering, but may also require the regulator to re-consider the boundaries of this exception.

Further, note that certain specific types of credit are governed by not just PSP 2 and the EMR. So in some instances there is also a need for reference to the FCA Consumer Credit Handbook ('CONC') and also the Consumer Credit Act 1974 (CCA) and linked statutory instruments. Under certain credit situations, highly prescriptive credit agreements have to be provided to individuals.[51]

---

[48] Regulation 2, Electronic Money Regulations 2011/99.

[49] Regulation 3 Electronic Money Regulations 2011/99. A second important category of exception is activities that predominantly cover payment instruments with limited scope of use. For instance, the purchase of goods or services only in the issuer's premises, or to buy only from a limited network of providers, or a limited range of good or services.

[50] Note this exception is replicated in paragraphs 2(k) and 2(l) of Part 2 of Schedule 1 of the PSR 2017.

[51] Article 21, Part 6 of the FSMA 2000 (Regulated Activities) (Amendment) (No. 2) Order 2013, SI 2013/1881, lists the fully or partially repealed CCA sections from 1 April 2014. An authoritative

11.14 Case study on Wirecard AG

It is inevitable that there will always be fraud associated with the use of payment services levering technology. Wirecard AG is an insolvent German company specialising in electronic payment processing, including mobile payments, and issuing e-money onto prepaid cards. In 2020 it emerged that €1.9 billion in cash was lost through unlawful accounting practices, for example misleading financial reporting. The main financial services provided by Wirecard AG were via its mobile payment App Boon. Based on a virtual Mastercard running on both Android and iOS, App Boon serves as an important current example of technology galloping ahead of regulation. For instance, in many European countries App Boon could be used via Apple Pay. Further, Wirecard AG had arrangements with both Alipay and Tencent to provide smartphone-based services to Chinese tourists holidaying in Europe. Although Wirecard AG was a Munich-based firm with a relatively modest headquarters office by City of London or Wall Street norms, digitally it was globally active on an immense scale.

Since the Wirecard AG debacle, the FCA has increased its resources into regulating and supervising payment services activities. The FCA has also commented that 'given the importance of the payments and e-money sector to consumers' everyday lives, it is important that firms are resilient and ensure customer funds are adequately protected to maintain trust and confidence in the sector'.[52] In July 2020, the FCA issued guidance focused on payment services and e-money.[53] These guidelines include three important changes:

- increased management of customer funds held in 'safeguarded' accounts with third-party banks, including the need to document reconciliation processes with an accompanying rationale to aid the distribution of funds if the firm becomes insolvent.[54]

---

practitioner-focused work on consumer credit is Goode, R (2021) *Consumer Credit Law and Practice* (LexisNexis).

[52] *Financial Times* (2021) 'UK FinTech Bosses Warn New Rules Will Stifle Start-Ups', 3 March 2021.

[53] FCA (2020) Finalised Guidance – Coronavirus and Safeguarding Customers' Funds: Additional Guidance for Payment and e-money Firms, 9 July 2020.

[54] This task is especially important because such accounts do not have the protection of the Financial Services Compensation Scheme (FSCS). For readers unfamiliar with the FSCS, under Section 213

- the need for senior managers to provide robust governance arrangements and effective procedures to identify, manage and monitor risks, in accordance with their conditions of authorisation or registration; and
- for APIs, Authorised Electronic Money Institutions (AEMIs), and Small Electronic Money Institutions (SEMIs) to have detailed wind-down plans.

As always there is a balance to be struck between protecting consumers versus stifling innovation because of higher compliance costs. With payment services growing in influence and scale, the new FCA rules certainly increase compliance costs. However, the indirect benefit is that more FinTech firms will assess their options and instead plump to apply for full banking licences. The established FCA and PRA banking rules will enable FinTech SMEs to plan with more regulatory certainty and also benefit from a closer comparison with traditional banks. In the light of the Wirecard AG incident that should create a wider pool of customers.

11.15 Buy now pay later

Buy now pay later (BNPL) firms are exempt from FCA regulation if the credit they offer is (a) on an interest-free basis; (b) with no more than 12 repayments; and (c) is totally repaid within 12 months of the date of the agreement.[55] On first considering BNPL some readers would be forgiven for thinking that this is a peripheral unregulated aspect of business. However, BNPL has become increasingly popular. Not only diverse products, but also dental fees and gym memberships can all rely on the exemption. For example, Klarna, a Swedish bank, allows customers to download its App and then purchase from many leading brands and stores, either online or in store, with the choice of paying back by instalments. Customers can choose to pay up to 30 days later or divide the

---

FSMA 2000, the UK regulators provide compensation via the FSCS. The current limit of compensation is £85,000 per account.

[55] Article 60F(2) of the Financial Services and Markets Act 2000 (Regulated Activities) Order 2001 (RAO).

total cost into three interest-free instalments.[56] Others prominent BNPL providers include Clearpay, LayBuy, Openpay and PayPal.[57]

In early 2021, the FCA published a report on consumer credit debt, based on, among other motivations, concern about consumer debt levels.[58] One of the key recommendations is to bring BNPL within the regulatory perimeter as soon as possible:

> The products and business models in the market, as well as those which may be developed in the future, can lead to harm. Regulatory oversight is appropriate to ensure that the product develops in a way which is beneficial to the end consumer. As a matter of urgency, the FCA should work with the Treasury to ensure the necessary amendments to legislation are made to bring BNPL products within the scope of regulation.[59]

The FCA unsecured credit review expressly indicates awareness that any rule changes need to be proportionate to avoid imposing overly burdensome regulatory compliance on hundreds of retailers. When BNPL providers are brought within the FCA perimeter,[60] which should occur in 2022, they will need to be authorised as credit brokers.[61] One likely scenario is that if a BNPL provider is a regulated credit broker its current network of retailers would be regulated under the FCA Appointed Representative Regime. This means the prime regulatory responsibility would be with the BNPL provider.[62]

---

[56] See www.klarna.com.uk/smoooth/.

[57] To avoid confusion, PayPal is synonymous with online money transfer. However, in 2020 it diversified into BNPL, including in the UK.

[58] Some of the data provided by BNPL providers to the FCA as part of its review indicated 25% of users are aged 18–24, 50% are aged 25–36, 75% of users are female, and 90% of transactions involve fashion and footwear: FCA (2021) Review into Change and Innovation in the Unsecured Credit Market (The Woolard Review), at 44.

[59] Ibid.

[60] The UK government seeks to achieve proportionate regulation by gathering industry-based evidence: HM Treasury (2021) Regulation of Buy-Now Pay-Later Consultation, at 3.1.

[61] Article 36A(1)(a) Financial Services and Markets Act 2000 (Regulated Activities) (Amendment) (No. 2) Order 2013 covers credit broking, namely 'affecting an introduction of an individual or relevant recipient of credit who wishes to enter into a credit agreement to a person ("P") with a view to P entering into by way of business as lender a regulated credit agreement (or an agreement which would be a regulated credit agreement but for any of the relevant provisions)'.

[62] Sections 2.3.6 to 2.3.11G PERG.

11.16 Future trends

In the HM Treasury review of payment services a key question posed to regulated firms, and other actors within the subsector, was what trends can be expected in the next 10 years?[63] As Figure 11.3 shows, there are three elements that explain the essence of payment services growth that in turn will determine how the new regulations narrow the technology gap while maintaining a balance between consumer protection and innovation. First, technology is enabling all these services to be delivered via APIs,[64] smartphone operation and intuitive Apps. Secondly, there is

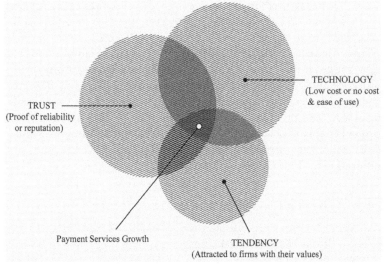

Source: © Iain Sheridan (2021).

Figure 11.3   *Payment services growth*

---

[63] HM Treasury (2020) Payments Landscape Review: Call for Evidence, Annex A, Question 17, at 36.

[64] Singapore-based readers will be aware of the commitment to increase the use of APIs in that jurisdiction. MAS has produced a detailed playbook, including standards relevant to payment services firms. ABS-MAS (2021) Finance as a Service: API Playbook.

a tendency by financial services consumers under 40 years of age,[65] to be characterised as less attracted to established banks and more attracted to disruptive businesses which signal alignment with their generational values.

Third, there is trust, in the sense of competence and reliability of service – charges are clear and money is not lost. This third element explains in part why the growth of payment systems from well-known trusted brands, such as Amazon and Apple, expand so rapidly. In short, the consumer is attracted by (a) cutting-edge technology; (b) disruptive brands; and (c) trusted digital solutions.

Three elements need to be present for the successful advancement of a payment services innovation. However, the fact that technology and trust can in combination be extremely influential creates the risk of anti-competitive payment services.[66] As just one example, and it is just that given that a number of the largest technology platforms wield immense financial influence, consider the position of Amazon. If its ecosystem is dissected, as captured in Table 11.3, based on its Amazoncash, insurance, lending and payments activities, it is already a significant participant in financial services.[67] The FCA, CMA and PSR may view these large technology platform offerings as a hindrance to competition and innovation for consumers.

11.16.1 The PSR's long-term strategic priorities

As payment services become increasingly important, then by extension so too will the PSR's practical strategic planning. Regulated firms that can plan ahead so that their offerings are aligned with regulator priorities affect not just costs and reputational risk but influence competitive advantage. In its proposed five year strategic plan, the PSR communicates

---

[65] Under 40 years of age is made up of several consumer groups with distinct characteristics, including Millennials (born 1981–1996), Generation Z (born 1997–2012) and Generation Alpha (born after 2012). However, all three of these groups are less attracted to established banks.

[66] Chapter 10 Competition includes substantial analysis and summaries on payment services.

[67] IBFED (2021) International Banking Federation Letter to the Basel Committee on Banking and Supervision, at 3–4.

Table 11.3   Amazon payment services

Amazon financial service	Activity
amazon pay	Allows a registered Amazon customer to buy goods and services from Apps and websites using the addresses and credit or debit card payment methods stored in their Amazon account.
amazon.com STORE CARD	Deferred interest card. No interest is charged as long as the card holder pays off the total amount outstanding based on pre-agreed six, 12 and 24 month contracts. Any amount outstanding at the end of the pre-agreed period is charged interest dated back to the date of purchase.
amazon protect	An additional insurance policy to cover accidental damage, malfunctioning or theft of electronic products purchased on the Amazon retail platform.
Amazoncash	Allows a customer to shop on the Amazon retail platform without using a credit or debit card.
amazon revolving credit lines	Credit lines for SMEs based on minimum monthly payments.

four strategic priorities to promote competition in the payment systems subsector:[68]

- ensuring users have continued access to depended on payment services, plus supporting effective choice of alternative payment options;
- ensuring sufficient on-going protection for users of the UK's payment systems;
- promoting competition in markets and protecting users where there is insufficient competition, including (a) between payment systems within the UK, and (b) in the markets supported by them; and
- ensuring the renewal and future governance of the UK's interbank payment systems support innovation and competition in payments.[69]

---

[68] PSR (2021) CP21/7, Consultation Paper – Our Proposed PSR Strategy.

[69] Ibid., at 1.14.

11.16.2 ESG

Perhaps the most overlooked issued by established financial services incumbents is the generational attitudes concerning ESG. For example, the younger the consumer the more likely there is a high personal value placed on climate change. The most cutting-edge technology from an established payment services brand may not be the choice of new consumers. Regulators will have to pay attention not just to the technical risks of a new technology and the fit and proper qualities of its leaders, but they will also need to factor in the tendencies of new consumers. Today's new FinTech SME is tomorrow's PayPal.

11.16.3 AI

Finally, in the context of AI, based on my discussions with experts attached to the Turing Institute, there is increasing focus on the priority of 'cooperative competences' for AI to flourish. In financial services this is mainly going to be required by agreement on machine learning interactions, for instance between ASPSPs and diverse TPPs. The payment services subsector relies heavily on cooperation, especially for open banking and secure authentication. Consequently, for the foreseeable future, there will be more regulatory complexity to cross-border transactions where AI forms part of payment services.

12. Machine learning

For many existing and potential clients the term AI captures their imaginations and provokes excitement. Conversely, for some clients AI maybe perceived as an Icarian flight albeit Icarus has delegated the flying to a machine. Whatever the general progress of AI, in technological substance what is being implemented in financial markets derives solely from a sub-field of AI called machine learning.[1]

12.1   Introduction

Machine learning use is becoming a pervasive strategic focus across the financial services sector. In a survey by JP Morgan, 72 per cent of the traders surveyed, a sample representing all asset classes, believed machine learning provides important data analytics for their daily trading activity.[2] Evidence of this trend can also be found in a joint Bank of England and FCA survey, which found that 56 per cent of respondents were using machine learning in some way.[3] Further, there is a widening range of applications. In the past, machine learning often revolved around compliance and fraud detection. But increasingly it is exploited in credit, customer engagement, general insurance, sales, securities and trading.[4]

As an exception to this perception of machine learning as a new-fangled strategy, it is overlooked that in the hedge fund industry machine learning use is well established. Some of the most successful hedge funds staffed with outstanding science, technology, engineering and mathematics

---

[1]   The use of the term AI in this chapter is reduced to a minimum. However, a high volume of valuable reference materials and international codes and standards will reference AI, so based on that reality it is still an often referred to term.

[2]   JP Morgan (2021) e-Trading 2020 Survey. See www.jpmorgan.com/solutions/cib/markets/etradingsurvey2021.

[3]   Bank of England and FCA joint paper (2019) Machine Learning in UK Financial Services, at 9.

[4]   Ibid., at 10.

(STEM) talent have been pioneer machine learning users for more than 10 years. So for these regulated firms this is not in any sense a new technology. For instance, Man Group have been focused for many years on using machine learning as a competitive advantage in trading, to predict investor decision making after gains and losses, and to understand the likely flow of investment.[5]

12.2 Key elements of machine learning

Readers may not be equally familiar with the boundaries and principles of machine learning, so it is sensible to first summarise these so that everyone can then follow the practical detail.[6] To begin with a definition, machine learning in the financial services sector refers to 'the development of models for prediction and pattern recognition from data, with limited human intervention'.[7] At the highest level of abstraction, machine learning is a tool supporting human decision making.[8] Machine learning models can provide either (a) classification, or (b) prediction. Machine learning has the potential power to classify or predict to the benefit of any aspect or event relevant to financial services, ranging from anti-fraud detection to derivatives trading. Over the last decade, significant advances in machine learning can be attributed to several reasons that have in combination propelled what was a neglected area of research to become one of the highest profile disruptive initiatives across the financial services sector, including established asset managers, investment banks, platforms and new FinTech firms.

---

[5] *Financial Times* (2020) 'Hedge Funds Exploit Technology to Reduce Cost and Waste', FT, Special Report Corporate Change and Technology, 15 December 2020.

[6] If you are reading this chapter with absolutely no knowledge about machine learning, Oxford University has produced an accurate and memorable two minute animation entitled 'What is Machine Learning?' Available at www.oxfordsparks.ox.ac.uk/content/what-machine-learning. Further, the Royal Society has an introduction with the same aim and title. See https://royalsociety.org/topics-policy/projects/machine-learning/videos-and-background-information/.

[7] Bank of England and FCA joint paper (2019) Machine Learning in UK Financial Services, at 3.

[8] Royal Society (2019) Machine Learning: The Power and the Promise of Computers That Learn from Example, at 19.

12.3   FinTech SMEs

First, given machine learning relies on data sets, the exponential increase in the volume of data makes machine learning increasingly viable. Combined with this volume of data, the varying forms of data make it hard to visualise its total quantities.[9] For instance, globally it is estimated that sent emails exceed 294 billion daily.[10] With ever-increasing cloud computing, smartphone and Internet of Things (IoT) device use, varied sources of data are growing exponentially.

Second, advances in the performance of machine learning algorithms have encouraged the financial services sector to invest in more technology projects. This algorithmic progress is based on new techniques and ways of learning from large data sets, drawing on concepts from computational neuroscience, computer science, physics and statistics. The mix creates computerised thinking, perception and action. Progress with hardware has also played a pivotal role, because machine learning has benefited from Moore's Law,[11] especially by the exploitation of Graphical Processing Units (GPUs) chips.[12] A significant acceleration in machine learning can be traced to 2012. In that year, Geoffrey Hinton, a professor of computer science and a vice-president of engineering at Google Brain,[13] entered a prestigious annual image recognition software competition.[14] His Toronto University team not only won the competition, it performed with an approximate efficiency of 10 per cent higher than the runner up.

---

[9]   Lawyers are sometimes stereotyped as pedantic wordsmiths, when in fact many are also highly numerate. So for legal counsel and compliance officers who like thinking in large numbers, daily global data growth is estimated to exceed 40 zettabytes (ZB), where 1 ZB equals $1,000^7$ bytes. In comparison, 1 gigabyte (GB) equals $1,000^3$ bytes or 1,000,000,000 bytes.

[10]   World Economic Forum (2019) How Much Data is Generated Each Day? See www.weforum.org/agenda/2019/04/how-much-data-is-generated-each-day-cf4bddf29f/.

[11]   Moore's Law is an insightful prediction named after Gordon Moore one of the founders of Intel. In his 1965 paper he argued that the number of transistors in an integrated circuit would double every year. This observation has proven quite prophetic given that from 1965 to 2012, transistors in an integrated circuit have been doubling every 18 months. See Moore, G (1965) 'Cramming More Components onto Integrated Circuits', *Electronics*, Volume 38, Issue 8 (April 1965), https://ieeexplore.ieee.org/document/4785860.

[12]   GPUs were originally designed for computer games applications, but have proven well suited to machine learning applications. GPUs are exceptionally adept at finding patterns in numbers.

[13]   Google Brain is the machine learning research team within Google.

[14]   The official name of that competition is the ImageNet Large Scale Visual Recognition Challenge. See http://image-net.org/challenges/LSVRC/index.

Third, there is the use of Big Data with machine learning. The term Big Data essentially refers to the collation and analysis of vast quantities of data primarily with the aid of algorithms.[15] A memorable way to dissect what Big Data means has been provided by machine learning experts from JP Morgan's Quantitative and Derivatives Strategy division. They analyse Big Data to incorporate '3Vs', namely (a) volume of data; (b) velocity of data in the sense of reception and transmission of data in near real-time or real-time; and (c) variety of data encompassing many different semi-structured and structured formats.[16] Big Data operations have the ability to collect large data sets for analysis, an activity that has significantly reduced in cost. This economic reality has been facilitated by the availability of cloud computing services, along with the improved interoperability of hardware and software.[17]

Yet while Big Data is transforming financial services its impact can be exaggerated. For instance, an eminent Harvard University statistics professor has pointed out that many current statistical measures covering errors and uncertainties are only meaningful when the sample data is perfect. He has observed that 'once we take into account the data quality, the effective sample size of a Big Data set can be vanishingly small'.[18]

Further, the importance of machine learning can be overstated. For instance, my own impromptu question posed to Stuart Russell, one of the world's leading AI experts, was did he judge a robust machine learning algorithm with a quality data set to be the ideal productivity option? He responded 'data is not all we have. We have [human] knowledge and should use it. So it does not at all follow [that] a quality data set is the ideal.'[19] Marcus Du Sautoy has echoed this sentiment in a thought provoking way for all legal counsel and compliance officers. He observed 'data will never be enough on its own. It has to come paired with knowledge

---

[15] www.ibm.com/software/data/bigdata.

[16] JP Morgan (2017) Big Data and AI Strategies – Machine Learning and Alternative Data Approach to Investing.

[17] An expert video summary of Big Data is available at www.ibm.com/cloud/blog/big-data?mhsrc= ibmsearch_a&mhq=big%20data. Also note Chapter 3 of this book is dedicated to cloud computing.

[18] Li Xiao Meng is the leading statistics professor at Harvard University. See 'Statistical Paradises and Paradoxes in Big Data', https://doi.org/10.1214/18-AOAS1161SF.

[19] Russell, S (2021) CogX Artificial Intelligence Conference, 16 June 2021. For readers new to AI and Machine Learning, Stuart Russell is one of the world's leading AI experts, and has won multiple awards and honours for his research work.

… It is here that human code [the human brain] seems better adapted to coping with context and seeing the bigger picture – at least for now.'[20]

12.4 The directing human minds

Figure 12.1 shows the essential elements of machine learning that require legal advice, legal audits and compliance supervision. Currently, 'computerised thinking, perception and action', based on computers and specialised algorithms,[21] are increasingly moving into the centre of financial services activity or at least as important supporting components.

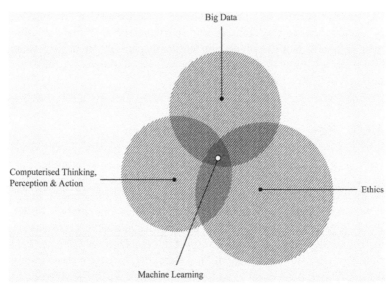

Source: © Iain Sheridan (2021).

Figure 12.1   Key elements of machine learning

---

[20] Du Sautoy, M (2019) *The Creativity Code* (Fourth Estate), at 95.

[21] Winston, P (2014) *Artificial Intelligence – Introduction and Scope* (MIT Open Courseware), presents a powerful incisive summary of AI as 'computerised thinking, perception and action'. Available at www.youtube.com/watch?v=TjZBTDzGeGg&t=1778s. A great pioneer of AI at MIT and lifelong AI expert, he passed away in 2019.

Whatever the machine learning influence on revenue or risk mitigation, this can never mean that ultimate responsibility, whether for funding, investing, risk management or trading, can ever be left to a machine. Human ethics must lead.

In the past, my analogy of machine learning algorithms has been that of the human anatomy.[22] Financial regulation is the human brain of any algorithm. The logical, mathematical input-output processes of the algorithm are the beating heart, under the initial training of one or more human brains. This heart is made up of code driven by computer processing power.[23] Yet this cardio comparison is imperfect, because machine learning algorithms self-improve. This self-learning quality implies cerebral-like intelligence that may seem to blur the lines of legal accountability. However, the digital heart is selected and, in the language of machine learning developers, 'feature engineered' by human decision makers to become increasingly efficient on its own. Ethics-based human brains complying with financial regulation may not always control, but they certainly direct and manage.

12.5   How machine learning works

From a practical viewpoint, machine learning concerns computer programs based on algorithms that improve in their classifying or predictive performance, where human involvement can vary from none to highly significant. Typically, machine learning achieves one of two things. Firstly, a prediction based on a real number; for instance, that tomorrow in the London Underground transport system there is a 65 per cent chance of delay on the Northern Line. Secondly, a discrete classification decision based on 'yes' or 'no' (1 or 0); for example, image recognition confirming that an image is either a cat or a dog.

---

[22]   Sheridan, I (2018) 'Financial Technology and Global Capital Markets – The Impact of Pro-enterprise Regulation and English Law', *CMLJ*, Volume 13, Issue 4, October 2018.

[23]   This analogy is not to ignore the important human intelligence required to adapt existing algorithms and invent new ones, something software engineers routinely do. But programming is a commercial activity governed by financial regulation that has to be interpreted by expert senior legal counsel and compliance officers.

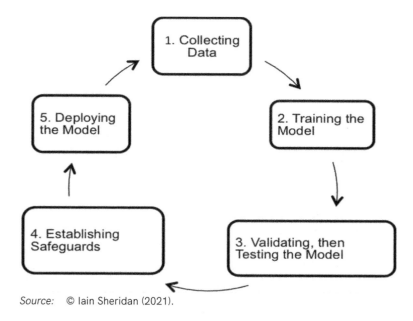

Source: © Iain Sheridan (2021).

Figure 12.2   The machine learning process

In terms of the cycle of machine learning development and deployment, Figure 12.2 captures the stages that are common across most machine learning models. First, the data set is collected. For a machine learning model to perform effectively, there needs to be a sufficiently large data set. Obtaining any data set is often a significant challenge. That sounds like a contradiction given the proliferation of data mentioned earlier, but the data has to be not only of the same quality, but also organised into the same format. That task may be relatively easy if it is all structured data, for example rows and column in spread-sheets. However, data sources will often be unstructured or supplied by a third-party. For instance, natural language processing of financial services customer voice data may have to first be converted into numerical values.

The complete data set must be spilt into three categories, namely (a) training data; (b) validation data; and (c) test data. It is vital to separate out the whole data set in this way so that the results are an unbiased estimate of the predictive performance of the chosen model. The training data set will typically be 70 to 80 per cent of the total data, leaving the smaller remaining percentage to form the validation and test data sets.[24] This careful splitting of training data, so that results do not fit with anticipated or estimated results can be checked, falls under the term 'robustness'.[25] However, machine learning robustness is a continuous process, because the nature of many machine learning methods applied in online environments can evolve. Over time, either the way the algorithm responds or the type of data or both can change. Put succinctly 'small changes to a [machine learning] system can be quickly replicated and deployed, with effects on a large scale'.[26] The way to detect and mitigate the risk of changes is by constant assessment and auditing[27] throughout the system's life cycle.[28]

Second, the training phase involves the vital technical skill to make logical decisions based on patient troubleshooting – trial and error. Successful machine learning training requires applying systematic engineering processes. In terms of specific methods used, it is evident that clustering, decision trees, natural language processing (NLP) and neural networks are popular choices for most appropriate algorithms in financial scenarios. Further, one method may lever another to maximise its aims.

Third, the engineer performs testing on the machine learning model, balancing the variables of bias and variance.[29] In Figure 12.3, the out-of-sample error, E out, refers to the test data results. The E out is the closest indicator of how the model will perform when implemented. Bias in this context means the best a model can achieve based on infinite data. Although an infinite amount of data is unlikely to exist in financial ser-

---

[24] So typically the validation data and test data can be 15–20 per cent each. But there are no set rules on the percentage split because it can depend on, among other things, the number of classification categories.

[25] Royal Society, (2019) Machine Learning: The Power and the Promise of Computers That Learn from Example, at 112.

[26] Ibid., at 122.

[27] See https://ico.org.uk/media/for-organisations/guide-to-data-protection/key-data-protection-themes/guidance-on-ai-and-data-protection-0-0.pdf.

[28] Both IOSCO and OECD reports prescribe on-going algorithm monitoring throughout the lifecycle of the AI model. See IOSCO (2020) The Use of AI and machine learning by Market Intermediaries and Asset Managers, Consultation Report, at 14/, www.iosco.org/library/pubdocs/pdf/IOSCOPD658.pdf; and OECD (2019) Recommendation of the Council on Artificial Intelligence, https://legalinstruments.oecd.org/en/instruments/OECD-LEGAL-0449.

[29] Mehta, P. (2019) A High-Bias, Low-Variance Introduction to Machine Learning for Physicists, Physics Reports, 810, at 11.

vices applications, the graphical representation of balancing bias versus variance remains an important insight into one of the key challenges facing a machine learning engineer. Variance refers to the fluctuation in performance of the training model because of errors in the finite training set.

The optimum model is an outcome where the test data has the lowest error rate and the maximum level of complexity – the lowest point on the E out curve. Here, Complexity means the number of parameters used in the model. At some level of complexity while the error rate decreases, there will be increased Variance. This Bias-Variance trade-off is a balancing process. Ultimately, the machine learning engineer needs to find the Optimum predictive performance based on more Bias with less Variance or less Bias and more Variance.[30]

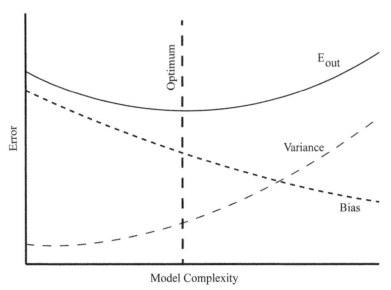

Source: Mehta, P. (2019) A High-Bias, Low-Variance Introduction to Machine Learning for Physicists, Physics Reports, 810, at 12. See www.sciencedirect .com/journal/physics-reports/vol/810/suppl/C.

Figure 12.3   *Bias versus Variance trade-off*

---

[30] Mehta, P (2019) 'A High-Bias, Low-Variance Introduction to Machine Learning for Physicists', *Physics Reports*, Volume 810, at 11–12.

Validating the model requires applying a variety of techniques. In a joint-survey by the Bank of England and FCA based on 106 regulated firm respondents, there is a full list of six testing techniques. These validation methods include benchmark-based testing and outcome-focused monitoring based on comparing the chosen machine learning model with a non-machine learning model.[31]

Fourth, there is a need to establish safeguards. Taken from the Bank of England and FCA joint-survey, Table 12.1 shows that the two most common forms of safeguard are (a) alert systems, and (b) a 'human in the loop'. Notably, 40 per cent apply guardrails, referring to systems that switch off the model automatically if it produces undesired outputs.[32] The respondents often used more than one type of safeguard, hence the total percentage is more than 100 per cent.[33]

Fifth, the final stage involves deploying the model. By which is meant the practical end user product as experienced by the regulated firm's clients, front office or risk management functions.

These five stages are a generalisation, given each regulated firm may split the process into additional stages, for instance because of complexity or for quality control purposes or both. Regardless of the number of stages, initial deployment is the end of the beginning because there will be on-going effort to improve the classification or prediction performance of the model. There is not only code to update, but also data. The expected improvement over time is a positive commercial aspect, but it also raises the likelihood of new risks. For instance, an engineer may have tuned the machine learning model to be a better predictor, but simultaneously introduced some bias into the system that needs to be assessed to check compliance with financial regulation and general lawfulness.[34] Amongst software engineers this challenge is often referred to as model drift.[35]

---

[31] Bank of England and FCA joint paper (2019) Machine Learning in UK Financial Services, at 25.

[32] Legal counsel and compliance officers might rationally ask why are guard rails not universally applied? Perhaps guardrails should become the machine learning equivalent of the prudent trader's stop loss.

[33] Bank of England and FCA joint paper (2019) Machine Learning in UK Financial Services, at 27.

[34] Ibid., at 25.

[35] As an interesting aside, in time insurance for AI, so that includes machine learning, may become mandatory, similar to motor car use where it is mandatory to have in place a third-party risk policy. See Turner, J (2019) Robot Rules – Regulating Artificial Intelligence (Palgrave Macmillan), at 114.

Table 12.1   *Percentage use of safeguards by survey respondents*

Safeguard used	Percentage of cases
Alert system	65
Human in the loop	63
Back-up system	57
Guardrails	40
Kill switches	30

12.6   Due diligence on potential liabilities

Whatever the precise number of machine learning stages, both legal counsel and compliance officers need to communicate with all contributing teams at each stage. Most prominently, this will include development operations engineers, data engineers and data scientists. Senior management responsibility for the machine learning algorithms, models and outcomes generally belong to the Chief Technology Officer remit or equivalent SMF formally recognised as responsible for technology in the SMCR documentation submitted to the FCA. However, legal and compliance functions have to complete on-going due diligence covering a number of aspects. Table 12.2 provides a preliminary framework of key aspects to accompany readers in their first meeting with the CTO. This liabilities list will need to be expanded on after completion of all due diligence and other peer review.

The key risk questions to answer before a machine learning model is deployed, and thereafter to mitigate model drift, are set out below.

- Under the FCA SMCR rules, do statements of responsibilities detail which SMF is responsible for algorithms?
- What is the input data?
- Is the input data private-only, public or a mix?
- Currently where is the data stored and where will it be stored on implementation?
- Under the Data Protection Act 2018 and the GDPR, have all data protection laws concerning data forming part of the data set been evaluated?
- Applying five key questions posed in a Bank of England Staff Working

Table 12.2   Potential liability chart

Liability issue	Senior Manager Function (SMF) or Service Supplier (delete as applicable)
Algorithm design	SMF or Service Supplier
Algorithm validation and model testing	SMF or Service Supplier
Software coding	SMF or Service Supplier
Training data	SMF or Service Supplier
Deployment in the business of the user	SMF or Service Supplier
On-going audit for algorithm drift from planned aim	SMF or Service Supplier

Paper, is the machine learning algorithm explainable?[36]
- Who is the coder of automated aspects of the contract?
- What are the risks and the risk levels of the machine learning algorithm?
- What are the assumptions, biases and weights processed by the algorithm?
- What critical method is applied to spot when the output of a machine learning model has drifted, so triggering a review of the system's robustness?[37]
- Currently, what English law and UK regulation governs the insertion and operation of automated processes?
- What English law and UK regulation, if any, is scheduled to govern the insertion and operation of automated processes?
- Under the finalised EU Artificial Intelligence Act have all the rules relevant to the risk level of the machine learning model been evaluated?[38]

---

[36] These five questions are covered later in this chapter. See Bracke, P et al. (2019) Bank of England Staff Working Paper No. 816 Machine Learning Explainability in Finance: An Application to Default Risk Analysis, at 3.

[37] This question is a paraphrase from the Technical Robustness and Safety section of 'The Assessment List for Trustworthy AI' published by the European Commission High-Level Expert Group, July 2020.

[38] The final draft proposals of the EU's Artificial Intelligence Act (AIA) were published in April 2021. Expect the final AIA rules, including any changes, to be made effective before Q2 2023. It is likely that many regulated firms exploiting machine learning will rationally need to factor in these rules in the

- What are the specific algorithms being used, if any, to automate processes in the contract?
- What is the identification code or number assigned to uniquely identify each algorithm?
- How often are the algorithms reviewed to mitigate delays, model drift or malfunctions?
- Is the machine learning system certified for cyber security?
- Is any algorithm or other AI-linked innovation causing or contributing to disorderly market behaviour?[39] and
- What aspect of the coding or model engineering, if any, is outsourced?

12.7 Data protection

As covered earlier in this chapter, although daily global data growth exceeds 40 zettabytes,[40] the quality of data sets slows down the true potential of machine learning to transform financial services. Data protection is an additional stymie to progress. Specifically, under the GDPR, data subjects[41] have rights that would apply in the context of regulated firms using machine learning to provide automated decision making,[42] including profiling.[43]

Automated decision making affecting individuals can only be made when (a) it is necessary for entering into or performing a contract; (b) if authorised by domestic law; or (c) based on the individual's explicit consent.[44] Regulated firms, for example the FinTech bank Starling, increasingly

---

design process phases. Not least because under Article 71(3) of the AIA, in some scenarios the consequences of breaching certain sections of the AIA is a fine based on 6 per cent of group turnover. See EC COM (2021) 206 final 2021/0106(COD). Available at https://eur-lex.europa.eu/legacontent/EN/TXT/?qid=1623335154975&uri=CELEX%3A52021PC0206.

[39] Article 17 MiFID II requires firms involved in algorithmic trading to avoid any such activity.

[40] World Economic Forum (2019) How Much Data is Generated Each Day? See www.weforum.org/agenda/2019/04/how-much-data-is-generated-each-day-cf4bddf29f/.

[41] Under Article 4(4) GDPR, personal data refers to any information concerning an identified or identifiable natural person – the data subject.

[42] Chapter 6 Data protection provides detailed reference to the GDPR.

[43] Under Article 4(4) GDPR, profiling refers to any automated processing of personal data about a person with the aim of analysing or predicting, among other things, their economic situation, health or reliability.

[44] Article 22(2) GDPR.

automate lending for customers via smartphones for rapid automated processing. Customer consent in compliance with the GDPR allows this to happen. However, there is the additional GDPR requirement to provide individuals at the time the personal data is obtained with 'meaningful information about the logic involved, as well as the significance and the envisaged consequences of such processing for the data subject'.[45] The response of an Oxford mathematics professor with a deep understanding of machine learning to Article 22 GDPR is 'good luck with that!'.[46]

From a regulatory guidelines angle, it is a challenge to determine precisely what may or may not constitute meaningful information. Reassuringly, advice from an EC working paper, also followed by the UK's ICO, makes clear that what is not required is any mathematical explanation. Instead the following five examples serve as helpful guidance on the expected information:

- planned or already chosen categories of data used in the decision making or profiling process;
- why these categories are considered pertinent;
- how any profile used in the automated decision making process is built, including any statistics used in the analysis;
- why this profile is relevant to the automated decision making process; and
- how it is used for a decision concerning the data subject.[47]

The ICO has also advised that human reviewers must be involved in checking that the system's recommendation is meaningful. Human reviewers must also have the authority to go against the computer's recommendation.[48]

---

[45] Article 13(2)(f) GDPR.

[46] Du Sautoy, M (2019) *The Creativity Code* (Fourth Estate), at 95.

[47] EC (2017) Guidelines on Data Protection Impact Assessment (DPIA) and Determining Whether Processing is 'Likely to Result in a High Risk' for the Purposes of Regulation 2016/679 (wp251rev.01), Annex 1, at 31. These guidelines derive from a working party of EU data protection authorities. It is endorsed by the ICO, which provides detailed guidance on these nine factors, including detailed reasoning for the high-risk indicators, and also examples of high risk processing likely to result in high risk.

[48] ICO and Alan Turing Institute (2020) Explaining Decisions Made with AI. In 2018 the UK government tasked these two organisations to collaborate on producing guidance for explaining AI decisions primarily with data protection laws, so GDPR and the DPA 2018 as the legal analytical framework. This 2020 publication is the result.

12.7.1 Data protection and pre-deployment of machine learning

The ICO's guidance on AI advocates best practice based on identification and mitigation at the design stage. For systems designers, and in turn legal counsel and compliance officers as risk managers of contracts, policies and regulatory compliance, AI robustness requires an increased rigour in the level of scrutiny to manage risk compared with traditional explicit rule-based algorithmic software systems.[49]

Under the GDPR, where personal data forms part of a system, prior to going live there may be a need for a DPIA[50] The following points encapsulate when a DPIA is required:

- if the processing of the personal data is 'likely to result in a high risk to the rights and freedoms of natural persons';[51]
- if the processing involves systematic and extensive profiling with significant effects;[52]
- if the processing involves large-scale use of sensitive data;[53]
- if the processing involves large-scale public monitoring;[54]
- if two or more of the nine EC working party criteria ('WP 251') apply;[55]
- if two or more of 10 ICO criteria apply;[56] or
- if one of the ICO criterion exists in combination with any of the WP 251 criteria.

Rather than list 19 criteria, for ease of reference Table 12.3 shows the nine WP 251 criteria with the four most relevant ICO criteria to financial services firms.

---

[49] Bank of England and FCA joint paper (2019) Machine Learning in UK Financial Services, at 6.

[50] Article 35 GDPR.

[51] Article 35 GDPR.

[52] Article 35(3)(a) GDPR.

[53] Article 35(3)(b) GDPR.

[54] Article 35(3)(c) GDPR.

[55] EC (2017) Guidelines on Data Protection Impact Assessment (DPIA) and Determining whether Processing is 'Likely to Result in a High Risk' for the Purposes of Regulation 2016/679.

[56] ICO (2021) When Do We Need To Do a DPIA? See https://ico.org.uk/for-organisations/guide -to-data-protection/guide-to-the-general-data-protection-regulation-gdpr/data-protection-impact -assessments-dpias/when-do-we-need-to-do-a-dpia/.

Table 12.3   *Key machine learning risk criteria*

Aspect	Authority
Automated decision making with legal or similar significant effect	WP 251
Data concerning vulnerable data subjects	WP 251
Data processed on a large-scale	WP 251
Evaluation or scoring	WP 251
Innovative use of technology or use of new technological solutions	WP 251
Matching or combining data sets	WP 251
Preventing data subjects from exercising a right or using a service or contract	WP 251
Sensitive data or data of a highly personal nature	WP 251
Systematic monitoring	WP 251
Data matching. By which is meant combining, comparing or matching personal data obtained from multiple sources	ICO
Denial of service. Decisions about an individual's access to a product or service	ICO
The use of innovative technologies, including machine learning	ICO
Large-scale profiling. Any profiling of individuals on a large scale[1]	ICO

Note: [1] See https://ico.org.uk/for-organisations/guide-to-data-protection/guide-to
-the-general-data-protection-regulation-gdpr/data-protection-impact-assessments-dpias/
when-do-we-need-to-do-a-dpia/.

Regulators can also provide a list of processing operations that do not require a DPIA, although the ICO has yet to do so.[57] In my view, a valuable list for regulated firms would include well-known machine learning models and techniques. However, given machine learning algorithms often have black box qualities, they are unlikely to ever be found on a regulator's list of exempted operations because of the challenges surrounding explainability, a topic discussed in the next section of this chapter.

---

[57]   Article 35(5) GDPR.

The minimum DPIA contents requirements are (a) a description of the envisaged operations; (b) a necessity and proportionality assessment; (c) a risk assessment concerning the rights and freedoms of data subjects; and (d) planned risk management measures and mechanisms.[58] If in the event the conclusion is the new technology is not high risk, it is essential to document the reasoning for not conducting a DPIA.

As part of the pre-deployment auditing process, legal counsel and compliance officers need to understand how machine learning systems architects and software engineers have traded-off privacy versus statistical accuracy. Privacy in this context is a broad, subjective term, but it may include the quantity of personal data required, sensitivity of the data, the extent that data might uniquely identify the individual, nature, scope, context and purposes of the processing, the risk of the processing to individual rights and freedoms, and the number of individuals forming part of the machine learning system.[59]

Statistical accuracy forms part of GDPR requirements, because each controller 'should use appropriate mathematical or statistical procedures for the profiling of individuals, including preventing discrimination on any ground'.[60] To clarify, machine learning would not be expected to be 100 per cent accurate nor 100 per cent sensitive. In a financial services context, for example credit card or loan applications, there is not going to be 100 per cent predictive precision on the probability of an applicant defaulting. Further sensitivity of accuracy, while expected above a minimum level, would be open textured. For example, if 10 out of every 100 credit card transactions by one credit card provider are actually fraudulent, and the machine learning system only classifies seven of out 100 as fraudulent, then this sensitivity rate of 70 per cent may be considered acceptable.[61]

The ICO propose that senior decision makers are presented with a graph depicting a 'production possibility frontier' graph, from which the trade-off between accuracy and privacy can be analysed and documented as part of a pre-production audit. Figure 12.4 shows such a graph, where the vertical axis is privacy and the horizontal one accuracy. These accu-

---

[58] Article 35(7) GDPR.
[59] ICO (2020) Guidance on the AI auditing Framework – Draft Guidance for Consultation, at 31.
[60] Recital 71 GDPR.
[61] ICO (2020) Guidance on the AI Auditing Framework – Draft Guidance for Consultation, at 48.

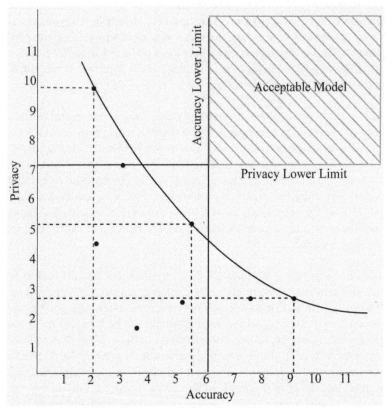

Source: ICO (2020) Guidance on the AI Auditing Framework – Draft Guidance for Consultation, at 34. See https://ico.org.uk/media/about-the-ico/consultations/2617219/guidance-on-the-ai-auditing-framework-draft-for-consultation.pdf.

Figure 12.4   The accuracy versus privacy trade-off

racy and privacy standards may form part of a high-level policy document produced by the Chief Technology Officer, or equivalent SMF of a regulated firm, relevant to all machine learning models. Clearly, the numerical measurement of both accuracy and privacy would have to derive from accepted methods of valuing each of these two variables from 1 upwards. In the Figure 12.4 example, the system architects and software engineers have recorded, marked with black dots, all the planned data sources and machine learning methods outside of the production possibility frontier

– the model cannot proceed. From an acceptable legal risk and legal audit viewpoint, the trade-off would be based on a privacy lower limit of 7, as depicted by the horizontal marker line, with an accuracy lower limit of 6.[62]

12.8   Explainability and common law

The FCA has remarked 'there is a growing consensus that algorithms need to be explainable, which makes balancing accuracy versus the ability to explain a fundamental challenge'.[63] To establish and maintain trust in the use of machine learning algorithms is fundamental to commercial relationships both individual and corporate clients. Clients are increasingly conscious that technology may produce unexpected outcomes based on the initial design or because of model drift from its original outputs.

In a Royal Society paper, a data scientist posed the challenges of explainable algorithms in this succinct way:

> Algorithms and machine learning techniques pose big questions around accountability and oversight. How can we achieve true transparency for algorithms written in code that few can understand? Or where constantly changing input data or their 'black box' nature means that it is difficult or even impossible to decipher how algorithms reach decisions? Or where for security or proprietary reasons algorithms cannot be published?[64]

A UK Supreme Court decision provides a two-stage test on the risk assessment expected from any professional adviser.[65] Recommendations by an adviser to an investor, must communicate (a) any material risks in the investment choices, and (b) any reasonable alternative. Therefore, there is a need to ensure material risks are captured in client consultations, marketing material, product explanations and written agreements. The Supreme Court interprets that material risks include assessing whether the specific person being advised is likely to see the risks as significant.

---

[62]   Ibid., at 34.

[63]   Chris Woolard, former FCA Strategy Director, presenting at the Alan Turing Institute Conference 'AI Ethics in the Financial Sector', London, 16 July 2019.

[64]   Drew, C (2016) 'Data Science Ethics in Government', *Philosophical Transactions of the Royal Society A, Mathematical, Physical and Engineering Sciences*, at 10.

[65]   *Montgomery v Lanarkshire Health Board* [2015] UKSC 11, at paragraph 87. This two-stage test is covered in more detail in Chapter 2 Accountability.

That implies the need for human-based communication between adviser and client.[66] This two-stage test has increasing importance, because material risks include potential biases from machine learning algorithms. There is also the risk of algorithmic drift away from what was intended, something that is more likely to occur if on-going checks are neglected. To take an example from Asian jurisdictions, a 2020 survey of 168 banks in Hong Kong and mainland China conducted by the HKMA found that only 68 per cent of regulated firms[67] using AI conducted regular reviews to identify AI-related risks.[68] Therefore, legal risk analysis has to include thinking through the level of material risk from machine learning algorithms when they initially form part of a financial service, and what risks could emerge over time.[69]

Further, the recent UK Supreme Court decision in *Manchester Mutual Building Society v Grant Thornton* has reconfirmed that to determine the scope of any professional adviser's duty of care, an objective test is applied.[70] The scope of a professional duty of care is determined on an objective basis by reference to the purpose or reason for which the advice is given. The case of *Caparo Industries v Dickman*, among other authorities, established this objective purpose of duty test when assessing the scope of the duty of care of professional advisers providing advice.[71] Importantly, in the *Manchester Mutual Building Society* judgment the UK Supreme Court disregarded the analysis from the case of *South Australia Asset Management Corp v York Montague Ltd*, which had previously made the distinction between when an adviser is merely providing 'information' compared with 'advice'.[72] The focus should be on identifying the

---

66 *O'Hare v Coutts* [2016] EWHC 2224 (QB), at paragraph 204.

67 To break down the sample, it was made up of 27 retail banks and 141 non-retail banks.

68 HKMA (2020) Artificial Intelligence in Banking – The Changing Landscape in Compliance and Supervision, at 22. To break down this sample, it was made up of 27 retail banks and 141 non-retail banks.

69 A succinct reference to some of the cases that provide detail on how courts interpret investment advice under FSMA 2000 can be found in *Financial Conduct Authority v 24hr Trading Academy Ltd & Another* [2021] EWHC 648 (Ch) per HHJ Richards, at 32. This case concerned, among other things, whether 'signals' sent via WhatsApp constituted investment advice. The four authorities relied on in this summary judgment were *Rubenstein v HSBC* [2011] EWHC 2304 (QB)[1]; *Thornbridge Limited v Barclays Bank Plc* [2015] EWHC 3430 (QB); *Re Market Wizard Systems (UK) Limited* [1998] 2 BCLC 282 (ChD); and *FCA v Avacade Ltd* (in liquidation) [2020] Bus LR 1897.

70 *Manchester Mutual Building Society v Grant Thornton UK LLP* [2021] UKSC 20.

71 *Caparo Industries plc v Dickman* [1990] 2 AC 605.

72 *South Australia Asset Management Corp v York Montague Ltd* [1997] AC 191.

specific purpose. The practical consequence is if machine learning forms part of a planned financial service advice, then any such offering demands bespoke terms of business agreed with the client.

My additional hunch is that past judicial treatment of sophisticated investors that already understand complex products may have some comparative value when assessing the future treatment of human advice augmented by machine learning provided to comparably knowledgeable investors. It has been commented on by the English High Court, in the factual background of derivatives product investment advice, that any assessment on the duties of care owed are likely to include a duty 'to explain why the opportunities were being presented and to provide such information as appeared appropriate and helpful to enable the client to make an informed choice'.[73]

If a machine learning model is provided as part of an advisory hybrid service, so human plus automated advisory service, the higher courts will no doubt return to the important earlier judicial commentary by Dame Elizabeth Gloster in *JP Morgan v Springwell*. This has already come close to happening. In 2020, preliminary hearings in the English High Court took place in a counter-claim by an investor for contractual misrepresentations concerning a Monaco-based investment manager's machine learning trading system.[74] Had this case proceed to trial, it may have produced an insightful court judgment commenting on the use of machine learning by investment managers.[75] Under English common law, the judiciary advance incrementally to account for new technology, but the presumption is continuity and predictability – part of the rule of law.[76] So machine learning principles diverging too far from existing common law are unlikely. However, when a future similar case proceeds to trial it will be illuminating to benefit from judicial commentary on the need to explain how a machine learning system works, and if so to what degree of detail.

---

[73] *J.P. Morgan Chase Bank & Ors v Springwell Navigation Corporation* [2008] EWHC 1186 per HJH Gloster, at 617 (iii), (Comm) (27 May 2008).

[74] *Tyndaris v MMWWVWM Ltd* [2020] EWHC 778 (Comm) (22 April 2020).

[75] Tony Beswetherick, a dynamic London-based commercial barrister that represented Tyndaris, confirmed to me in June 2021 that the case did not proceed to trial.

[76] Bingham, T (2011) *The Rule of Law* (Penguin), at 45–46.

12.8.1 Explainability and technical transparency

At AI conferences, some systems architects and software engineers can incorrectly subsume explainability into discussions about technical transparency.[77] In fact explainability is distinct from technical transparency. Explainability refers to the obligation of regulated firms to provide a rationale for decisions made by machine learning algorithms to clients and customers so that each can trust the use of machine learning as an influential factor in some aspect of financial decision making.[78] So, rather than a technical explanation, the regulated firm summarises the information and logic behind a decision.[79]

Beyond data protection law requirements covering individual data subjects, there is a need constantly to analyse and audit to whom any explanation is provided. In the 2018 House of Lords' investigation into AI, an expert in electronic commerce law put the reality in this way: 'What people need to know about how an AI system is operating, and why it is making particular decisions, will often be very different depending on whether they are developers, users, or regulators, auditors or investigators.'[80]

12.8.2 Explainability and target audiences

How can legal counsel and compliance officers contribute to auditing, drafting and other legal risk tasks to increase the quality of explanations to targeted audiences? Helpfully, a Bank of England Staff Working Paper provides six stakeholder categories as follows:

- professional developers, so all involved in developing and implementing an machine learning model;
- first-line model checkers determining the quality of the model;
- management, so logically that will include one or more senior man-

---

[77] The Alan Turing Institute and the Information Commissioner's Office (ICO) have jointly produced lengthy guidance on explainability. See The Alan Turing Institute and ICO (2020) Explaining Decisions Made with AI. The focus of this publication is individuals, but given many financial services clients are individuals it is a valuable source of broader, collective knowledge.

[78] International Regulatory Strategy Group et al. (2019) Towards an AI-powered UK: UK-based Financial and Related Professional Services, at 25.

[79] House of Lords (2018) AI in the UK: Ready, Willing and Able? – Written evidence from IBM, Simul Systems Ltd, Imperial College London and Professor Chris Reed, at 39.

[80] Ibid.

agers documented in a regulated firm's Statement of Responsibilities[81] and Management Responsibilities Maps;[82]

- second-line model checkers, from a controlled function, which may be compliance or risk or both;
- conduct regulators, ordinarily the FCA; and
- prudential regulators, so normally the PRA.

These six categories are enough to provide a framework for the first version of an internal legal policy document, albeit tailored to an asset manager, investment bank, platform or FinTech firm. In my view, there are three additional aspects concerning such a draft structure. First, the document needs to be continuously updated, with sensitivity to lessons learned and evolving technologies. Practically, this requires a diary alert linked so that such an update task actually happens, for example by setting a quarterly review. Second, any quality determination by first-line checkers must follow the regulated firm's chosen policies on (a) *ex ante*, and (b) *ex post* explanations. By which is meant distinguishing between explanations that can be made in advance of a machine learning auto-mated process (*ex ante*), and explanations after the decision (*ex post*) by reference to testing the model's performance in the same circumstances.[83]

12.8.3 Explainability and senior managers

Third, it is sensible for senior managers to document as part of FCA SMCR requirements, a detailed policy document specifying the types of *ex ante* and *ex post* explanations tailored to the specific financial ser-vices of the regulated firm. There is a tension here between commercial strategy and legal risks. For instance, *ex ante* or *ex post* explanations would be strong evidence against any legal liability. Yet unfortunately for common place neural networks models, discussed later in this chapter, such explanations are not possible.[84] An eminent professor of computer science has incisively observed you can often trust that people 'know what they are doing if they can explain to you how they arrived at an answer or a decision. However, "showing their work" is something that deep

---

[81] FCA SUP 10C.11G.

[82] FCA SYSC Rule 25.2.3.

[83] House of Lords (2018) AI in the UK: Ready, Willing and Able?, Written evidence from Professor Chris Reed, Professor of Electronic Commerce Law, Queen Mary, London University, at 38.

[84] Reed, C (2018) 'How Should We Regulate Artificial Intelligence?' *Philosophical Transactions of the Royal Society A*, at 9.

neural networks – the bedrock of AI systems – cannot easily do.'[85] The earlier referred to Bank of England Staff Working Paper proposes that the concept of a meaningful explanation emerges from answering the five questions listed below.

- Which features mattered in individual predictions?
- What drove the actual predictions more generally?
- What are the differences between the machine learning model and a linear one?
- How does the machine learning model work?
- How will the model perform under new states of the world? (that are not captured in the training data)[86]

12.8.4 The computer says no, because

While taking into account on-going concern that the provider of a financial service will be unable to explain many machine learning models, the constant evolution of technology makes this a pivotal legal risk issue. Encouragingly, there are already software packages that allow for explanations of supervised machine learning. For instance, if a client SME submitted a loan application that is rejected there would be scope to use techniques such as SHAP that can break down why the machine predicted a loan default, resulting in a rejection of the application.[87]

Such quantitative explanation models allow the client to visualise, by diagram and graph outputs, how their default prediction compared with approved loan applications. The client can see which variables are predictive of the decision to approve a loan or not. Given the potential for machine learning to widen access to credit by introducing processes with no or reduced human bias,[88] such insights from SHAP and equivalent techniques may prove helpful in avoiding erosion in client trust and preventing regulatory breaches.

---

[85] Mitchell, M (2019) *Artificial Intelligence – A Guide for Thinking Humans* (Pelican), at 127.

[86] Bracke, P et al. (2019) Bank of England Staff Working Paper No. 816 – Machine learning Explainability in Finance: An Application to Default Risk Analysis, at 3.

[87] Such an explainability technique is called SHapley Additive exPlanations (SHAP).

[88] Turiel, J, and Aste, T (2020) 'Peer-to-Peer Loan Acceptance and Default Prediction with Artificial Intelligence', *Royal Society Open Science*, 7. In this article the researchers summarise how their machine learning model can significantly improve credit risk by lowering the default risk of issued loans by 70 per cent.

To finish off this section on explainable machine learning, some commentators have argued persuasively that it is unhelpful, even to a degree misleading, to label any communication about the machine learning model as an explanation.[89] They propose instead to use the words 'summary' or equivalent. This may, at first glance, seem pedantic. Yet pedantry is the mark of competent legal drafting in the context of liability. Therefore, we may see a change to 'summary' in both new legislation and regulated firm drafting choices to reflect a more obtainable aim of providing clients and customers with an overview.

12.9   Algorithmic trading and machine learning

In essence, algorithmic trading concerns computerised trading with no or limited manpower in the trading process. Under MiFID II rules it refers to 'trading in financial instruments where a computer algorithm automatically determines individual parameters of orders such as whether to initiate the order, the timing, price or quantity of the order or how to manage the order after its submission, with limited or no human intervention'.[90] It is estimated that 75 per cent of equities trading and 40 per cent of foreign exchange trading already rely on algorithmic processes across capital markets.[91] Machine learning is not only increasing in trading volumes, but also in sophistication of operations. For instance, providing predictive capabilities to feed into trading decisions for equities or fixed income products across multiple stock exchanges.

Earlier in this chapter there was reference to the challenge of machine learning algorithms preventing transparency because regulated firms will rationally avoid disclosing the competitive advantage of their proprietary algorithms or create potential security vulnerabilities.[92] However, current regulation already requires regulated firms to disclose their strategies if the regulator so requests. Specifically, under MiFID II, Article 17(2),

---

[89]   Rudin, C (2019) 'Stop Explaining Black Box Machine Learning for High Stakes Decisions' https://arxiv.org/pdf/1811.10154.pdf.

[90]   See Article 4(39) MiFID II.

[91]   Bank of England (2017) 'The Promise of FinTech – Something New Under the Sun?', speech by Mark Carney, former Governor of the Bank of England, 25 January 2017.

[92]   Drew, C (2016) 'Data Science Ethics in Government', *Philosophical Transactions of the Royal Society A, Mathematical, Physical and Engineering Sciences*, at 10.

a regulator[93] 'may require the investment firm to provide, on a regular or ad hoc basis, a description of the nature of its algorithmic strategies, details of its trading parameters or limits to which the system is subject'.[94] Further, the FCA market abuse rules require that a firm must provide within 14 days, among other things, the following at the FCA's request:

- a description of algorithmic trading strategies;
- trading parameters or limits of the system;
- evidence of compliance with MAR 7A.3.2R (systems and controls) and MAR 7A.3.3R (business continuity and system tests); and
- details of the testing of the firm's systems.[95]

It is notable that at the consultation phase ISDA concluded that 14 days is too short a period to produce such detail, and that the deadline should be extended to 30 days.[96] Unfortunately that was rejected. In the context of machine learning combining with algorithmic trading the demands of an FCA request could be too much. It would, in my view, be prudent for legal counsel and compliance officers to discuss and document how their client proposes to deal with this 'what if' scenario in this short time period.

12.10 Balancing compliance with protecting IP

Regulated firms have to balance financial regulation compliance versus the protection of IP in the form of trade secrets.[97] Given algorithmic trading may often include potentially unique strategies, explaining the details of the testing may divulge IP to the regulator, which may in turn be leaked to competitors. This is not to imply that any financial services regulator would ever recklessly breach its duty of confidentiality.[98] However, there would inevitably be conscious or unconscious leakage of valuable

---

[93] In the UK this regulation is ordinarily found under just FCA rules. However, PRA rules transposed under MiFID II are also relevant to Capital Requirements Regulation (CRR) firms. See PRA CP9/16, March 2016.

[94] Article 17(2) MiFID II. FCA MAR 7A gives effect to Article 17(2) MiFID II.

[95] FCA MAR 7A.3.7R.

[96] ISDA Response to FCA's MIFID II Implementation under FCA CP15/43, at 22.

[97] Chapter 9 Innovation protection covers the management of intellectual property.

[98] Indeed under Article 76 (1) MiFID II there is a specific duty of professional secrecy imposed on competent authorities.

proprietary strategies because employees move back and forth from regulators to regulated firms.[99]

12.11 Machine learning and satellite imagery

An extensive JP Morgan report provides multiple examples of established opportunities to combine diverse data sources with machine learning technologies, with the aim of making better decisions in financial markets.[100] This includes data from social media, e-commerce transactions, web search trends and many others. Machine learning increasingly incorporates data from satellite sensors. This would allow asset managers, corporate financiers and research analysts to make more precise decisions with minimal effort. For example, Descartes Labs is a company using geospatial data and satellite imagery. With their software, a pixel of mineral rich land can be pinpointed using satellite imagery. The image of a targeted land of 10 hectares (24.71 acres) might be represented by one screen pixel for comparing the spectral similarity of minerals found in other land. For instance, an automotive or mining sector analyst in an asset manager or investment bank might want to research into lithium supplies. This element is found in batteries running Tesla cars and similar vehicles. Lithium is commonly found in remote parts of Argentina, and the Descartes Labs product allows comparisons against similar pixels of land anywhere else in Argentina, elsewhere in South America or globally.[101]

12.12 Machine learning and force majeure

Beyond corporate finance due diligence and investment analyst research, the global, real-time nature of many satellite platforms can dynamically combine with both classification and prediction machine learning

---

[99] ISDA Response to FCA's MIFID II Implementation under FCA CP15/43, at 21.This commercial point was raised by ISDA in its response to the FCA's consultation on MAR 7A, when it remarked: 'ISDA members would like to understand if the intention of the FCA is to capture the detailed cases of each type of test ... which may include proprietary information detailing the behaviour of the algorithm'.

[100] JP Morgan (2017) Big Data and AI Strategies – Machine Learning and Alternative Data Approach to Investing, at 136–213.

[101] See www.descarteslabs.com.

models. For instance, the monitoring of extreme weather is a memorable example of how machine learning will influence financial services decision making.[102] It has been observed that with the aid of such machine-driven early warning systems 'knowledge can be deployed not just in addressing problems as they arise but in pre-empting problems in the first place or in containing their escalation'.[103]

Specifically for legal counsel this combination of satellite and machine learning technology changes the management of both force majeure and material adverse change (MAC) clauses in contracts.[104] However, force majeure case law is well established, so my intention is to apply this discrete area of law to illustrate how machine learning would work and how it changes both legal obligations and drafting. Under English law, a force majeure event is undefined in statute, but generally treated under case law as a broad concept of 'events beyond the control' of the parties that entitle the cancellation or suspension of the contract.[105] For example, parties to a commercial contract may agree on a force majeure clause that includes tropical cyclones as a qualifying force majeure event.

Tropical cyclones typically occur between 5 and 30 degrees of the equator when the sustained winds reach 119kph or higher.[106] In Asia they are usually referred to as a typhoon, and in the US as a hurricane. If a cyclone travels over a city it is likely to cause loss of electricity supply, potential trading platform disruption, and even the closure of stock exchanges. Current technology enables cyclones to be monitored by satellites for several days before they are forecast to pass over populated areas.[107] There

---

[102] My contribution in an earlier book used the example of typhoons off the coast of Hong Kong. That book also includes a detailed introduction to machine learning and a chapter on AI and financial services by the global law firm Linklaters. See Kerrigan, C (ed.) (2021) *Artificial Intelligence and Law* (Edward Elgar Publishing).

[103] Susskind R, and Susskind, D (2017) *The Future of the Professions – How Technology Will Transform The Work of Human Experts* (Oxford University Press), at 226.

[104] *Travelport Ltd & Ors v WEX Inc* [2020] EWHC 2670 (Comm), at 171. While there are not too many English cases on MAC clauses, this decision summarises English case and also reference to an illuminating US case.

[105] See *Chitty on Contracts*, 34th edn. (2021), at 15–152. The effect of a force majeure clause is a matter of construction. See Treitel, G (2014) *Frustration and Force Majeure*, 3rd edn. (Sweet & Maxwell), at 12-026.

[106] www.oceanservice.noaa.gov/facts/cyclone.html.

[107] For examples of infrared satellite images that really capture the formation of a cyclone see the US Joint Typhoon Warning Center images at www.meteoc.navy.mil/jtwc.html.

is a complex interplay of variables, especially air velocity, competing weather systems, density, humidity, pressure and temperature. Recent satellite imagery processed by machine learning models have also revealed that the rainfall rate within the eye of the storm, air temperature flowing away from the eye, and ice water contents of clouds within the cyclone can in combination forecast rapid intensification in the next 24 hours.[108]

Turning to the contract drafting implications, it is clear there needs to be precision about what is the trigger for a force majeure cyclone event. At the same time, the drafting benefits from flexibility to allow for more accurate machine learning models in the future. For example, parties can mutually agree that when a machine learning computer algorithm predicts a 90 per cent confidence that a storm will pass over a specified urban area within 24 hours, the force majeure clause can be relied on. The party relying on a force majeure clause must factor in two aspects. First, the frustrated party relying on the force majeure clause has the burden of proof.[109] Second, English courts expect the frustrated party to specifically prove there were no reasonable steps to avoid or mitigate non-performance.[110] Therefore, a logical way of providing clarity on the timing of attempted mitigating steps is for both parties to agree to an AI clause that includes words along the lines:

> *Force Majeure* includes market disruption caused by a cyclone reaching or exceeding 119kph over the metropolitan area of [insert city name] based on the 24 hour predictions of mutually agreed machine learning methods.[111]

From a technology viewpoint, Figure 12.5 captures how a machine learning neural network system predicts when a cyclone is predicted to be a force majeure event.[112] As an illustration it applies equally to the hurricane season in the US, and the typhoon season off the Korean peninsula. The engineers developing the machine learning model may be in-house employees or external contractors or both. Whoever the developer is,

---

[108] NASA Jet Propulsion Laboratory (2020), A Machine-Learning Assist to Predicting Hurricane Intensity. See www.jpl.nasa.gov/news/a-machine-learning-assist-to-predicting-hurricane-intensity.

[109] *Chitty on Contracts*, 34th edn. (2021), at 1229.

[110] *Mamidoil-Jetfoil Greek Petroleum Co SA v Okta Crude Refinery AD* (No. 2) [2003] EWCA Civ 1031.

[111] This proposed draft force majeure clause first appeared in my chapter on 'Commercial Contracts' in another book. See Kerrigan, C (ed.) (2022) *Artificial Intelligence and Law* (Edward Elgar Publishing).

[112] Diagram 3 is adapted from Wilks, Y (2019), AI – Modern Magic or Dangerous Future (London: Hot Science).

they start by introducing the initial training data inputs on past cyclones ('Training Data').

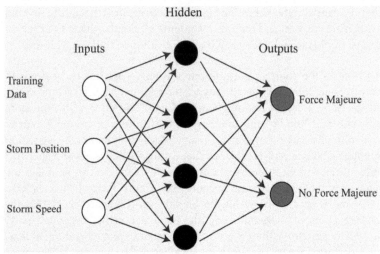

Note: *Tensorflow* provides a browser-based sandbox that enables you to get an immediate insight into how machine learning parameters are adjusted to achieve classification or regression results. This will aid envisioning the cyclone example. Available at: https://playground.tensorflow.org/.
Source: Adaptation of Wilks, Y (2019) *AI – Modern Magic or Dangerous Future* (Hot Science).

Figure 12.5   A neural network predicting a force majeure event

The pivotal data relied on is trusted government meteorological scales measuring 1 to 10, where a No. 8 or above is a force majeure event. Further, it has to be factored in that many cyclones may approach land as a No.8, but then change direction or reduce in speed to below the force majeure level. The Training Data is inputted to the machine learning neural net structure. The Training Data is made of results the algorithm can confidently rely upon as examples of:

- correctly predicted No. 8 cyclones over the relevant city;
- No. 8 cyclones off the relevant coastal area that decrease to below 119kph; and
- No. 8 cyclones off the relevant coastal area that bypass the relevant city.

12.13 Backpropagation of errors

Training Data is improved by the backpropagation of errors achieved by an algorithm that responds to the output data. An eminent computer science professor at Oxford University has summarised that the 'backward propagation of errors', often shortened to 'backpropagation' or 'backprop', refers to the transmission of error information provided by the neural networks output calculations based on the data. An error rate is calculated and transmitted back through the neural network before the next iteration.[113] The backpropagation algorithm is based on a calculus formula called gradient descent of a cost function.[114] At the highest level of abstraction, the essential aspect of the calculations can be described as shown in Equation 12.1.

$$error\ rate = actual\ output - expected\ output \qquad (12.1)$$

The *error rate* is calculated from the output and immediately transmitted back through the neural network so that the result can alter weights in one or more network layers before the next output calculation is made. Applied correctly, backpropagation is a key benefit of supervised machine learning, and has been described as inspired by the human brain's ability to make calculations, spot errors and learn from the errors before making the next calculation. In the specific context of neural networks 'there are many values to set as well as complex design decisions to be made, and these settings and designs interact with one another in complex ways to affect the ultimate performance'.[115] The adjustment and optimisation of performance are often collectively referred to as parameter or hyper-parameter tuning. By which is meant finding the right settings for the model.[116]

---

[113] Wooldridge, M (2020) *The Road to Conscious Machines: The Story of AI* (Pelican Books), at 183.

[114] A full explanation of backpropagation requires university-level calculus. Readers seeking such an in-depth mathematical explanation, see Michael Nielsen, Neural Networks and Deep Learning http://neuralnetworksanddeeplearning.com.

[115] Mitchell, M (2019) *Artificial Intelligence – A Guide for Thinking Humans* (Pelican), at 111.

[116] Often the most important hyperparameter is the learning rate, which determines how quickly or slowly the backpropagation algorithm used in a neural network model adapts to changes in weights.

12.14 The power of neural networks

The neural network can assist in predicting if a force majeure No. 8 level cyclone event is likely to occur. Such predictive calculations provide additional proof that a potentially frustrated party to a contract monitored the risk, then decided that no mitigation was necessary at certain time periods before an unexpected force majeure event because of the predicted lower wind storm speed over the urban area or predicted storm path away from the urban area. Alternatively, that the computer predicted a No. 8 storm over the urban area and the frustrated party can take timely mitigating action based on this prediction. Machine learning combined with satellite technology means under English common law, the duty to mitigate a specified force majeure event is objectively triggered. The quantitative prediction of an imminent force majeure event provides a mutually agreed notice period for the frustrated party to mitigate the situation.

If any of the foregoing cyclone prediction summary seems speculative, in fact there already exists a proven, more sophisticated prediction model. As published in a 2019 paper in *Nature's Scientific Reports*,[117] a deep learning system has been developed to predict (a) the eye of the storm's location when passing over the Korean peninsula, and (b) the shape of the typhoon's cloud structures. *Nature Scientific Reports'* published results show this deep learning model was able to predict 42.4 per cent of typhoon centres with absolute errors of less than 80km. The average error was 95.6km. The notice period provided by this machine learning system was based on six-hour intervals.

12.15 Competition and machine learning

There are currently numerous anti-competitive risk issues associated with algorithmic technology and machine learning.[118] For instance, algorithmic trading has the potential to be opaque and exploitative. Established financial regulation provides principles upon which legal counsel and

---

[117] Rüttgers, M et al. (2019) 'Prediction of a Typhoon Track Using a Generative Adversarial Network and Satellite Images', *Scientific Reports*, https://www.nature.com/articles/s41598-019-42339-y.

[118] There is a whole chapter of this book focused on anti-competitive issues, including detailed reference to machine learning and price collusion. See Chapter 10 Competition.

compliance functions competently advise front office and other staff.[119] Critical human judgement has to be applied to analysing new technology and the boundaries of acceptable conduct by authorised market participants. The CMA is already aware that reinforcement learning pricing algorithms competing in simulations are showing the ability to learn collusive strategies with punishment for deviation.[120]

12.16 Final points

The introduction and maintenance of any machine learning model that affects the profits and reputation of a regulated firm requires early, robust challenging. If readers make reference back to the earlier Figure 12.1 illustrating 'Computerised Thinking, Perception and Action', 'Big Data' and 'Ethics', their collective monitoring can be achieved in two ways. First, that machine learning design requires an initial phase of modelling and testing before progressing onto rigorous testing, where 'proper testing implies built-in contestation – in science as in law'.[121] Stephen Roberts, MAN Group Professor of Machine Learning at Oxford University, has underlined that financial services is not an exception to best practice, commenting that 'AI needs to be a science discipline, which means keeping to scientific principles'.[122] Marcus du Sautoy captures this need for scientific rigour with his memorable words, 'the machine may be learning but you need to make sure it's learning the right thing'.[123]

Second, the sublimely astute Mireille Hildebrandt also advises that lawyers must 'learn to speak law to statistics'.[124] By which is meant effective challenging requires sufficient technical understanding of machine

---

[119] Section 2.1, FCA Individual Conduct Rules. For example, under fundamental FCA rules all conduct is based on acting with integrity (Rule 1), care and diligence (Rule 2), fairness to customers (Rule 4) and proper market conduct (Rule 5).

[120] CMA (2021) Algorithms: How They Can Reduce Competition and Harm Consumers, at 2.85.

[121] Hildebrandt, M (2018) 'Algorithmic Regulation and the Rule of Law', *Philosophical Transactions of the Royal Society A*. Professor Hildebrandt is the author of over 100 articles many of which are focused on computer science and law.

[122] Professor Stephen Roberts presenting at the Alan Turing Institute Conference 'AI UK – Machine Learning for Finance' seminar presentation, London, 24 March 2021.

[123] Du Sautoy, M (2019) *The Creativity Code* (Fourth Estate), at 94.

[124] Hildebrandt M (2018) 'Algorithmic Regulation and the Rule of Law', *Philosophical Transactions of the Royal Society A.*, at 9.

learning and the computer architecture that enables it to function, which includes familiarity with the terminology of machine learning. Machine learning methods expand and nuance annually, which is potentially consistent with the competitive advantages any asset manager, investment bank, platform or FinTech entrant firm seeks. However, lawyerly rigor to ask difficult, meaningful questions about the scientific basis of any machine learning model is an important contribution.

In sum, the vital contribution to make is to pose questions based on the right level of technical fluency to then recommend the right legal risk options and solutions. Both legal and compliance functions need to be part of the risk management team to mitigate the technical effects of machine learning fuelled by Big Data. All financial regulation legal counsel and compliance officers have to increase their understanding of machine learning to remain competent.

13. Quantum computing

Some readers will be familiar with *Monty Python's Flying Circus* catch-phrase 'And Now for Something Completely Different'. In that epony-mous film and television series, the actor John Cleese repeatedly employs this catchphrase as a humorous segue. While there is nothing remotely amusing about QC, my advice is to read this chapter with this catchphrase constantly in mind. Quantum computers apply principles of quantum physics, so this technology is not intuitively understood.

13.1 Introduction

At first glance, the commercial emergence of QC seems a science fiction. Yet the interest and investment by some global financial services busi-nesses reveals a self-fulfilling ambition comparable to the NASA moon landings. It is known that Barclays, BBVA, Caixa Bank, Goldman Sachs, JP Morgan and Standard Chartered already have dedicated QC teams researching its potential for financial applications and regularly pub-lishing some of their results.[1] The overall scale of human resource and investment by global technology companies such as Google, Honeywell and IBM suggests that the commercial service of cloud-based QC will occur by the end of this decade.[2]

From law and regulation viewpoints, QC has to be grasped to identify what obligations and risks need to be considered. This chapter explains the fundamental concepts of QC, and then covers the main areas of exist-ing relevant or imminent law and regulation. Expect to receive a message soon from your asset manager or investment bank client along the follow-ing lines: 'Our strategic acquisitions team is researching the commercial

---

[1] *efinancialcareers* (2020) Quantum Computing at Goldman Sachs and JP Morgan. See www.efinancialcareers.co.uk/news/2020/12/quantum-computing-at-goldman-sachs-and-jpmorgan.

[2] See https://quantumai.google/; www.honeywell.com/us/en/company/quantum; and https://quantum-computing.ibm.com/.

potential of quantum computers. They believe these machines have the potential to be exponentially quicker. I was wondering, what are the laws and regulations on QC relevant to our regulated firm?'

13.2 QC explained

QC presents a radically different alternative technology based on the properties of quantum mechanics.[3] A succinct definition of QC refers to the design and theory of computer systems that depend on quantum effects for their operation.[4] A quantum computer manipulates quantum objects, for example photons. Any subatomic particle can be manipulated, but the most popular to date have been photons, electrons and ions.[5]

13.3 Superposition

The key QC concept of superposition cannot be fully explained by reference to an existing understanding of classical mechanics.[6] Nevertheless, initial insights derive from contrasting classical computer with quantum machines. All classical computers rely on electromagnetically driven calculations, where processing with logic gates revolves around the binary digit output of either a 1 or 0. Electromagnetism drives a classical computer's results, from a CERN supercomputer to every smartphone – 11010111010011110101. In contrast, Paul Dirac, pioneer of quantum mechanics, encapsulated superposition as a phenomenon where a subatomic particle is 'partly in two or more states' at the same time.[7] More recently, two Silicon Valley QC experts have succinctly explained that

---

[3] The *Oxford Dictionary of Physics* (2019) (Oxford University Press), at 487, defines quantum mechanics as 'a system of mechanics based on quantum theory which arose out of the failure of classical mechanics and electromagnetic theory to provide a consistent explanation of both electromagnetic waves and atomic structure'.

[4] The *Oxford Dictionary of Physics* (2019) (Oxford University Press), at 481.

[5] *WIRED* magazine has produced a short six-minute video summary entitled 'Quantum Computing and Quantum Supremacy, Explained'. See www.youtube.com/watch?v=QF7QfE6qgTM.

[6] The term classical physics refers to the principles and rules that govern all phenomena with the exception of quantum phenomena, including Newton's motion equations and Maxwell-Faraday theory on electromagnetism. The general rules of classical physics are called classical mechanics. See Susskind, L, and Hrabovsky, G (2013) *Classical Mechanics – The Theoretical Minimum* (Penguin), at chapter 1.

[7] Dirac, P (1930) *The Principles of Quantum Mechanics* (Oxford University Press), at 8.

'a quantum bit representing 0 or 1 can neither be viewed as "between" 0 and 1 nor can it be viewed as a hidden unknown state that represents either 0 or 1 with a certain probability'.[8]

An eminent Oxford physicist has memorably contrasted classical mechanical movement versus quantum movement. His analogy is an apple in a fruit bowl. In classical mechanics we can look at an apple in the bowl and measure its precise location. Quantum mechanics is entirely different, because we cannot know the exact position or state of motion of the apple.[9] The imaginary apple is in a superposition. If a line was drawn splitting the bowl into left (1) and right (0) sections,[10] the quantum physicist can calculate that the apple is 60 per cent in 1 and 40 per cent in 0. In quantum mechanics the apple's position is based on probabilities.[11] By which is meant a qubit, a unit of information in QC,[12] has simultaneous probabilities of being in more than one state.

13.4 A practical experiment to demonstrate quantum principles

A practical way to understand quantum superposition is to observe polarised light. It is established that light travels in waves, where the light moves, or vibrates, in a truly random way in 'any direction on the plane perpendicular to its motion and the amplitude and direction of vibration on this plane is the light ray's polarization'.[13] On an everyday level, we apply our understanding of polarisation by choosing to wear sunglasses to absorb or block the glare of the sun.

---

[8] Rieffel, E, and Polak, W (2000) 'An Introduction to Quantum Computing for Non-physicists', *ACM Computing Surveys*, Volume 32, Issue 3, 300–335, at 303. See www.science.smith.edu/~jfrankli/250s13/QuantumComputingForCS.pdf.

[9] Ferreira, P (2006) *The State of the Universe* (Phoenix), at 141. This phenomenon is known as the Heisenberg uncertainty principle.

[10] In classical mechanics, if the apple appeared to visibly sit in the exact centre of the bowl, a precise measurement would show it is either in the left (1) or right (0) part.

[11] Another popular analogy of superposition is that of a spinning coin on a table top. While the coin spins it cannot be characterized as either heads or tails, but it is a mixture of the two states – a superposition.

[12] *Oxford Dictionary of Physics* (2019) (Oxford University Press), at 460.

[13] Ferreira, P (2006) *The State of the Universe* (Phoenix), at 255. Also see Rees, G (2015) *Physical Principles of Remote Sensing* (Cambridge University Press), at 15–18.

With a small sheet of polarised film cut into three squares an experiment can be conducted to quickly observe the phenomenon that photons travelling through a polarised sheet can only do so in one orientation (see Figure 13.1). It is important to remember that actual quantum computers often function by measuring the orientation of photons.

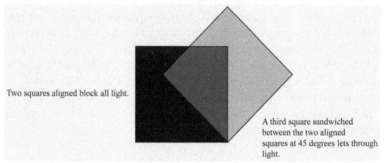

Two squares aligned block all light.

A third square sandwiched between the two aligned squares at 45 degrees lets through light.

Source: Bernhardt, C (2020) *Quantum Computing* (MIT Press), at 14.

Figure 13.1   Three polarised squares

This experiment takes one minute, but in my experience yields a long-term insight into quantum behaviour. First, shine a light source, such as a lamp or torch, through one polarised square onto a piece of recycled paper or a wall. Photons vibrating in every direction will travel towards the polarised square. However, only photons that are perpendicular or can orientate themselves perpendicular to the electromagnetic field created by the polarised square pass through. By which is meant all photons travelling horizontally compared with a vertically oriented polarised square travel through the electromagnetic field.

The key aspect to focus on with this experiment is that photons can either travel through the electromagnetic field covering each polarised square or not. The photons are either oriented correctly or not. Based on my experience of reading a number of articles on polarisation, thinking about a polarised square as a type of 'filter' or 'sieve' does not aid understanding of quantum behaviour. It is better to focus on the principle that photons are either oriented to pass through an electromagnetic field or are blocked.

When a second polarised square is placed over the first one, two notable things can be observed. If the second polarised square is also vertically oriented, so rotated to have the same polarisation, the amount of light passing through is approximately the same. Conversely, if the second polarised square is rotated 90 degrees then placed directly over the first one all the visible light is blocked. The zero probability of light passing through the polarised squares oriented at 90 degrees to each other is based upon (a) only horizontally travelling photons can pass through the first vertically aligned polarised square, and (b) all of the remaining horizontally travelling photons are absorbed by the second horizontally oriented polarised square.

When the first two polarised squares are oriented at 90 degrees absorbing all the light, insert a third polarised square at 45 degrees between the first square and the second square. When this third polarised square is sandwiched at 45 degrees, visible light passes through the overlap area of all three squares.[14] The result of more light intensity from three polarised squares shows the quantum nature of photons. Based on the random unpolarised nature of the photons, approximately one eighth, so 12.5 per cent, of their total number travel through the three polarised squares. This is because the sandwiched third polarised square angled at 45 degrees creates a 50 per cent probability of photons passing through it onto the third polarised square where there is a 50 per cent probability of the remaining photons (25 per cent) passing through. The result is that approximately 12.5 per cent of the light comes through the overlapping area of the three polarised squares.[15]

This short practical experiment of observing photons travelling through three polarised sheets provides an insight into the different way quantum computers function. Rather than measuring with the certainty of Newtonian classical mechanics to 'know both where the apple is and how (and where) it is moving', quantum physics is a world of uncertainty requiring the application of probability.[16]

---

[14] Bernhardt, C (2020) *Quantum Computing* (MIT Press), at 11–15. These pages provide a detailed practical explanation of this simple experiment.

[15] Applying Malus's Law, $cos^2 \theta$, the percentage intensity of light can be predicted for any angle of polarising material. For readers unable to obtain a polarized sheet to cut into three squares, Harvard University's Natural Sciences Faculty provides an excellent summary of this experiment with clear diagrams and images. See https://sciencedemonstrations.fas.harvard.edu/presentations/malus-law.

[16] Ferreira, P (2006) *The State of the Universe* (Phoenix), at 141–142.

Table 13.1   *16 configurations of four bits*

0000	1111	0011	0101
1000	0010	1001	0100
1100	0001	0110	1101
1110	0111	1010	1011

13.5   QC computational power

As captured in Table 13.1, the potential computational power of QC is of practical importance to regulated firms. Imagine a classical computer that can only process four bits of information at a time, Table 13.1 records all 16 possible configurations. In a classical computer each operation would have to be individually processed.

Astonishingly, in a quantum computer four qubits[17] can simultaneously process the 16 configurations.[18] The number of qubits q, determines the total number of states because – 2x2x2x2 = 2^4 =16. Just four qubits acting at once process all 16 numbers.[19]

The most significant aspect of superposition is that qubits perform calculations on an exponential scale. Therefore, five qubits can make 32 simultaneous calculations (2^5), seven qubits can make 128 simultaneous calculations (2^7) and 10 qubits can make 1,024 simultaneous calculations (2^{10}). As IBM has commented in a paper analysing how to exploit QC in

---

[17] An actual quantum computer can manipulate photons as qubits. Popular alternative particles used in quantum computers as qubits are electrons. An important QC aspect to clarify is that when a qubit is measured it collapses into one of the two states – 1or 0. Therefore, a qubit is measured the same as a classical bit – 1 or 0. In the photon polarisation experiment each polarised square measured the photons based on one of two states – horizontal (1) or vertical (0).

[18] Stewart, I et al. (2018) 'Committing to Quantum Resistance: A Slow Defence for Bitcoin against a Fast Quantum Computing Attack', *Royal Society Open Science* 5: 180410, at 3. See http://dx.doi.org/10.1098/rsos.180410.

[19] Grover, L (1999) 'Quantum Computing – How the Weird Logic of the Subatomic World Could Make It Possible for Machines to Calculate Millions of Times Faster Than They Do Today', *The Sciences*, July 1999, at 4.

financial services contexts, this advantage means its computational power approximately doubles when only one qubit is added.[20]

13.6 Entanglement

A second powerful and related concept of QC is entanglement. In brief, this additional unique aspect of QC refers to 'a quantum state of two or more particles, where the probabilities of the outcome of measurements on one of them depend on the state of the other – even though there is no interaction between them'.[21] To be clear, there is no magnetic pull or push, nor any other force known to physical science acting between them. To highlight the existence of entanglement, the current record for measuring entangled particles is 1203 kilometres or about 747.5 miles apart.[22]

The quantum concept of entanglement is unintuitive, again because it does not follow anything we know about classical computing and classical physics. If some readers have been generally reading about quantum mechanics, they will have quickly come across Einstein's memorable description of entanglement as 'spooky action at a distance'.[23] Given there is no magnetic force acting between the qubits and the relationship remains constant regardless of distance, it is indeed a weird aspect of quantum physics. There is no causation, but there is a proven correlation.[24]

My initial reflections about entanglement involved a cold towel wrapped around head plus a retreat to a quiet study. But as a cautious, questioning lawyer it is important to seek scientific proof. I found it in what has been called the 'Vienna Experiment'. In summary, in 2015 a leading quantum physics team set up an extremely robust experiment to send photons from a laboratory under the Vienna *Hofburg* castle via an optical fibre to two separate rooms spaced 58 metres apart. For physicists, the results

---

[20] IBM (2021) Exploring Quantum Computing Use Cases in Financial Services, at 1. See www.ibm.com/downloads/cas/2YPRZPB3.

[21] Rae, I, and Napolitano, J (2016) *Quantum Mechanics* (CRC), at 348.

[22] *New Scientist* (2017) 'Chinese Satellite Beats Distance Record for Quantum Entanglement'. See www.newscientist.com/article/2134843-chinese-satellite-beats-distance-record-for-quantum-entanglement/.

[23] The original Einstein quote was in German, *spukhafte Fernwirkung*, and translates as 'spooky remote effect'.

[24] Bernhardt, C (2020) *Quantum Computing* (MIT Press), at 69.

of this proof of entanglement experiment are categorized as technically 'loophole free'.[25]

Theoretically, entanglement works regardless of the distance between the sub-atomic particles. Recently, a 500 kilometres fibre optic cable between two Chinese cities has been used to establish a secure quantum data link.[26] The current distance record for measuring entangled photon particles is 1203 kilometres or about 747.5 miles, achieved from space to ground stations on Earth.[27]

If two qubits are entangled,[28] the measurement of the first qubit will provide quantitative information about what will happen when measuring the second qubit. The predicted outcome of measurements on one of them depends on the state of the other, even though there is no interaction between them. Entanglement provides QC with the unique computing power to predict the measurement of a twin qubit regardless of its location. Quantum encryption across computer networks, for example a network carrying bank transfers, will rely on quantum entanglement as a secure encrypted key.[29]

It is important to note that in the context of practical implications for the financial services sector, entanglement is not at an advanced stage of control by researchers to be useful. Currently, large-scale entanglement is unproven, so for legal counsel and compliance officers this phenomenon needs monitoring to gauge how it progresses or not.[30] Arguably, when it does progress global payment services and trading platforms would be transformed.

---

[25] Zeilinger, A et al (2015) Significant-Loophole-Free Test of Bell's Theorem with Entangled Photons, *Physical Review Letters*, 115, 250401 (2015).

[26] *New Scientist* (2021) Quantum Data Link Between Two Cities, 26 June 2021, at 23.

[27] Yin, J et al (2017) Satellite-based entanglement distribution over 1200 kilometers, *Science*, 16 June 2017: Vol. 356, Issue 6343, at 1140–1144.

[28] When qubits are unentangled, the measurement of one has no effect on the other. See Bernhardt, C (2020) *Quantum Computing* (MIT Press), at 60.

[29] *New Scientist* (2021) 'The Quantum Internet is Coming', at 38.

[30] Tichy, W (2017), 'Is Quantum Computing for Real? An Interview with Catherine McGeoch of D-Wave Systems', *Association of Computing Machinery*, (July 2017), at 14.

Table 13.2   Key QC concepts

QC concepts	Explanation
Quantum decoherence	The interaction of qubits with something from the environment not part of the computation, which causes a distorting, negative effect. The higher the quantity of qubits, the more likely the system fails. This is considered the greatest challenge to building reliable quantum computers.[1]
Error correction (fault tolerance)	The operation of a quantum computer is extremely sensitive to external noise from electromagnetic fields, heat and vibration. Quantum computers chips operate at -273° Celsius (0.015 Kelvin) as a protective measure, but any change in temperature disturbs computations. Error correction is currently an unsolved significant limitation on the performance and scalability of QC.[2] From a legal viewpoint the existence of errors above contractually agreed percentages will result in disputes.[3]
Quantum supremacy	A point in the long-term future when a quantum computer can outperform the most powerful classical computer.[4]

Notes: [1] Rieffel, E, and Polak, W (2000) 'An Introduction to Quantum Computing for Non-physicists', *ACM Computing Surveys*, Volume 32, Issue 3, 300–335, at 304. [2] Ibid., at 309. [3] The issue of operational viability is especially important, because in any financial services context the near perfect reliability of classical computers is taken for granted. This will require some careful and novel drafting. [4] *New Scientist* (2019) Quantum Supremacy – Special Report, at 6.

13.7   Other key QC concepts

There are several other unique QC concepts recorded in Table 13.2. Similar to the concept of entanglement, legal counsel and compliance officers do not need to know these in technical depth, but they may be required to pinpoint and record potential areas of legal and regulatory risk. These key QC concepts should allow anyone to grasp the fundamentals, then advise regulated firms about (a) when QC is authoritatively predicted to become a threat, and (b) on-going updates on the original (a) prediction.

13.8 Legal analysis of post-QC cryptography

Compared with classical supercomputers the practical advantages of QC continue to be a source of debate. However, in the context of current merger activity involving QC technologies there are already two applicable laws. As covered earlier in Chapter 10 Competition, under an amendment to the Enterprise Act 2002 a turnover test determines potential enforcement action or the blocking of a planned acquisition or merger. The turnover level would have to exceed £1 million concerning (a) QC research; or (b) any services employing QC communication or simulation; or (c) quantum resistant cryptography.[31] Additionally, regulated firms and start-ups seeking to expand in the financial services sector with a turnover figure below the £1 million threshold may still be investigated at the discretion of the Secretary of State on the grounds of public interest. In this context, quantum cryptography initiatives may experience special attention regardless of their turnover level.[32]

If QC has the potential to crack existing cryptography standards and create immense financial services systemic risk, the above £1 million threshold test is an ill-suited approach. There will be QC firms that generate low or no turnover, but have millions of pounds of investment resulting in considerable advancement in QC performance.

13.8.1 The National Security and Investment Act 2021

Fortunately, the flawed £1 million threshold test added to the Enterprise Act 2002 has been superseded by the introduction of the NSIA 2021.[33] The NSIA 2021 creates a mandatory notification regime for both domestic and foreign investment in the UK across 17 sectors, including 'quantum technologies'. The original draft NSIA 2021 definition of 'quantum technologies' was initially so broad it included research activities, but these are now exempt. The revised draft definition of quantum technology covers the following:

- quantum communications;
- quantum connectivity;

---

[31] Section 23A Enterprise Act 2002.
[32] Section 42 Enterprise Act 2002.
[33] The NSIA 2021 was made effective from 4 January 2022.

- quantum imaging, sensing, timing and navigation;
- quantum information processing, computing or simulation; and
- quantum resistant cryptography.[34]

Whatever the final NSIA 2021 definition of quantum technology, its use in the financial services sector will be scrutinised for assessment to determine if there is a risk to national security.[35] If a proposed acquisition or merger is considered to pose an unacceptable risk to national security the NSIA 2021 provides the power to block the transaction. These triggering percentages apply to both share ownership percentages and percentages of voting rights in shares.[36] In both situations, the thresholds of percentages of an entity requiring mandatory notification are:

- from 25% or less to more than 25%;
- from 50% or less to more than 50%; or
- from less than 75% to 75% or more.[37]

In addition, there are another two acquisition situations that require mandatory notification. First, where the acquisition of voting rights enable a person to 'secure or prevent' the passing of any class of resolution under the entity's constitution.[38] Second, where an acquisition enables the person to materially influence the policy of the entity. Material influence may be achieved alone or in combination with other interests or rights held by the person.[39] So in many instances under these two broader

---

[34] UK Department for Business, Energy & Industrial Strategy (2021) National Security and Investment: Sectors in Scope of the Mandatory Regime Government Response to the Consultation on Mandatory Notification in Specific Sectors under the National Security and Investment Bill, at 80.

[35] Controversially, the NSIA 2021 provides no definition of 'national security'. From a foreign investment viewpoint, that uncertainty may deter cross-border M&A transactions. The City of London Law Society and The Law Society of England and Wales provided joint evidence on this weakness as part of the consultation phase of the NSIA 2021. See The City of London Law Society/The Law Society (2020) House of Commons Public Bill Committee, Joint Response of the Company Law Committees of The City of London and The Law Society, at 2.

[36] Importantly, The City Code on Takeovers and Mergers (the 'Code'), deriving its statutory basis under Chapter 1 of Part 28 (Sections 942 to 965) of the Companies Act 2006, will not have specific amendments covering how the NSIA 2021 interacts with the Code. However, the Code Committee has produced valuable guidance of what it expects professional advisers, including lawyers, to advise clients to do. This guidance is summarised in Takeover Panel RS 2020/1 (2021) Conditions to Offers and the Offer Timetable, at 1.18.

[37] Section 8(2)–(5) NSIA 2021.

[38] Section 8(6) NSIA 2021.

[39] Section 8(8) NSIA 2021.

acquisition scenarios the declaring party may be the person or entity that originally held an insignificant percentage shareholding or percentage voting rights, but over time acquires increasing influence to secure or block voting decisions or play a significant role in a change of policy.

13.8.2 Acquiring QC assets

Under the NSIA 2021, the Secretary of State also has the power to notify an acquirer, qualifying entity or any person it considers appropriate, to determine if the acquisition of an asset may give rise to a national security risk.[40] The specific language used in the NSIA 2021 is a 'call-in notice' that a national security assessment will be undertaken.[41] The range of assets covered includes algorithms, databases, designs, formulae, plans, drawings, software, source code, specifications and trade secrets.[42] So in the context of QC where an invaluable breakthrough may derive from an individual patent holder or small start-up entity, an invention may be subject to the same level of scrutiny compared with the acquisition of an established company with QC expertise.

In my view, a technical risk that legal counsel and compliance officers need to be especially diligent to spot is the combination of algorithms and software to replicate some aspects of QC in a classical computer. Based on fast, intuitive thinking this should fall outside the NSIA 2021 perimeter. But, in fact, so-called 'quantum emulation' is specifically included. Under the definitions of quantum information processing, computing and simulation there is the inclusion of the 'use of a classical computer to represent the internal state and operations of a quantum computer'.[43]

13.8.3 Failing to notify

If a relevant acquisition of a QC asset or entity proceeded without notification it would be void.[44] Further, it is a criminal offence to do so,[45] car-

---

[40]   Section 1(1) to (4) NSIA 2021.

[41]   Section 1(3) NSIA 2021.

[42]   Section 7(5) NSIA 2021.

[43]   UK Department for Business, Energy & Industrial Strategy (2021) National Security and Investment: Sectors in Scope of the Mandatory Regime Government Response to the Consultation on Mandatory Notification in Specific Sectors under the National Security and Investment Bill, at 80.

[44]   Section 13(1) NSIA 2021.

[45]   Section 32 NSIA 2021.

rying a maximum sentence on indictment of five years' imprisonment.[46] From a civil penalty perspective the consequences are also potentially severe based on a maximum £10 million fine, or if it is a higher figure, 5 per cent of global turnover.[47] Directors can also be found guilty of the same offences committed by a body corporate based on their consent, connivance or neglect.[48]

13.8.4 NSIA 2021 operates retrospectively

Another important aspect of the NSIA 2021 is its retrospective effect. The Secretary of State has the power to intervene and issue a call-in notice concerning an acquisition or transaction that occurred up to five years in the past.[49] This five year period does not apply if an acquisition has been completed without UK Government approval, nor if false or misleading information is provided in applications or notices provided to the Secretary of State that form parts of assessment processes.[50] Further, from the date when the Secretary of State is aware of the triggering event, there is a time limit of six months to issue the call-in notice.[51]

13.9 Quantum resistant cryptography

The motivation driving UK competition law to focus on quantum resistant cryptography is an area of QC that requires on-going understanding of the issues and monitoring by legal counsel and compliance officers. It is a future technical risk which means it is not on today's legal or compliance function 'to do' list.[52] However, as the UK Department for Business, Energy and Industrial Strategy succinctly put it 'quantum computers, when fully scalable machines do come, are expected to pose a significant

---

[46] Section 39 NSIA 2021.

[47] Section 41(1)(a) NSIA 2021.

[48] Section 36(1) NSIA 2021.

[49] Section 2(2)(b) NSIA 2021.

[50] Section 22(5) NSIA 2021.

[51] Section 2(2)(a) NSIA 2021.

[52] A current task for legal and compliance functions to assess is how 'digital services providers', as defined under the Network and Information Systems (NIS) 2018 Directive, are taking proportionate technical and organisational measures to manage post-quantum cryptographic risks. See the Network and Information Systems Directive, 2016/1148.

threat to the cryptographic systems which underpin much of our existing cyber security'.[53]

QC presents a specific threat of unknown timing. This is because a key strength of one QC algorithm, namely Shor's algorithm, is its ability to find the factors of large numbers, something it does exponentially faster compared with all known classical algorithms.[54] The private key element of public key cryptography,[55] such as RSA,[56] relies on the difficulty of factoring the product of two large numbers. The theoretical risk is that a future QC system will be created with sufficient qubits to apply Shor's algorithm to break public key cryptography that is used to encrypt messages over the Internet, including bank transfers and trading data.[57] So there are numerous risk implications for the financial services sector.

From a technical viewpoint, QC cannot reliably decrypt public key cryptography until error correction is achieved. By which is meant the QC architecture must have control over environmental noise to function.[58] Achieving error correction may take a decade or more to control. From an on-going practical legal risk viewpoint, lawyers need at least five years' clear notice from independent leading QC experts that quantum computers are predicted to decrypt RSA and similar public key cryptography schemes. This is because the regulated firm will need sufficient time to upgrade hardware, firmware and software. In short the arrival of QC means potentially multiple high-risk projects for which the time to complete could easily be underestimated.

Whatever the progress of QC it deserves cautious monitoring. While senior management responsibility for encryption is logically that of the

---

[53] UK Department for Business, Energy & Industrial Strategy (2021) National Security and Investment: Sectors in Scope of the Mandatory Regime Consultation on Secondary Legislation to Define the Sectors Subject to Mandatory Notification in the National Security and Investment Bill 2020, at 64.

[54] Stewart, I et al. (2018) 'Committing to Quantum Resistance: A Slow Defence for Bitcoin against a Fast Quantum Computing Attack', *Royal Society Open Science* 5: 180410, at 3–4.

[55] MacCormick, J (2020) *Nine Algorithms That Changed the Future* (Princeton University Press), at 167–168.

[56] The RSA patent granted to MIT can be seen at https://patents.google.com/patent/US4405829. Although note GCHQ had been applying its own classified public key algorithm before RSA.

[57] Knight, P, and Walmsley, I (2019) UK National Quantum Technology Programme, *Quantum Science Technology*, 4 405026, at 4–6.

[58] Rieffel, E, and Polak, W (2000) 'An Introduction to Quantum Computing for Non-physicists', *ACM Computing Surveys*, Volume 32, Issue 3, 300–335, at 328.

Chief Technology Officer or equivalent SMF formally recognised as responsible in the SMCR documentation, lawyers need to be involved in three immediate things. First, a post-quantum cryptographic plan needs to be agreed and recorded by the Chief Technology Officer. Such a plan would need to include an understanding of the level of risk posed by commercially available QC based on specific qubit thresholds. Currently, it is estimated that to break Shor's algorithm a quantum computer would need in excess of 20 million qubits.[59]

Second, the period for re-assessment of that plan has to be based on one or more metrics that trigger its revision in terms of dedicated resources. For instance, the authoritative published results on the number of qubits in a quantum computer exceeding 1,000, 5,000, 10,000 and so forth. Currently, quantum computers built by Google and IBM have less than 200 qubits,[60] although IBM has already revealed that by 2023 it plans to make commercially accessible a machine with 1,000 or more qubits over the cloud.[61] Third, auditing that the right levels of internationally respected standards are followed. Currently, the US NIST provides extensive guidance on quantum safe ways to replace RSA, which includes contributions from the UK NCSC.[62]

13.10 Is QC the Millennium Bug of the 21st century?

It is important to also mention that the commercial self-interest of some businesses in the QC industry could easily produce a replication of some of the scaremongering surrounding the Y2K problem, colloquially known as the Millennium Bug. As a reminder for some readers, the Y2K event

---

[59] Gidney, C, and Ekera, M (2021) How to Factor 2048 Bit RSA Integers in 8 Hours Using 20 Million Noisy Qubits. See https://arxiv.org/pdf/1905.09749.pdf.

[60] IBM has built a quantum computer with 127 qubits and hope to achieve 400 qubits by the end of 2022. See *New Scientist*, 'New Quantum Leader?', 20 November 2021, at 7.

[61] Tearsheet (2021) Understanding Quantum Computing's Potential in Financial Services with Goldman Sachs' Will Zeng and IBM's Stefan Woerner, at 11.34 to 11.40. See https://tearsheet.co/podcasts/understanding-quantum-computings-potential-in-financial-services-with-goldman-sachs-will-zeng-and-ibms-stefan-woerner/.

[62] Knight, P, and Walmsley, I (2019) UK National Quantum Technology Programme, *Quantum Science Technology*, 4 0405026, at 4.

turned out to be unfounded,[63] although, the comparison is imperfect because Y2K was a specific date, and QC decrypting public key cryptography could occur in five, 10 or 20 years' time. Regardless of the timeframe, QC is not a threat to be forgotten – it is only a question of when.

13.11 Financial services marketing

Acknowledging the considerable attraction of QC as a means of augmenting financial services and the performance of financial instruments, it is inevitable that established regulated firms and new entrants will provide marketing that communicates its use. Already the *Financial Times* has published articles from investment banks confident about their imminent use of QC to enhance investment performance. Given the valuable addition of QC as a marketing signal of serving clients with cutting-edge technology, financial regulatory promotion requirements need to be at the front of both lawyer and compliance officer minds before approving the release of all material covering QC. While financial promotion rules vary with considerable detail depending upon the level of client sophistication and regulated financial service offered, in general terms UK transposed and EU MiFID organisational regulations require, among other things, that marketing information:

- is accurate and always gives a fair and prominent indication of any relevant risks when referencing any potential benefits of an investment service or financial instrument;
- presents risk information in a prominent way, and in a font size that is at least equal to the predominant font size used throughout the information provided;
- the information is sufficient for, and presented in a way that is likely to be understood by, the average member of the group to whom it is directed, or by whom it is likely to be received; and
- the information does not disguise, diminish or obscure important items, statements or warnings.[64]

---

[63] Anderson, R (1999) The Millennium Bug – Reasons Not to Panic. See www.cl.cam.ac.uk/~rja14/Papers/y2k.pdf.

[64] Article 44 MiFID 2017/565. See https://www.legislation.gov.uk/eur/2017/565/article/44. These same financial promotion rules are replicated in FCA COBS 4.5A.3, at www.handbook.fca.org.uk/handbook/COBS/4/?view=chapter.

13.12 Pricing and risk simulations

For current classical computers, the time spent processing Monte Carlo simulations is considerable, because it may require the computer to run millions of samples to provide answers. Monte Carlo methods simulate the probability of a range of outcomes based on independent risk variables, such as the rolling of dice or the tossing of a coin. Using multiple calculations of random numbers 'the results produce a distribution of samples that is a fair representation of the target probability distribution'.[65] For instance, with a Monte Carlo simulation you can simulate the rolling of one dice for 5,000 and 10,000 times. The 10,000 times simulation is likely to provide the most accurate predictive representation.[66]

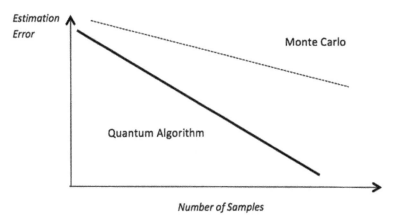

Number of Samples

Source: Adaptation of IBM (2021) Getting Your Financial Institution Ready for the Quantum Computing Revolution, at 3. See www.ibm.com/thought -leadership/institute-business-value/report/quantumfinancial.

Figure 13.2   *Monte Carlo speed-up*

---

[65] Barbu, A, and Zhu, S (2020) *Monte Carlo Methods* (Springer), at 1–2. For a seminal paper see Boyle, P (1977) 'Options: A Monte Carlo Approach', *Journal of Financial Economics*, Volume 4, 323–338, https://doi.org/10.1016/0304-405X(77)90005-8. For instance, with a Monte Carlo simulation you can simulate the rolling of one dice for 5,000 and 10,000 times. The 10,000 times simulation is likely to provide the most accurate predictive representation.

[66] For an interactive online overview also see www.ibm.com/cloud/learn/monte-carlo-simulation.

In contrast, 'quantum computers have the potential to sample data differently, providing a quadratic speed-up for these types of simulations'.[67] A recent example of this is evident from a dedicated team at Goldman Sachs that used QC to speed up derivatives pricing by 1,000 times.[68] As Figure 13.2 illustrates, quantum computer algorithms require far fewer samples to provide accurate results, plus when more samples are used the error rate diminishes.[69] The Goldman Sachs QC team, plus a similar team from ETH Zurich, IBM and JP Morgan, both underline that Monte Carlo simulations consume extensive computational resources.[70] Therefore, the successful application of QC to derivatives pricing would be valuable across the financial services sector. Of course both these research teams are at the bottom of a Himalayan QC challenge, because fault tolerance and quantum scale up to many qubits has yet to be achieved.

13.13 Portfolio optimisation

A second major financial services application of QC is portfolio optimisation, referring to the process by which risks are minimised for a specified expected return and returns are maximised for a specified risk.[71] Put succinctly, both minimising risk and achieving the desired rate of return. A team of researchers led by the QC manufacturer QC Ware[72] recently examined a range of important finance areas to determine if quantum speed-ups are viable. In the context of portfolio optimisation their conclusion mirrored those of the other Goldman Sachs and JP Morgan QC teams already discussed. Quantum hardware needs to progress with connectivity, error correction rates, and greatly increased numbers of qubits to achieve a practical speed-up.[73]

---

[67] IBM (2021) Exploring Quantum Computing Use Cases for Financial Services, at 5. Available at www.ibm.com/thought-leadership/institute-business-value/report/exploring-quantum-financial#.

[68] Chakrabarti, S (2020) A Threshold for Quantum Advantage in Derivative Pricing. Available at https://arxiv.org/abs/2012.03819.

[69] IBM (2021) Getting Your Financial Institution Ready for the Quantum Computing Revolution, at 2–3. Available at www.ibm.com/thought-leadership/institute-business-value/report/quantumfinancial.

[70] Stamatapoulos, N (2020) 'Option Pricing Using Quantum Computers', *Quantum Journal*, at 1. Available at https://arxiv.org/abs/1905.02666.

[71] Markowitz, H (1952) 'Portfolio Selection', *The Journal of Finance*, Volume 7, Issue 1, at 77–91.

[72] https://qcware.com/.

[73] Bouland, A et al. (2020) Prospects and Challenges of Quantum Finance, at 35. Available at https://arxiv.org/abs/2011.06492v1.

13.14 Combining QC with machine learning

A third significant potential use is QC combined with machine learning.[74] The computational processing time to train some neural network machine learning models can often take weeks. Therefore, it is unsurprising that important actors, for example IBM Research, invest in how QC can potentially support machine learning by accelerating certain computational tasks. In financial markets, the QC is already being assessed over how it can potentially enhance AML and trading applications.[75]

13.15 Conclusions

Not all moon-shots reach their target, but QC appears to have the right mix of investment and talent to be applied successfully in under 10 years' time. While the estimated time of arrival of many practical QC financial services applications is uncertain, this reality alone presents regulators with an opportunity to prepare clear, proportionate rules based on the evolving drivers of its use.

If there is a lesson to be learned from classical computing it is the following. In 1971, the first CPU microchip, the Intel 4004, contained 2,300 transistors. In 1996, 25 years later, the Intel 386 microprocessor contained 275,000 transistors, so just over 100 times more processing power. Currently, the transistors in an above average smartphone exceed 2 billion transistors.[76] In total, over just four decades, the number of transistors has increased more than 1 billion-fold.[77] The essence of this growth, known as Moore's Law, is illustrated in Figure 13.3. From a cryptographic view-

---

[74] Chapter 12 Machine learning provides a detailed explanation of how machine learning works, relevant regulations, and its practical application in the financial services sector.

[75] Tearsheet (2021) Understanding Quantum Computing's Potential in Financial Services with Goldman Sachs' Will Zeng and IBM's Stefan Woerner. Available at https://tearsheet.co/podcasts/understanding-quantum-computings-potential-in-financial-services-with-goldman-sachs-will-zeng-and-ibms-stefan-woerner/.

[76] Oxford University provides a range of visually memorable graphs of the exponential increase in transistors on microchips since 1970 entitled 'Exponential Progress – Moore's Law'. Available at https://ourworldindata.org/technological-progress.

[77] To clarify, the number of transistors does not technically result in a precise increase in processing power because other factors, such as the architectural design of the chip, influence its speed and use of electricity. An everyday analogy is automotive engines. The power of a motor car engine size is

point alone, QC needs cautious monitoring, so that technical progress on its computational power forms part of both SMCR documentation and practical risk implementation.

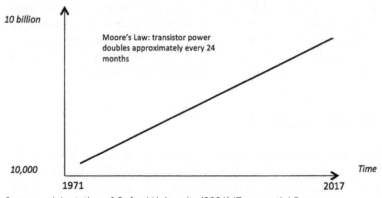

Source: Adaptation of Oxford University (2021) 'Exponential Progress – Moore's Law'. See https://ourworldindata.org/technological-progress.

Figure 13.3   Transistors per microprocessor

Currently, QC is a fledgling, prototype technology with significant error tolerance issues. Nevertheless, this presents several on-going challenges for lawyers and compliance officers. First, lawyers must have an acute understanding of how the NSIA 2021 impacts both asset and entity acquisitions. Second, financial promotion rules require assessing how commercial opportunities can be captured accurately without misleading existing and potential clients on the impact and role of QC.

Third, there is a need to horizon scan legal and regulatory changes relevant to QC. For example, given the often immense energy resources required to power QC these changes would logically include ESG regulatory disclosures.

A running thread throughout this book is the gap between technology and human understanding. With QC there are no excuses. Technology

---

expressed in horse power, but the design and materials used in the making of the engine all play their part.

either improves or is made obsolete by something that is better. Until QC becomes obsolete it cannot be ignored by legal counsel and compliance officers. Indeed QC has already shown its astonishing potential. Ultimately, QC has been added to the legal and compliance function list of 'things to understand' so that its progress and any accompanying risks can be competently monitored. I hope this chapter, combined with interrelated chapters,[78] support evolving QC legal risk management goals.

---

[78] Especially Chapter 2 Accountability, Chapter 3 Cloud computing, Chapter 10 Competition, Chapter 5 Cyber security and Chapter 12 Machine learning.

Index